T0039628

THE ONE TRUE

Barbecue

FIRE, SMOKE, AND THE PITMASTERS
WHO COOK THE WHOLE HOG

RIEN FERTEL

PHOTOGRAPHS BY DENNY CULBERT

TOUCHSTONE

NEW YORK   LONDON   TORONTO   SYDNEY   NEW DELHI

Touchstone
An Imprint of Simon & Schuster, Inc.
1230 Avenue of the Americas
New York, NY 10020

First Touchstone hardcover edition May 2016

TOUCHSTONE and colophon are registered trademarks of Simon & Schuster, Inc.

For information about special discounts for bulk purchases, please contact Simon &
Schuster Special Sales at 1-866-506-1949 or business@simonandschuster.com.

The Simon & Schuster Speakers Bureau can bring authors to your live event. For
more information or to book an event, contact the Simon & Schuster Speakers
Bureau at 1-866-248-3049 or visit our website at www.simonspeakers.com.

Interior design by Jill Putorti

All photographs by Denny Culbert

Manufactured in the United States of America

10   9   8   7   6   5   4   3   2   1

Library of Congress Cataloging-in-Publication Data

Fertel, Rien, 1980– author.
  The one true barbecue : fire, smoke, and the pitmasters who cook the whole hog /
by Rien Fertel ; photographs by Denny Culbert.
pages cm
Includes bibliographical references and index.
1. Cooks—Southern States—Biography. 2. Barbecuing—Southern States—History.
3. Southern States—Social life and customs. I. Culbert, Denny, photographer. II.
Title.
TX649.A1F47 2016
641.5092'2—dc23
[B]
2015033791

ISBN 978-1-4767-9397-9
ISBN 978-1-4767-9399-3 (ebook)

*Dedicated to those who worked in the
restaurant kitchens I grew up in—the women and men
who raised me, fed me, and taught me how to work and play.
I wish I remembered all of your names.*

Contents

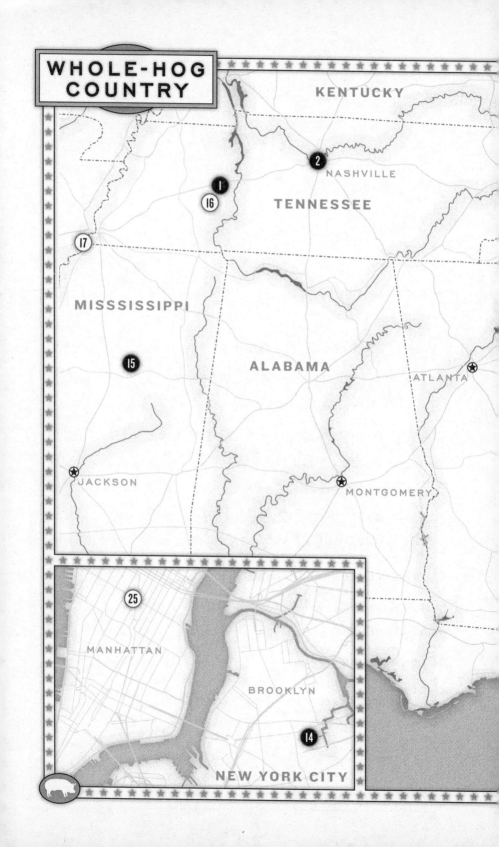

WHOLE-HOG COUNTRY

KENTUCKY

NASHVILLE

2

1

16

TENNESSEE

17

MISSSISSIPPI

ALABAMA

ATLANTA

15

JACKSON

MONTGOMERY

25

MANHATTAN

BROOKLYN

14

NEW YORK CITY

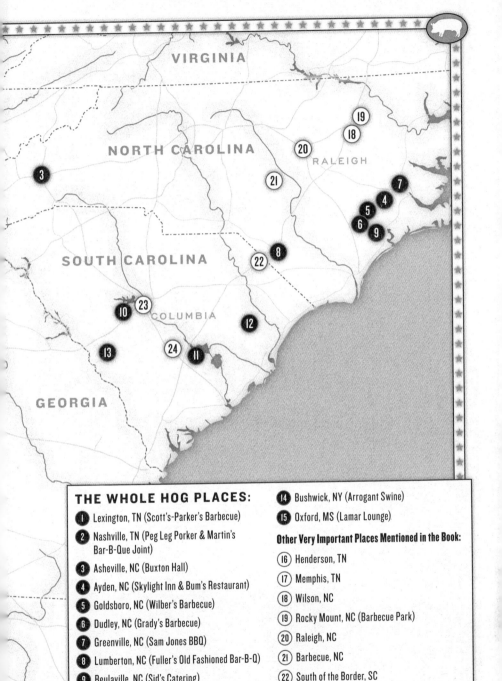

THE WHOLE HOG PLACES:

1. Lexington, TN (Scott's-Parker's Barbecue)
2. Nashville, TN (Peg Leg Porker & Martin's Bar-B-Que Joint)
3. Asheville, NC (Buxton Hall)
4. Ayden, NC (Skylight Inn & Bum's Restaurant)
5. Goldsboro, NC (Wilber's Barbecue)
6. Dudley, NC (Grady's Barbecue)
7. Greenville, NC (Sam Jones BBQ)
8. Lumberton, NC (Fuller's Old Fashioned Bar-B-Q)
9. Beulaville, NC (Sid's Catering)
10. Batesburg-Leesville, SC (Jackie Hite's Bar-B-Q)
11. Holly Hill, SC (Sweatman's Bar-B-Que)
12. Hemingway, SC (Scott's Bar-B-Que)
13. Hell's Half Acre, SC (Scott's Bar-B-Que)
14. Bushwick, NY (Arrogant Swine)
15. Oxford, MS (Lamar Lounge)

Other Very Important Places Mentioned in the Book:

16. Henderson, TN
17. Memphis, TN
18. Wilson, NC
19. Rocky Mount, NC (Barbecue Park)
20. Raleigh, NC
21. Barbecue, NC
22. South of the Border, SC
23. Columbia, SC
24. Orangeburg, SC
25. Madison Square Park, NYC (Big Apple Barbecue Block Party)

INTRODUCTION

A Dying Breed

*S*ome people count sheep to lull themselves to sleep, but Ricky Parker counted hogs to remind himself of his own existence.

Whole hogs. Prodigious beasts, 180 to 200 pounds apiece. Fed and fattened to his specifications, slaughtered at the local abattoir, head and offal removed and ready for roasting and smoking in his cinder-block pits. This is what Ricky called barbecue. Whole-hog barbecue. The only barbecue that he and all of Lexington, Tennessee, ever knew. The one true barbecue: a hog, slow simmered over hickory coals and ash, its flesh and fat and skin primed for the cleaver and chopping block after twenty-plus hours. Bathed in smoke and massaged by fire. He served five, ten, as many as two dozen hogs a day, every day but Sunday, sometimes running out of fresh meat for chopped barbecue sandwiches well before noon.

Ricky couldn't say for sure how many hogs he'd prepped since 1976, when he began tending the pits at Scott's Barbecue, the year Early Scott took the thirteen-year-old boy on as an apprentice and, eventually, son. It was immediately clear to Scott that no one could smoke hogs like Ricky. He was a pitmaster, body and soul, born to the rough trade. He would master pit, fire, and hog. Shovel, sauce, and spice. He would master barbecue. The young Ricky could remain on his feet for twenty hours straight: cleaning the pits, stoking the fire, shoveling coals, smoking hogs, serving customers. And the customers liked Ricky: courteous, handsome, a bit wild. Dedicated to finishing the job and doing it well, Ricky would eat standing up—"I eat on the run," he liked to say—and rarely if ever slept for more than three hours a night. Sleep didn't come easy when you were cooking with live flame. He'd close his eyes and experience terror-filled dreams of his pit catching fire, his hogs rendered inedible, the Henderson County Fire Department arriving too late to save his smokehouse, which now lay a conflagrated heap of charred timbers and sheet metal. Ricky would rather stay awake to watch the fire.

His eating and sleeping patterns, or lack thereof, remained constant through the summer of 2008, when I first watched Ricky Parker smoke a pig. At first sight of him—slender and gangly, his skin bronzed from working in close quarters to fire—I questioned how he could possibly find time even to dress himself, energy enough to shave that perfectly sculpted Van Dyke beard. Three hours of sleep and working like this? How can he be standing? How can he be alive?

But Ricky assured me that this was all a part of the whole-hog pitmaster's life. He repeated a boast that he recited to just about everyone who came to interview him: "I got to buy four or five pair of shoes a year. I do a lot of walking, a lot of pacing." He told me that he was married to his work more than he was to his wives, past and present. He spoke in self-mythologizing tones. He was special, an original, a dying breed. For all he knew, he was the last of the great pitmasters, a man who strove to smoke as many hogs as humanly possible.

Ricky counted sleep in hours and shoes in pairs, but, above all else, Ricky counted his life in hogs.

Annually, beginning with my first visit in 2008, I'd make a pilgrimage to eat Ricky Parker's barbecue. Each year, as I ate my chopped pork sandwich, he'd tell me about a future date circled on his mental calendar: July 4, 2013, the holiday weekend over which he aspired to cook one hundred whole hogs. One hundred! Hardly an arbitrary number crudely culled from a beer-fueled backroom bull session, but the apogee of human achievement. The age of modern Methuselahs. In sports, the most notable of statistical achievements. One zero zero. A symbol of perfection. One hundred pigs. One pitmaster's dream. Three digits' worth of whole hogs. A century of swine.

Ricky Parker knew with some certainty that no pitmaster, living or dead, had ever reached that number. Through a complex formula of weather data, gasoline prices, hog futures, and unemployment rates, Parker calculated that 2013 would be his year. He could stop counting hogs after this achievement. He could slow down, ease into retirement, pass the pitmaster's shovel off to his son, Zach. He might even learn to sleep.

But until then he would keep on cooking. Because no one could smoke hogs like Ricky. No one worked to make barbecue like this anymore. Few cared like Ricky Parker, the world's greatest pitmaster, the man who counted hogs to keep both himself and barbecue alive.

CHAPTER 1

Hungry

I make my stand upon pig.
—CHARLES LAMB

*T*hough I was born and raised in the South, I grew up entirely barbecueless. My birthplace of Lafayette, Louisiana, the hub city of Cajun culture, occasionally harbored a franchise chain out of Texas or Tennessee, but none endured for very long or, for that matter, served up any meat that any self-respecting Texan or Tennessean would deem to be quality barbecue. Louisianans, especially those in Cajun country, are a people raised on the hog but not barbecue. A few links of boudin, a pork, rice, and spice-filled sausage, best eaten still warm while sitting on the hood of your car or truck, is my favorite snack. We consume plenty of cured pork products, like tasso, andouille, and smoked sausage. Although it's a disappearing custom, Cajun families still gather for a harvest-season pig slaughter and curing called a *boucherie* that, accompanied by music, dancing, and too much alcohol, extends over a weekend. Elsewhere in Cajun country, men roast suckling pigs, called *cochon de lait*, or "pig in milk" in French, a rite of spring in a handful of small towns.

Growing up in the suburbs, I hazily remember seeing a barbecue pit in the backyard of my family home, not that it saw much use. Neither of my two dads, my birth father nor my stepfather, fired up the Weber for a Sunday rack of ribs, much less to char-grill a hamburger. Not that my two brothers and I were raised on a meat-free diet. Because my mother managed a steakhouse, we were a beef family, spoiled with the riches of steak. I worked as a busboy at her restaurant throughout my teenage years, and, on a whim, I can still conjure up the scent of seared steaks sizzling in pools of molten butter, as if the essence of beef had seeped into my skin.

Throughout my college years, while living in New Orleans, on several occasions en route to concerts or to visit friends, I detoured through hellish Atlanta traffic for Styrofoam takeout trays of charred and fatty bones from Fat Matt's Rib Shack. Later, and further afield, I road-tripped to the Hill Country surrounding Austin with the sole intent of tasting a half dozen or so sausages and beef briskets, each more fat capped and smoke ringed than the next, to round out a gluttonous vacation that was very nearly pleasurable enough to make me consider moving to Texas. Eventually, I moved up to New York for a graduate degree and dined at Blue Smoke, a posh Murray Hill–area restaurant that covered the breadth of the nation's barbecue cultures, complete with a complementary wine list.

For me, barbecue, in all its forms, existed as a vague notion. Real barbecue truly remained a mystery, lingering, like smoke, at an intangible distance. But in the summer of 2008 I traveled throughout Memphis recording oral histories—capturing the narrative histories and the personal stories behind the food—as a freelancer for the Southern Foodways Alliance, a University of Mississippi–based organization devoted to, as their mission states, "documenting, studying, and celebrating the diverse food cultures of the changing American South."

I saw this documentary project as an opportunity to connect with my southern roots.

———

So there, in Memphis, I consumed as much barbecue as I could find: twice, three times, and, at least once, five times in a single day. I gnawed on the famous dry-rubbed ribs at Charlie Vergos' Rendezvous, the downtown grande dame of barbecue restaurants. I snacked on barbecue nachos alongside college students at the crowd-pleasing Central BBQ. I guiltily gulped down a terrible chopped barbecue sandwich at an indoor shooting range, where Second Amendment advocates took practice shots at paper targets printed with the face of Hillary Clinton. I ate all the only-in-Memphis specialties: barbecue rib tips, barbecue bologna sandwiches, barbecue Cornish game hens, and barbecue spaghetti.

By the time I left Memphis I liked barbecue—certainly didn't love it—and had eaten enough of the stuff to think that I understood it. To riff on T. S. Eliot's "The Love Song of J. Alfred Prufrock," I had known smoked sausages, briskets, porks; I could measure out my life with plastic sporks. The art of barbecued meats seemed simple enough, I thought: meat meet heat.

But it was on a trip beyond the city to Siler's Old Time BBQ in Henderson, Chester County, Tennessee, that I realized that, concerning barbecue, I didn't know a damn thing.

I arrived at the barbecue house just in time to catch the yellow, rust-worn Chevy pickup back into a gravel-lined gap between the kitchen and the pit house. A single pale-pink trotter stuck out of the truck's bed, pointing accusatorially at the driver and the concealed-carry weapon permit sticker on the back window. Ronnie Hampton dipped out of the cab and ambled toward me. He wore a camouflage baseball cap sunk low over half-open eyes and crooked nose, his tongue steadily rolled a toothpick, and he seemed to exist in a perpetual state of drowsy awareness that only old dogs can channel. He ignored my presence, my wide-eyed ogling of his truck's cargo, and unlatched the tailgate to reveal three hogs stacked and shrink-wrapped in glossy black contractor-sized garbage bags. They looked so much like body bags—three Mafia-dispatched corpses ready for disposal in New Jersey's Pine Barrens—that I had to remind myself that this was just barbecue.

This is just barbecue.

Except it was not the sort of barbecue I recognized to be barbecue: a rack of ribs smoking on the Weber grill; licking sugary sauce from sticky fingers; baseball, backyards, and the Fourth of July.

This was an animal. Still bleeding, though just barely.

I leaned in closer. Amidst a pile of spent Gatorade and beer bottles, a spare tire, and a length of weed-whacker twine, each body bag—imperfectly wrapped, or perhaps too small to hold the carcass—spilled out its contents of flesh and fat and blood. The hogs had been split along the spine, their internal organs and heads removed. The flabby neck meat, remaining attached to the right-side shoulder, hung flapping like a massive, fatty tongue against the truck's bed. Raw meat met rust. Sanguinary fluids merged with a decade's buildup of grease, tar, and mud.

There's a reason geneticists and other biotechnologists believe that surgeons will soon be harvesting organs from genetically modified pigs for human transplantation: inside and out we are very much the same. These poor pigs looked remarkably human.

Alive and breathing just a couple of hours ago, the hogs still radiated heat, adding unwanted degrees to an already steamy July morning. The flies had arrived before I did, buzzing back and forth between the skin—patchily jaundiced and cantaloupe mottled—and the exposed flesh. Feasting.

Chris Siler came bursting out of the kitchen's back doors with a knife in hand. The new owner of Siler's Old Time BBQ, here in Henderson, Chester County, Tennessee, was as lumbering as Hampton was whip thin. Under a black chef's apron he wore a red T-shirt and a pair of bright blue Wrangler overalls with oversized pockets.

Dragging the first hog to the tailgate's lip, Siler tore open the plastic wrapping. With the pig on its back, he used his left hand to pry open the cavity. Wiping the sweat from his face, he then gently ran the blade, sinking no deeper than an inch, along where the animal's backbone—now split in two—once united and divided the animal. As he reached the hog's midsection, streams of blood began issuing from some unseen wellspring, pooling in one side of the curved rib cage. This pig had been alive earlier this morning. Sweat dripped from the tip of Siler's nose and forehead, commingling with the blood.

He grabbed a trotter, and concentrating on his knife work—biting his tongue between teeth and lips—he rotated the blade around the midpoint of the hog's four feet, marking superficial circular incisions into the skin. Ronnie Hampton reentered the scene, his black-gloved right hand holding a reciprocating saw. He had Siler's five-year-old son in tow.

This was the exact moment young Gabriel came to see. As his father held down the hog's bottom half, Hampton began grinding away at the front-left trotter. The saw spat out bone, blood, and sinew. Gabriel skipped around the truck, screaming, laughing, delighting in the joy of another pig getting made ready for the pit.

He stopped to tell me—taking the lollipop from his mouth—that he could not wait until he was big and strong enough to lift a hog.

The saw and the meat, combined with the promise of smoke and fire, did more than excite a version of southern exoticism within me; these rituals unlocked a deeply held memory. I was instantly and quite uncomfortably put in mind of my mother, who, in one of my earliest recollections, I can see slashing through a short loin with an electric band saw. Her thriving steakhouse—this was before the days of pre-packaged, Cryovaced steaks—cut the following day's quota of New York strips, filets, and rib eyes. When any given employee became a no-show, my mom took up his position, even if that meant being the butcher. It was brutal, violent work, not maternal in the least. The next fifteen minutes went by in the blur and whine of the saw blade. By the time Gabriel had stopped reveling in the rendering of pig flesh, twelve disembodied trotters stood macabrely piled in the truck's bed. I was sickened. I was thrilled. I was hungry.

I walked inside to order a barbecue sandwich.

The dining room of Siler's was a jumble of southern stereotypes, minus the rusted tin sign advertisements, worn farm equipment, and other vintage bric-a-brac that define the Cracker Barrel aesthetic. There were stacks of Wonder bread buns piled high along the painted cinder-block walls, a plastic plant in each corner, and squeeze bottles full of barbecue sauce on every table. On the walls, inspirational Christian curios mingled with pig iconography and family photographs. The Ten Commandments hung over the cash register. Most of the clientele had long passed the minimum AARP age, but that would be appropriate as Siler's Old Time BBQ was Henderson, Tennessee's last authentic barbecue joint and one of the last surviving wood-cooked whole-hog pit houses in the entire South.

I paid for my barbecue sandwich and took a seat at the table, brushing a sesame seed from the red-gingham-clothed table.

My sandwich appeared as a grease-slicked, wax-papered parcel speared with a toothpick. I unwrapped the barbecue bundle to find a rather sad-looking plain white hamburger bun leaking what appeared to be ketchup. Disappointed by what aesthetically amounted to fast food rubbish, I rotated the wax paper clockwise to get a look at the sandwich's backside. There, teasingly poking through the two halves of bread, was a single, sly tendril of meat. Tossing the top bun aside, I uncovered a baseball-sized mound of mixed white and dark pork: thick, ropey strands of alabaster flesh curling serpentine around chunks of smoke-stained shoulder, some pieces of which still contained black-charred bits of skin. It was all smothered in a heavily pepper flecked coleslaw containing little else but chopped cabbage and ketchup.

Using my hands, I started forking the meat into my mouth. Each bite seemed to reveal a different part of the pig. I could discern, with tongue and teeth, the textural differences between the soft, unctuous belly meat and the firm, almost jerky-dry shoulder. The slaw added softly alternating rushes of sweet and heat to each smoke-tinged taste.

In Memphis I had eaten barbecue more times than I'd like to count, but this was the first time I truly tasted barbecue. Every bite transported me to a South I partially recognized but had never really known: a porky place, a swine-swilled space, a region where barbecue was "ever so much more than just the meat," as the southern historian and journalist John Egerton once penned. I was tasting history, culture, ritual, and race. I was eating the South and all its exceptionalities, commonalities, and horrors—a whole litany of the good, the bad, and the ugly. Everything I loathed and everything I loved about the region I called home.

This was not just barbecue, this was place cooked with wood and fire.

As I took another bite, while rolling this possible connection over in my mind, Chris Siler joined me at the table. "I've been doing barbecue for a few years now," he announced by way of introduction, but also a testament to his expertise. He warned me that he talked too much, which he proceeded to do, not that I minded.

He grew up in the type of southern town where you know your history and won't ever forget your last name—Silerton, the smallest incorporated town in Hardeman County, little more than a farm hamlet of a hundred or so residents, where, as he described, "they're all kin to me one way or another." It was in those lean years following the Civil War that two sets of four brothers, eight Siler men and their accompanying Siler families, set out from Siler City, North Carolina, to resettle in the timber forests east of Memphis. They followed a previous generation of Carolinians who had trekked to west-central Tennessee following Andrew Jackson's Native American removal policy. There, Silers begat more Silers. Eventually the Gulf, Mobile and Northern Railroad showed up, hungry for hardwood lumber. But it didn't take long for the timber trade to dry up, the woodlands laid bare. The Silers traded forestry for hog and cattle farming.

Chris Siler was not born on a farm, he made sure to emphasize, but "in between farms." His father long ago left the family trade to open an auto body shop in the nearby town of Bolivar, but still felt it important to expose the young Siler to the farm life, or, as he termed it, to "lease out" his son. He'd pasture the cattle: separating calf from cow, keeping the land evenly grazed. For two weeks each winter he'd have to clean out the dairy barn—"the really nasty downside" of it all.

The dividends from working on his uncle's hog farm far outweighed those of the dairy. In the fall they would slaughter a hog. The hind legs would be sugar-cured and hung in the family's old-fashioned smokehouse—honey hams for next year's holiday season. The hand-crank grinder took care of the rest. "They would line me and my cousins up and every one of them would take a turn until their arm gave out." Two to three days were spent grinding the shoulders, loin, and belly; spicing the meat with red pepper; stuffing casings and forming homemade sausage links.

The whole time during our interview he exuded a buzz of boundless, youthful energy, politely excusing himself from the table to greet customers, fix sandwiches, herd his two young children away from my tape recorder, and warmly direct his employees. He appeared able to do all of these duties and more within just a minute's time. This energy was matched with a serene religiosity. He hinted at a trouble-filled past—drugs, alcohol—and a born-again redemption. Now thirty-three years old, with a family and a business, he felt imbued with a purpose to serve barbecue and thank the Lord every day for the opportunity.

After I finished my sandwich, he jumped up to grab me a taste of what he called "a happy accident," his latest experiment in sauce making. He returned holding a square tray laden with a pair of massive, fatty, meaty pork ribs. "I had a goal when we opened up that I was going to change the ribs. I wanted something that would make our ribs stand out where it would be something that people would want more. Instead of just going back to using our regular sauce, I just decided one day I was going to get back here in the back and take a mixing bucket and see what happened." He started throwing ingredients in his plastic bucket: spices, vinegar, those elements found in a traditional barbecue sauce. Because sauces in West Tennessee are sugary, he needed some nectar. He wanted something different but familiar, a punch of sweetness that embodied this place and himself. Instead of reaching for the jug of corn syrup from Piggly Wiggly—the staple cheap sweetener for barbecue sauces across the nation—he sent an employee to C&R Grocery, the little country store and gas station across the street, to fetch a gallon of locally produced sorghum molasses. "When I got done I had something that I really liked, and I cooked a rack of ribs and gave it away as samples and, you know, we had people standing at the counter sucking on the bone." Rib sales had nearly doubled since he changed the sauce recipe.

Golden lacquered, with meat separating from bone, the ribs looked so sticky, I got the feeling that if I looked at them too hard, my eyes would cement shut. They emanated a multidimensional perfume of rich sugars and that earthy medicinal funk common to sweet sorghum. This was not the syrup some southerners drizzle on their morning griddlecakes, according to Siler, but an industrial-strength molasses, colored "nearly black. Very, very, very dark. Too dark and too thick to sell by itself. At room temperature it's almost solid."

This guy, these ribs are gonna be famous, I thought to myself. This approach—taking a locally sourced historical ingredient and pairing it with a conventional recipe—went beyond ordinary barbecue. This was some cheffy, Culinary Institute of America–trained, forward-type thinking, without any hint at trend surfing.

"It's very expensive to make because of the sorghum," Siler said. "They make a year's supply in the month of September. Now I'm out, and I've done run the country store across the road out, so I'm trying to get ahold of them to see if they had any leftovers still put up."

Just in case, I swiped my finger across the surface of the paper tray until I had licked the plate clean.

———

Siler led me back outside. On the path to the smokehouse, he nodded toward his pitmaster, the man he referred to as his "full-time cook," and sighed, "I wish I could find a way to pay him more." Ronnie Hampton sat in quiet repose on an upturned tree stump, staring at a boisterous fire, smoking a cigarette.

Two rows of waist-high cinder-block-formed pits lined each side of the building. Siler lifted up a thick black plastic tarp that covered a sheet of metal corrugated roofing material, together acting as the pit's makeshift lid. He then delicately removed three stacked cinder blocks, one by one, like dislodging oversized pieces from a game of Jenga, to reveal a bed of coals. The sinuous aroma of pork filled the structure, mixing with the sound of dripping fat sizzling on coals. He crouched down to show me how the hogs rested skin side up on a metal grate welded together to resemble a slatted bed frame of sorts, hovering over the fire. He pointed to four shovels leaning against the wall, the pitmaster's tools of the trade.

Siler explained that well before loading the hogs onto the pits, Hampton had, using a mixture of hickory and oak wood for fuel, started a pair of fires in two overturned oil drums, burn barrels, just outside. Then, with the hardwoods burned down to charcoal, the pitmaster had spread a bed of cinders on the floor of each pit. His work really swung into gear with the hogs finally loaded in. Over the first hour and a half, he "fired" the hogs every thirty minutes. Then he shoveled load after load of coals every forty-five minutes until the fat started dripping. And every hour after. The entire smoking process took twenty-four hours.

Here in Chester County, this was the way "everybody has always done it," Siler said with pride. "Sticking with the old way, people like that."

Chester County was the perfect location for a whole-hog barbecue culture to develop. It was a place where "we were only completing the work that our fathers had begun. . . . We had just one money crop—cotton," as local memoirist S. E. Reid characterized the agriculturally focused existence of area residents during the late nineteenth century. "We didn't make much of a living," he wrote. "We just breathed." A tiny rural farming community, surrounded by even smaller agricultural outposts (like Silerton, located a dozen or so miles to the southwest), the town of Henderson acted as the county's central hub, a locus where farm families could gather, eat, celebrate, and just breathe.

And there was not a more natural place to breathe the sweetly loamy Tennessee air, no finer spot to get off the farm without escaping the farm, than this grove of hickory and oak trees off a bend on the rural highway. This was getting out of the country to get into more country. Here, stretching back over 150 years according to Siler, farm families—sometimes more than a thousand individuals—converged to smoke hogs over hardwood coals in earth-dug pits. Most of the attendees of these weekend barbecue jubilees were kinfolk by blood or marriage. The men stayed up—restlessly talking, carousing—past midnight and into the morning, shoveling fire. Fifty-gallon cast-iron kettle pots brightly simmered with sauce. The next day, they would feast under a pavilion while enjoying the fruits of their labor. "You hear people tell stories of things like that," Siler said. "I just have heard people talk about when they used to cook here."

These are the stories that still circulate over chopped barbecue sandwiches among old-timers here, the unrecorded history of Henderson and Chester County, the legend that informs the name of the restaurant: Old Time BBQ.

In the real old times, way before Old Time, a real brick and mortar restaurant was eventually built in the hickory and oak grove. Established in the 1960s, Nobles Barbecue reputedly would sell on average sixty to eighty whole hogs a week. After tracking down Pat Nobles Jones, the niece of founders Glenn and Dorothy Nobles, to glean a bit of the long-shuttered restaurant's history, she told me, "Everything's different, hon, everybody's dead." She pronounced this last word with three syllables, "day-ee-da," as if to emphasize just how very dead everybody was. "You could've gotten lots and lots of information from them." I had arrived too late. "Honey," she told me, "that's almost a thing of the past."

Almost.

But with a little prodding, everyone, I have found, has a barbecue story. To paraphrase Faulkner, barbecue's past is never dead; it's not even past. "You could smell that barbecue, it just smelled so good," Mrs. Jones remembered. "Many cars would just stop because they would smell—it's sort of like smelling yeast bread cooking, it makes you hungry for a piece of bread. Same way with that barbecue, that hickory chip burning, you smell the pit, you know, the open pit." She continued without my prompting. "It's some good memories of back then, where you'd just pull in at an unusual hour and just hoped that the hogs were ready. But you know, you could count on those men. If they tell you what time it be ready, it would be ready. They had it down to a true art. They didn't need a clock, they just knew."

I asked Mrs. Jones who did the cooking, for there always must have been someone to cook the hogs. Their names came pouring out of her memory. There were the Crowes, Jerry and Leon. Charles Stovall helped out around the pit and might still be living, she said; must be around eighty-five years old. These men, like Hampton and Siler, were all white. But there were, working at different times, two African Americans, Bill Howard and Pic Massengill. The names of these and other pitmasters, black and white, had all been largely forgotten to history. They cooked dozens of hogs a week. Each month these men fed thousands of customers who, more than likely, did not even know their names.

For an indeterminable amount of time, one of these men was Ronnie Hampton. He had worked these same pits on and off for eight years at least, maybe a decade, likely much longer. No one could agree on the exact number of years. It might be said that Hampton transcended time. He was the pitmaster here; he had always been the pitmaster. He first started working for Bobby Sells, when the place was called Bobby's Bar-B-Q. Sells sold the business to his son-in-law, a Baptist minister named Chad Sellers, who maintained the name and the pitmaster. In early 2008, after a half-dozen years selling barbecue, Sellers passed the business on to

Siler, his former store manager, and moved his wife and five children to Nepal to help spread the Gospel. Through each sale, every change in ownership, Ronnie Hampton stayed on.

Several times throughout my day at Siler's Old Time BBQ, I glanced back at Hampton and considered asking him a few questions. But after twelve hours, I had not heard a word from the man, had not witnessed him open his mouth except to exhale cigarette smoke. I guessed it would have been easier to get a hog to talk than Ronnie Hampton. With the pits maxed out, nine hogs to cook with shovel after shovel of fire and coals, it felt like I would be trespassing on not only the pitmaster's time, but his meditative state. When not stoking the pit or the fire, Hampton remained stationed a few feet from the burn barrels. Each of the repurposed oil drums had seen such an infinitude of infernos that they were contracting, collapsing in on themselves like two terrestrial black holes. I never saw him eat, I never saw him consult a watch. An internal clock seemed to drive him each time to take up his shovel.

I left without talking to Hampton, but something stayed with me from that day forward. With a belly full of barbecue, I departed Siler's unsated, hungry for sustenance of another kind. I would seek out the last of the whole-hog pitmasters, in hopes of hearing a story or two about the one true barbecue.

CHAPTER 2

The Ballad of Ricky Parker

The whole hog is the perfect blend of barbecue: every little bit of the animal can be consumed in a single, decadent, maybe even gluttonous bite. "You got a little bit of everything," Ricky Parker liked to say. Ricky gave the world his all by providing everything the pig had to offer. This is what made the offerings of Scott's Barbecue distinctive: this everything, the very wholeness of whole-hog barbecue itself.

It may seem self-evident, but it is this "everything" that provides the whole hog with its name. Except for the head, trotters, and guts, the entire pig is smoked and roasted to become the whole-hog barbecue. The first written appearance of the phrase "whole hog" occurs in a small slice of verse, "The Love of the World Reproved; or, Hypocrisy Detected," by the eighteenth-century English poet William Cowper. In the first lines of the poem, the Islamic prophet Muhammad (here, "Mahomet") issues his decree declaring that his followers abstain from pork.

There is a part in every swine
No friend or follower of mine
May taste, whate'er his inclination,
On pain of excommunication.

Muhammad's command confuses his people. Exactly which unholy part was the Prophet referring to? And if that forbidden fruit was to be determined, could the rest of the animal be consumed? After a debate, Muhammad's followers decide to put the controversy to a taste test.

But for one piece they thought it hard
From the whole hog to be debarr'd,
And set their wit at work to find
What joint the prophet had in mind.

Some chose the hog's belly, the others its fatback. A few brave eaters noshed on the head, while some were content with chewing on the pig's tail. Eventually, the whole beast is consumed, and the fools "eat up the hog" only to all become, as the reader well knows, sinners in the eyes of the Prophet.

Cowper's tale is satirical to the point of cross-cultural blasphemy, but it is also a bit of sleight of hand: in the poem's second half the poet offers the reader a deeper commentary on the human condition. No matter what church or belief system we belong to, we are told to "renounce the world," to shun material possessions, to avoid a life defined by the trivial. But each and every one of us picks his poison. One person's hobby or obsession might be considered the most mortal of sins to a friend or neighbor:

While one as innocent regards
A snug and friendly game at cards;
And one, whatever you may say,
Can see no evil in a play;
Some love a concert, or a race,
And others shooting, and the chase.

We hate and love, denounce and follow our passions and one another, until, little by little, according to Cowper, "the world is swallowed."

The world of whole hog drew me in, consumed me, swallowed me whole, just as I would swallow the worlds of Chris Siler, Ricky Parker, and many others to come. I would consume many a pig, just as a customer at Scott's Barbecue could eat up the hog.

Ricky Parker's menu offered two sizes of wax-paper-wrapped sandwiches—regular and jumbo—alongside barbecue sold by weight (priced at $7.50 per pound when I first visited) and stuffed into a paper tray decorated in red and white gingham. Ordinarily, the meat arrived cleaver-chopped to a medium coarseness. But whether delivered by bun or tray, the barbecue could be ordered crudely hacked, finely minced, or pulled, straight no chaser, from the hog.

Depending on one's tolerance for heat, the barbecue could be dressed with sweet, mild, medium, and hot homemade sauces, all made fresh by Ricky Parker. Most locals ate their sandwiches topped and dripping with coleslaw, which came in two varieties: the standard mayonnaise-heavy version, called white slaw, and a red variant made with ketchup and vinegar. Sandwiches could be further tricked out with fat rings of raw Vidalia onion.

Scott's sold a few varieties of potato chips, often stocked some fried pies made by a John Gordon from his house up the road, but there were no other sides except baked beans, which were burdened, in the best way possible, with heapings of barbecued pork.

Smoking whole hogs allowed Ricky to provide eaters with any edible portion of the pig; in addition to portion sizes and spice levels, customers, as if peering through the window of a butcher shop's display case, could select their individual cuts to get the taste and texture they wanted. At Scott's, one could eat a different barbecue sandwich every day of the week. The combinations and permutations were near limitless.

For example, a customer could request the wetter, fleshier meat from the inside of the shoulder, or the crusty exterior bark charred by flames. One could go even deeper, literally, into the very heart of the pig, to demand the meat from the undersides of the ribs, or the rib bones themselves; the jowly flesh nearest the neck, or the delicate tenderloin. Cuts could be mixed and matched—a pulled part from this, a chopped bit of that—to imagine the perfect sandwich.

Over a ten-minute stretch perched at Scott's lunch counter one summer afternoon I witnessed the full range of possible orders. Through the Plexiglas window that separates the meager prep area from the dining room, customers shouted rapid-fire lists of ingredients and techniques, combinations that ranged from the mundane to the extraordinary, the unusually healthy to the distressingly heart hazardous.

A quarter pound of plain barbecue, please.

Regular barbecue, white meat, extra chopped, no fat.

Jumbo, dark, pulled with a lotta fat on it, mayo slaw, extra hot.

Occasionally, a customer would drop terms that reminded me of the so-called "secret menu" at In-N-Out Burger, a West Coast fast food chain where a rabid fan base fetishizes an in-the-know lan-

guage of keywords and food hacks. At Scott's, these orders sounded foreign, like they could not possibly come from a pig.

A medium middlin'. Or, even more bizarre: You got any catfish today?

Middlin' is what most people commonly refer to as bacon, the fatty underside of the hog, which earned its vernacular nickname for its location at the animal's midsection. The catfish is a rarer cut of swine, a six-by-three-inch strap of meat embedded under the tenderloin with the shape and fleshy shade of a catfish fillet and arguably the most tender part on the hog, a dozen times more succulent than the meat from those fishy mud dwellers for which it is named. Because a pig only yields two sandwiches or so worth of this cut, customers were known to leave Scott's empty-handed and hungry if they couldn't fulfill their catfish fix.

But there would always be another opportunity for a bite of catfish tomorrow, another shot at the big score. Or the next day. Or the day after that. Or never, if you didn't ever arrive early enough, say well before the noontime surge. "Root, hog, or die," the adage goes: fend for oneself, fight for sustenance and survival, or starve. There are only so many parts on a pig, only so much barbecue in a whole hog. Root, hog, or die.

———

Ricky Parker stood slight of frame. Lanky and rail thin, he looked no larger than the hogs he lifted each morning onto his pits. But the pitmaster, like his barbecue, contained multitudes.

Ricky defined his own mythos. To hear him tell it, his life resembled an as-yet-unwritten country and western song: "The Ballad of Ricky Parker." And though he didn't like to sit down and pore through the particulars of his life, once he began spilling his own

history, he would talk like he walked: fast and out of control. I never knew which of his stories to believe—dates changed, details popped in and out of each telling. It became clear that the trauma that went hand in hand with hard living was a matter of course.

He was born in Memphis in 1962, to a sharecropping family that crisscrossed the country with the seasonal harvests. Joe and Callie Parker dragged their five children from apple orchards in Michigan to wintertime Florida orange groves and back again. Ricky remembered picking fruit with his sister and three brothers for a few hours before the opening school bell rang and returning to the fields after class. He was bred to work, he told me, born to run. The family settled in Lexington, Tennessee, the seat of Henderson County, an agricultural town situated exactly halfway between Nashville and Memphis along Highway 412. At the age of thirteen (sometimes he said sixteen), Ricky walloped his old man with a baseball bat while defending his mother from another round of liquor-fueled abuse. Ricky returned from school the next day to find his belongings on his family's front porch. He escaped across town and took what jobs he could get: bagging groceries, mowing lawns, pumping gas.

At the Morgan's Service Station he was discovered by Early Scott, a former school bus driver who fifteen or so years earlier traded a pair of yellow buses to his brother for Scott's Barbecue. Scott was a rowdy man, a man with a third-grade education who was driven to drink and prone to violence and bizarre behavior. He once sliced a man clear across the belly for attempting to steal a twenty-five-cent bottle of Coke. Because he did not believe in banks, he'd absentmindedly bury jars full of cash—fifteen thousand here, twenty thousand there—around his barbecue restaurant's property and would often resort to hiring guys with metal detectors to root out the mislaid loot. Still, Scott was an honorable man to work for. A man with no

children of his own who might have been searching for a son to take over his barbecue business. "It's time to put the boy to work," Scott told Ricky's dad, who, after the beatings and neglect, was still the boy's father. And Joe Parker complied. No one said no to Early Scott.

Ricky grew up a typical child of the 1970s. He loved karate and was known to be an eight-wheeled speed demon at the roller rink. A photograph from the era shows Early Scott, portly and proud, grouped with his wife, Dorothy, and two unnamed workers posed in front of his restaurant. All four smile for the camera. Off to the left side, separated from the group, Ricky, wearing those oversized, tinted early eighties-style glasses, looks uncomfortably shy. He stands with his hands pressed deep into his pants' side pockets as if he could find some deeper truth hidden there.

This photo was taken before he grew out his signature Van Dyke beard. Before he started smoking Swisher Sweets cigars. Before the marriages, kids, and divorces. Before the obsessive work hours. Before being the man he would become, he worked nights and week-ends at Scott's Barbecue, an assistant in the pit house, while attending Lexington High. He couldn't try out for the baseball or basketball teams, missed just about every party, and couldn't score more than a second date because he did nothing but sweat and toil for Early Scott. He quit school just three months shy of graduating. It was then that Scott, his mentor and adopted father, told Ricky that he had learned enough about learning. Now he would learn about life.

But birth fathers are hard to forget and even harder to forgive. Ricky installed the same baseball bat that he used to whoop his dad and win his freedom on a wall of the pit house, visible only to him, where it would hang as a totem, a mythological reminder of what came before. It was as if he were the reincarnation of Sheriff Buford Pusser, the Tennessee lawman made famous in the *Walking Tall* films, who patrolled McNairy

County, just thirty miles from Lexington, often fighting vice and crime with just the aid of a baseball bat. Over time, saturated by years of smoke and grease, Ricky's own bat would turn from its natural ash-wood grain to a lustrous black, like a shoe polished to a mirror's sheen, so glossy that it appeared to glow amid the darkness of the pit house.

A first-time spectator could mistakenly judge Ricky's hog-cooking method to be as simple as throwing fatty meat on a fire. But just an hour in his smokehouse made it clear that Ricky's apparent primitiveness was as deceptively simple as the three-chord blues. From the sow's litter to the crafting of his sauces, Ricky had systematically mapped and quantified every step of the process.

Unlike just about every barbecue establishment throughout the country, whole hog or not, Ricky did not buy his pigs at market or barn sale. He didn't rely on a packing company to deliver his meat by refrigerated truck or run down to the local slaughterhouse and say, "Gimme a two-hundred-pound hog." Ricky knew his hogs from the moment they were born.

I asked him what kind of hogs those were.

"Pacific pigs," I heard him say.

"Pacific pigs?"

"Pah-cific pigs."

I couldn't believe what I was hearing: he imported his hogs from the West Coast? Maybe whole hog wasn't so locally defined.

"Where do you get them?" I hesitated. "California?"

Ricky rolled his eyes and repeated what he'd been saying this whole time, but now really vocalizing that first S sound: "Spah-cific." It turned out I was just dumb, unused to hearing Ricky's vibrant West Tennessee accent.

"I've got a certain type of boar and a certain type of gilt," he explained as if illustrating the birds and the bees: one pig prized for his muscle content, another for her fatty marbling. Together with his trusted hog farmer, Roger Gill, Ricky had tinkered with the genetic makeup of his hogs until settling on a half-Duroc, half-Yorkshire breed that delivered a rather lean 3 percent fat content—thus providing the optimum yield of sellable meat—while still furnishing a sufficiently blubbery three-quarter-inch fat cap along the hog's back. Ricky's careful consideration of hog anatomy was a thoughtful reaction against the historical entanglements of the American hog industry. Three decades earlier, when he began working in the pit house under Early Scott, barbecue-ready hogs weighed in with a 10 percent fat content. But since 1987, the National Pork Board began marketing their product as "the Other White Meat," fulfilling nationwide demand for a more flavorful alternative to chicken and turkey, while keeping the cholesterol levels at a minimum. To sate the consumers' demands, commodity farmers and wholesalers genetically reengineered the American hog to achieve a fat content nearing zero. Whole hogs became more wholesome.

The average Roger Gill–farmed hog weighed in close to the 300-pound range when nearing only its sixth month on the planet Earth. A quarter or more of that total live, or "on the hoof," weight would be lost on the slaughterhouse floor, with the removal of the internal organs and head, leaving a carcass with a "hanging" or "tag" weight of approximately 200 pounds. Edible meat constituted about 70 percent, or 150 pounds, give or take, of that carcass, minus the skin, bones, and cartilage. But that raw flesh, its protein-packed cells brimming with water and other liquids, would literally boil off most of its weight throughout the long cooking process. Thus the original tag weight would yield only 30 to 40 percent after roasting, or about 70 pounds of sellable meat. Other whole-hog pitmasters made do with smaller pigs, often tagged in the 150-pound range.

I asked Ricky what it took to reverse engineer his pigs to get to that 3 percent fat yield that made them so marbled, meaty, and colossally grand. "Well, that I can't say," he politely demurred, before implying that it was a secret blend of supplements added to the hogs' corn-based diet that packed on the pounds.

He was more forthcoming with most other aspects of his trade. Only hickory wood heated his pits: skinny three-foot-long planks— tossed-off barrel staves, I would come to find out—that he bought from a sawmill in nearby Savannah, Tennessee. It took just over half an hour to burn a four-by-six-foot pile of hickory planks down to coals and ash, ready to heat the hogs. He used a long-poled shovel to scoop the incinerated hickory from the fire pit, just steps outside the smokehouse, and deposit layer after layer of the fiery fuel source under the hogs, all the while making sure to disperse the embers flat and even across the pit floor.

Those pits looked like most any other I've come across: a simple cinder-block construction, built waist high and running the length of the room. Inside the two rows of pits, thick steel bars, spaced every six inches, formed a latticework to hold the pigs over the void. He insulated the top of the pits with vast sheets of corrugated cardboard, like refrigerator boxes but sturdier, thicker, and heavier, that he had made to order from a container manufacturer down the road. After exhausting every last ember from the fire, he'd begin to cover the pits with the corrugated slats, none of which were large enough to completely cover a single pit, so he'd arrange them, layer upon layer, to form a sort of jigsaw puzzle made from cardboard sheeting. When finished, only faint whispers of smoke escaped, coiling around certain joints and corners among the tangled mass of cardboard. Though he had no thermometer with which to measure, he knew that the pit's internal temperature would hold steady at around 225 degrees.

Without having sat through a single physics class, he could more than untangle the basic principles of thermodynamics, atmospheric pressures, and beyond, without the benefit of timers, thermometers, or other instruments. He called this common sense, but few pitmasters have ever understood the science behind barbecue like Ricky Parker. He could explain the insulation strengths of cement blocks versus corrugated cardboard; expound on the occurrence of air pockets and drafting within his barbecue pits, and their effects on smoke; and illustrate how dips and surges in external temperature, humidity, or precipitation would affect the time it took to produce a perfect piece of meat.

But there was another tool, an unquantifiable know-how, in Ricky's pitmaster skill set: patience. Despite his limitless energy levels, the pairs of shoes he wore out each year, and the number of hogs he'd cook over a lifetime, Ricky's livelihood was defined by a capacity to ease, and never rush, his hogs to doneness. If each of us on the planet Earth is capable of something greater, imbued with and defined by an extraordinary talent—a superpower, even!—that allows us to achieve something bigger, this was Ricky's: the ability to oppose the slowness of time. When watching Ricky, it was almost as if the faster he ran, the quicker he hustled about the pit house, the slower the minutes turned to hours and dusk turned to dawn. His hogs might have cooked for sixteen, eighteen hours in real time, but in Ricky time those hogs might have been immersed in smoke and heat for twice that amount. He could do the work of four men, could squeeze two evenings into one, and could coax more smoke out of a piece of hickory wood—one day he might even fit one hundred hogs into a weekend!—but he would never tire, never lose patience.

This is what made Ricky a true master of the pit.

CHAPTER 3

The Once and Future King of Barbecue

There are no ideas in the South, just barbecue.
—PAT CONROY

The route from west-central Tennessee to the birthplace of barbe-cue roughly follows a straight line across the two-thirds girth of this country's southern belly. Interstate 40 leads east through Nashville and Knoxville, jogging up and over a snaked path into North Car-olina and across the Great Smoky Mountains to Asheville, where the road unsnarls and the elevation dips from such great heights that the Appalachians seem able to wash into the distant, unseen sea. But out of the mountains the highway gently plateaus into the Piedmont region, and I feel safe when the first town name I see is named Hickory. I imagine that I can almost smell the barbecue, even though I know that there couldn't possibly be good barbecue, real barbecue, in a town called Hickory. That would be too easy. So I drive on.

Still hungry, I speed past the old tobacco cities—Winston-Salem, Greensboro—that have been rendered smokeless by a cigarette industry that had dried up and moved to sunnier climes farther south. Past Lexington, where the people eat chopped hickory-smoked pork shoulders, damn fine barbecue, at a handful of establishments. But not what I'm searching for, not whole hog. I split Durham and Chapel Hill, pursuing the interstate to Raleigh, where I continue farther east on US 264, which cuts hard, narrow, and flat through the new riverine-soaked landscape. Looking out from my car's windows, eastern North Carolina opens up: all thickset piney woods and verdant farmlands flashing by in harmonic tableau. Despite the best intentions of the lofty pines, the land here is dead level, unhesitantly horizontal, ideal for the cultivation of large swaths of tobacco, cotton, and soy. Perfect for baseball, for carving outfields into the farmland, instead of paving over for basketball courts as they have done in the university towns just west. And suitable for swine farming, for the large-scale production and eating of pig meat.

I first drove this route in late November 2011 several years after wrapping up my Tennessee barbecue project. My colleagues at the Southern Foodways Alliance pitched a documentary survey of North Carolina 'cue. Waist deep in writing a dissertation and with its deadline fast approaching, I initially resisted. What did barbecue have to do with my study of nineteenth-century Creole literature? Not much—nothing, in fact. But there was a craving, a hunger both gastronomical and intellectual. What is out there in North Carolina? Would there be whole hog?

I signed up for a month on the road.

For companionship and to share driving duties, I invited my friend Denny Culbert to join me. An Ohioan turned Louisianan who would soon marry my best friend since childhood, Denny is a gifted photographer. He also loves to eat. We made a perfect pair.

For transportation and housing, my parents loaned me their brand-new Solera RV, which we goofily christened the Barbecue Bus. Our home on wheels kept us out of questionable interstate exit motels, but most campgrounds and state parks were either out of our budget or closed for the coming of winter. So we resorted to the scenic parking lots of Walmarts, many of which permit free and relatively safe RV overnighting.

Covering the state from west to east, we ate our weight in barbecue, grew sick on smoked pork. After just four days on the road, locals would often follow us with their noses before stopping to inform us that we "smelled like barbecue." Pork grease and wood smoke had soaked into our clothes, our hair, our bedsheets. We woke up each morning in a different town but the same damn Walmart parking lot. I vowed when we were finished to never again eat barbecue.

But since that first visit to North Carolina, I've retraced this route four times, from my home in New Orleans to the flats of eastern North Carolina, a two-thousand-mile round-trip pilgrimage that I endeavor to make each and every year. A journey into the heart of barbecue.

Crossing into this other Carolina, I tick off town names like mile markers: Zebulon, Middlesex, Wilson, and finally Farmville, the gateway to Pitt County. As home to three of the country's last dozen or so whole-hog establishments that still use wood, smoke, and fire, Pitt County, North Carolina, could not be better named, for it is the literal and spiritual capital of whole-hog barbecue. This agriculture- and livestock-rich region serves as a bastion, or pit, as it were, where the nation's oldest vernacular barbecue tradition has been slowly smoking for nearly two centuries.

Arguably America's most revered barbecue joint—whole

hog or not—is a half-hour spin from Farmville, outside down-town Ayden and down a series of two-lane rural highways that bisect uninterrupted fields of leafy soy. As you approach from the south, a half mile down the road, glinting silvery white in the noonday sun and just barely visible through a small copse of trees, rises the great shining beacon of barbecue: the dome of the "Bar-B-Que Capital of the World." Constructed of wood and aluminum, the cantilevered cupola is campily modeled after Washington, D.C.'s own congressional building, complete with an American flag perched at the pinnacle that flutters in the wind borne across an adjacent field of shallow-plowed collard greens growing thick and yellowed like tobacco leaves. A bold architec-tural element that crowns an otherwise characterless redbrick and metal-roofed building, the capitol dome signals that I have arrived at the Skylight Inn.

————

Four tenets, each as serious and sacred as Holy Scripture, govern the Skylight Inn. Each item in the Skylight credo is painted in bold capital letters on a large wooden billboard that stands in the shadow of the capitol dome. Listed at top, the Skylight Inn, and by proxy its hometown of Ayden, North Carolina, is THE BAR-B-Q CAP-ITAL OF THE WORLD. Moving clockwise, the second reads that the men of THE JONES FAMILY are this capital's founding fathers and statesmen. Third, the Joneses are UPHOLDING A FAMILY TRADITION OF WOOD COOKED BAR-B-Q SINCE 1830. And finally, IF IT'S NOT COOKED WITH WOOD IT'S NOT BAR-B-Q. The tenets circle a simple stenciled portrait of an unsmiling gentleman in a 1950s-style pom-padour and wide-lapelled shirt, who is identified as PETE JONES, BAR-B-Q KING.

Chefs, restaurateurs, and other denizens of the culinary realm have, for better or worse, long promoted the Great Man theory of history, a nineteenth-century idea that men—charismatic, intelligent, and heroic men (think Napoleon, Washington, and Churchill)—have governed with such authoritative power that one could say they've helped sustain the Earth's orbit around the Sun. Same, perhaps to a lesser degree, goes for chefs Bartolomeo Scappi, Alexis Soyer, Paul Prudhomme, and David Chang (not to mention Julia Child, Madhur Jaffrey, and Alice Waters), who have each altered the course of what we cook and how we eat. But nowhere in America do the great culinary heroes stand taller, are more lionized, than in the barbecue business. These great pitmen and masters transcend space and time by breaking from their limited, not to mention provincial, spheres of influence to become first regionally renowned, then nationally and internationally worshipped. Though many are long gone, their faces still peek out from menus, highway billboards, and franchises. They are men become legends, the true kings of barbecue: John "Big Daddy" Bishop, Arthur Bryant, Louie Mueller. And in the annals of barbecue, where there are hundreds of self-styled Barbecue Kings, Pete Jones—his legend earned, self-made, or shaped simply by the fact that he wrestled with the world that is whole hog—just might stand an inch or two taller than the rest.

Most all Ayden locals know and recognize the world's barbecue capital only under a single name. Ask an old-timer directions to "the Skylight Inn, please, sir," and you will likely be met with a genial wink and smile before being gently guided to Pete Jones Barbecue (no possessive needed, just those three nouns sand-wiched together as if it were his full and proper name). If you've stopped a more surly sort of local, he might even throw out the last part and give a short and sharp "Pete Jones" while pointing the way.

Back in 1947, as Pete Jones worked to finish framing the roof of his planned barbecue house, a small plane buzzed overhead, circling in for a landing at an adjoining airstrip. The pilot told the nineteen-year-old Jones that an exposed section of the building's interior, visible from between the sheets of uninstalled plywood roofing, looked like he was building a barbecue shack with a skylight. And though, from the beginning, family and friends questioned Jones's judgment, the moniker stuck.

The audacity of naming a pit house with a fancified and incon-gruous name like the Skylight Inn likely struck Jones as good business sense. It was an inn in the traditional sense: a rustic road-house, located along a travelers' highway, that offered food, drink, and respite. On the menu besides barbecue there were hamburgers, hot dogs, and beer. It was close quarters, with bar stools and a jukebox—not "even room for a good fight, to be right honest with you," according to Samuel Jones (Sam to his friends), the Skylight's daily operational manager and grandson to Pete.

Without fail, the legend of Pete Jones Barbecue begins and ends with the story of the capitol dome and the "Capital of Barbecue" slogan. Family members, customers, and print sources by the hundreds, if not thousands, have told and retold the same tale: In the late 1970s, *National Geographic* sent a reporter and photographer on a cross-country trip to discover America at its most authentic. While searching for eastern North Carolina's best barbecue, they stumbled upon the Skylight Inn, their own personal Shangri-la, where they tasted smoked swine so sublime that they declared it "the Bar-B-Q Capital of the World." Its secret discovered and broadcast to the world, travelers started making the hour-plus long detour from I-95, and the Skylight Inn's business soon skyrocketed, a success that Pete Jones commemorated several years later by enlarging the kitchen, adding two extra dining rooms, finally adding air-conditioning, and erecting the capitol dome.

In reality, Thomas O'Neill and Ira Block's reportage, published by the National Geographic Society in 1980 as *Back Roads America: A Portfolio of Her People*, speaks volumes more to the commercial acumen of Pete Jones and the process that goes into the making of a barbecue king. One mid-spring morning, after finding a highly recommended barbecue joint in nearby Farmville closed, O'Neill and Block traveled to the outskirts of Ayden to find the Skylight Inn. There, writes O'Neill, Jones "welcomed me as if I had reached the final destination of a pilgrimage. 'You've come to the right place,' Jones said. 'You don't need to look any farther.' Whereupon he reached into a box and presented the hungry traveler with a white shirt that read, 'AYDEN, BAR-B-Q CAPITAL OF THE WORLD,' and on the reverse, 'THE WOOD MAKES IT BAR-B-Q.'" It could always be said of Pete Jones that the man knew how to sell barbecue and sell himself.

Born Walter Bruce Jones a year before the Great Depression, Pete grew up in an agricultural-based life and economy that had already experienced a decade of downturn due to an overreliance on growing cash crops—cotton and tobacco—instead of farming food. The Joneses were area pioneers and landowners in a land of sharecroppers and tenant farmers. His mother, Josie Dennis, descended from a thriving barbecue dynasty. Her father, Bill Dennis, and brothers, Emmett and John Bill, each ran his own barbecue businesses in town, while her great-grandfather Skilton Dennis is said to have started the region's, if not the nation's, first whole-hog barbecue trade in 1830. From an early age, Pete liked to say that barbecue was in his blood, and under the tutelage of his uncle Emmett, he learned the craft of his mother's family. Pete was a slight man with small hands—as a baby, his mother called him Little Bo Pete for his diminutive size, and soon no one ever called him anything but—yet he was able to manage the weight of the hogs and control the fire beginning at the age of seven. A dozen years later, he managed to convince his father to let him build a barbecue restaurant across the street from their homestead, on a pretty plot of family farmland. A few years into running the Skylight, he married his sweetheart, Emmy Lou Pierce, in the front seat of his car, with the pastor squeezing in to perform the service and each of their mothers present to offer their blessings from the backseat. Pete Jones was always in a hurry to get to work.

The barbecue business remained the heart, but hardly the sole moneymaker, for Pete Jones. He was gifted with a knack for turning his hobbies into profitable ventures. He sold flowers by the roadside, farmed tobacco, and had a pilot's license (hence the airstrip next door); he bred and sold a wide variety of animals—exotic fish, chickens, hunting and field trial dogs. For decades Jones owned racehorses that ran on tracks throughout the country, but he was always too busy to watch them in competition (though he most certainly showed an interest in the prizewinning purse that a horse could bring his way). He had only a third-grade education and, likely due to dyslexia, his wife would have to read his business contracts to him, but the man knew how to make money. His parents raised him "as a work object," according to his son, Bruce, "not a child that was loved." Or, as his grandson Sam tells it, Pete Jones "could trip over a stick and there'd be a hundred-dollar bill under it." There were always new ventures—new sticks to stumble over—and more money to borrow to support his hobbies and his family, so Pete Jones never bought wedding bands for him and his wife. He never took Emmy Lou and his two children on vacation. It wouldn't be right to treat himself while indebted to others.

But he did show up at his barbecue business—seven days a week, from six in the morning until two the following morning—wearing his standard uniform: collared shirt, dress pants, and a white apron. He would stand behind the counter, taking orders and exchanging small talk with not a one. Business was business, and customers were customers. Pete Jones wasn't one for chitchat, he didn't want to talk crops or the weather; he only wanted to turn his barbecue into cash: "What size plate do you need: small, medium, or large?" Throughout the day, he would take short breaks, during which he'd walk to the far end of the short counter and smoke

Camel cigarettes. Only then would he make time to talk hunting and fishing with his friends and regulars. Later, when health code regulations forbade smoking near food-prep areas, he'd accept his docked letter grade while telling the health inspector that he'd keep the Camels around because "tobacco built this business."

Of course, it was the barbecue that Pete Jones cooked and served that truly built his business. The method is simple; there are no secrets. Split hickory and oak logs are burned down to embers. Those coals are shoveled under whole hogs that rest butterflied on metal rods, skin and fat side up, lined snout to tail, snout to tail, snout to tail on the pit, single file, like fallen toy soldiers. The hogs' exteriors are moistened with water and rubbed with salt. As they cook, the liquid lard is siphoned off and collected, destined for the next day's cornbread. Smoked overnight and through the next morning, the pigs, their meat and fat rendered into a luscious golden brown, are flipped onto their backs for a final hour of cooking, during which the skin swells, blisters, bubbles—or "blows," in the local pit-speak—to form a crackling-like consistency.

Most everyone associated with the Skylight Inn describes the process using the word "nothing"—as in, There's nothing on it. There's nothing in it. There's nothing to it. This is nothing fancy. But there is something to be said for nothing.

And nothing definitely becomes something when that smoked meat is prepped before serving. This is the theatrical denouement of the Skylight's whole-hog technique, when the meat is not pulled, not slivered nor shredded, and certainly never tartared. Rather, with two finely honed cleavers, a three-inch-thick sugar maple butcher's block, and a whole hell lotta sweat and noise, the chopper—and that is his official title—does exactly that: hand chops smoked meat into barbecue.

The chopper chops and spices a hog quarter at a time (alternating between shoulders, the greasiest section, and the drier hams), tenderly tenderizing while vigorously massaging the meat into uniformity, a medley of quarter-inch-sized morsels of muscle and fat and crisped skin. His station is located dead center: set back behind the serving counter; underneath the neon-lit Pepsi-sponsored menu, and picture-framed in white trim. The chopper's setup, not to mention the racket he produces, makes him look not unlike a DJ confined to his booth. Finished, he pushes the final product across his board to an adjacent chopping block to add to the small hill of chopped and spiced barbecue ready for serving. Sometimes, during the onslaught of a lunch rush, the barbecue mound reaches the chopper's chest. The message is clear: chopped whole-hog barbecue is the Skylight way. "Every time that cleaver hits the board, it's like another guarantee of fresh barbecue," Sam, who manages the Skylight, told me. The chopping is also a performative spectacle that, at first turn, seems out of place in this humbly diminutive, sparsely decorated, Savior-praising, family-owned and -operated restaurant in the backwoods of North Carolina. When the chopper is on break or has chopped all of the meat, it feels like something is missing from the dining room—like a birdless sky. There is a deafening silence.

Most every lunch shift, the chopper on duty is Mike Parrott, a sharply metal-looking dude—all angles and elbows, tattoos and spiked facial hair—who is as distant as possible from the southern working-class aesthetic of the Jones family. While on the clock and at the butcher's block Parrott wears earphones, streaming heavy metal and classic rock, which completes his look, while providing a drum rhythm to replicate with knives and chopping board. Holding a pair of cleavers, he looks eminently dangerous. But he talks and, especially, laughs, cackles really, in a soft, nasally midwestern accent that draws people in. He's the quiet drummer from your favorite teenage heavy metal band; the guy who could rage behind his drum kit for forty-five minutes before returning to a state of offstage placidity; the one whose name you don't remember, or never knew.

The music coming from his earphones on this visit was deafeningly loud—it sounded like early Metallica. "I try to keep the rhythm going," he told me. "Make it a little entertaining for the public out there." His cleavers were recently custom-made: the spines of each steel blade a few inches longer, the handles a cool gunmetal black. *Thwock . . . thwock . . . thwock . . . thwock . . .* Parrott's chop began as a tough rhythmic staccato before sonically morphing into a steady drumline beat *tak . . . tak . . . tak . . . tak . . . tak . . . tak . . .* and finally *takka . . . takka . . . takka . . . takka . . .* into a full-on rave-up. As he pounded out a drum solo, I watched as he chopped a side of pork into shape, but not without a good amount of loss: within minutes my reporter's notebook was splattered in meat drippings, Denny's camera lens was greased with fat. "He always goes off the deep end," Sam Jones said of his best chopper. "It's never kiddie pool with him." Parrott likes performing for a crowd: the meat and knives and ersatz drum solos—the chopper's role is built for him, a role that would not be possible without the demands and display of Skylight barbecue.

Pete Jones liked to describe his business as nothing more than "four walls and barbecue." Whether a customer came from down the road or downtown New York to eat this barbecue (and most every day finds residents from both coming to dine), Pete Jones Barbecue should strike everyone as being, in the words of a favorite family adage, "as country as cornbread." But the Skylight Inn's clever affectations—the capitol dome and the window-framed chopper—betray and reveal a greater truth about barbecue in general and whole-hog barbecue in particular. And that is this: barbecue is all about the spectacle.

Knives down, Parrott picked through the once-chopped meat, sorting out and discarding veins and gristle and flecks of bone. The "bad stuff," he called it, the nasty, tough, and too chewy; the indigestible parts that "you don't wanna eat." Now with a single cleaver in hand, he scraped the last gelatinous bits and membranous tissue from the interior of the hog quarter's skin, then flipped the pig hide right side up, its surface crisp and puffed from the application of searing heat on the pit, its color caramelized to slightly blackened. The pigskin rang with the sound of shattered glass under a light stroke of the cleaver's blade, splintered into a smattering of shards. A few light chops reduced any remaining pieces to size. Incorporating the skin into the meat, he gave the fold a second quick chop, priming the meat to be sauced.

The Skylight Inn does not use a barbecue sauce, that often tomatoey, syrupy, spicy-sweet condiment that most Americans associate with and serve atop and alongside their smoked meats. Here the meat not only speaks for itself but boastfully asserts its historical import and culinary prominence in a stubborn East Carolina drawl. Akin to how a four-star restaurant like Le Bernardin extols its own straightforward preparation and flavoring of fish (just salt, pepper, oil, and heat), only spice and vinegar enhance the wood-smoked meat. Each chopped quarter is sprinkled with a handful of salt, then a fistful of black pepper. There are no written recipes, measuring cups, or calculations; instead the chopper is chef: knowledgeable, trusted, and mostly always right in his apportion of spice. Next come splashes of White House brand apple cider vinegar and

Texas Pete, a Tabasco-esque cayenne and vinegar hot sauce that, despite its name, hails from North Carolina. Both are poured from plastic gallon jugs, arms held high, the liquids cascading like twin waterfalls into the meat. The chopper then used his two blades like paddles to mix the shoulder and ham, spice and sauce. From quarter side to the final mix, the whole process takes about twenty minutes. "The main thing," Parrott believes, "is to just make the first piece taste like the last piece. You want the whole season to be beautiful."

This is the magic hour, when spice meets meat, ambrosia melds with nectar—when smoked and chopped pork becomes barbecue, when barbecue transcends its own simplicity and becomes simply beautiful. When nothing becomes truly something.

My order of barbecue arrived in a medium-sized paper tray printed with the standard red on white gingham pattern and overflowing with chopped meat. A thin slab of dense, unleavened cornbread rested flat on top of the barbecue. And on top of that, a slightly smaller tray filled with a pale-green, mayonnaise-heavy coleslaw. This all came stacked and swaddled in a rip of wax paper and capped with a plastic fork stuck through the top, so that when I finally sat down and anxiously folded back the paper to unwrap the stack of meat, bread, and slaw, it resembled both the precursor to and the perfected version of an ice-cream sundae.

I dug in.

Bruce Jones, the present-day co-owner of the Skylight Inn— a title he shares with his cousin Jeff Jones—also preaches full-time as a Baptist pastor. Round in the face, with ears nearly as prominent as a sow's, he is a carbon copy of his father, Pete

Jones, and a man as dedicated to his church as his father was to his barbecue. From the age of four or five he was drawn to the pulpit, announcing to everyone that he wanted to be both a cowboy and a preacher when he grew up. "I ain't got no problem with you being a cowboy," his father would reply. There was no money in the ministry. Besides, Pete Jones was not a churchgoing man; he even kept the Skylight open on Sundays, an affront to the sensibilities of just about everybody in town. But at seven, Bruce stepped in front of a speeding car along the highway that separated the family home from the Skylight. After Pete Jones found his boy facedown in the road, and before the doctor told him that his son would not live to see the sun rise, he spoke to the gathered few: "If anybody in this crowd knows how to pray, would you pray for my boy?"

The accident caused Pete Jones to stop guzzling beer and roughhousing. He canceled plans to open a dance hall behind the Skylight. He closed his business on Sundays, reserving the day for church service, morning and night. On turning twenty, Bruce Jones answered his calling to become an ordained Freewill Baptist preacher, but he never stopped working at his father's barbecue place. From his pulpit at the King's Crossroads Original Free Will Baptist Church, Pastor Jones remains, as stated in the church's literature, "an old fashion preacher who preaches old fashion morals, standards, convictions and the old time religion from an old fashion KING JAMES BIBLE." Reading these words during a Sunday-morning service I attended reminded me of the Skylight's emphasis on antiquated barbecue techniques. In fact, it soon became difficult to separate the warm and charismatic pastor from the man, clothed in a simple red apron, who served me barbecue just the afternoon before. He preached on hell and preached on sin and, on this Father's Day, he made me cringe when he spoke at length about the obligatorily subservient position of women in the Christian home. He compared traditional gender roles to the ingredients in his wife's biscuits—"All things work together for good"—but all I could think about was how well each bite of barbecue, slaw, and cornbread worked in combination. Each mouthful met and melded tastes and textures: spice with a vinegar pucker, the creaminess of mayo with the fattiness of pork, crackling skin with the welcome dryness of the cornbread. Standing at his wooden pulpit Pastor Jones looked no different, at least from my viewpoint while seated in the farthest row, than the chopper at his butcher's block.

A week later I asked Bruce Jones if he had to decide between the pit and the pulpit, which profession he would choose. He looked at me as if I had just blasphemed the name of God and said, "It wouldn't be a choice." But, he continued, "I was still raised by my dad, who said when folks came through that door, they were looking to see a Jones. And I believe that."

The Joneses of Ayden, the sons and daughters of the Bar-B-Q King, are true believers. Believers in the Baptist Church, in Jesus Christ as Savior, and the Bible as the infallible Word of God. But it is their unwavering faith in the righteousness of another, thoroughly unholy trinity that speaks to their passion for barbecue, a passion that may best be described as fundamentalist. Wood smoke, chopped hogs, and vinegar: this is barbecue. As defined by the Jones family, throughout eastern North Carolina, and across four centuries of American history: this is barbecue. "By definition, in the dictionary, barbecue is the whole animal cooked over hardwood coals," Sam Jones, Bruce's only son, explained. "And so we take the pig, in that respect, and make what our family just truly believes is how barbecue ought to be." That's all there is to cooking Jones-family barbecue: belief rooted in history and tradition.

Belief, however, as many a thinker has told us, at best will often lead to self-deception and at worst down the road to fanaticism. From Ayden to Los Angeles, Brooklyn to Little Rock, every pitmaster believes that his barbecue is just how it ought to be. But the Jones men claim historical precedent, law laid down centuries ago to form a true and definitive definition of barbecue.

For proof, to find an answer to the question, What is the essence of barbecue?, we could turn to the etymological experts. And sure enough, the *Oxford English Dictionary*'s entry for "barbecue"—from the Spanish *barbacoa* and the Haitian *barbacòa*, but not, as was once frequently alleged, the French phrase *barbe à queue*, or "beard to tail"—defines the noun as "1. A rude wooden framework, used in America for sleeping on, and for supporting above a fire meat that is to be smoked or dried. 2. An iron frame for broiling very large joints. 3. A hog, ox, or other animal broiled or roasted whole. 4. a. A large social entertainment, usually in the open air, at which animals are roasted whole, and other provisions liberally supplied. b. A structure for cooking food over an open fire of wood or charcoal, usually out of doors, and frequently as part of a party or other social entertainment." The *OED*'s fifth and final definition—"An open floor on which coffee-beans, etc. may be spread out to dry"—seemingly works beyond the purview of barbecue as we know it but was most certainly the original meaning of the word *barbacòa* (sometimes *babeque*), used by indigenous Taíno peoples throughout the Caribbean. The first usage of that word in print, according to one scholar, appears in Englishman Richard Hakluyt's translation of an earlier chronicle of the Spanish explorer Hernando de Soto's Florida expedition (1539–40), which came across "a loft made of canes, which [indigenous Floridians] build to keep their maiz in, which they call a barbacoa."

That loftlike structure likely resembled a scene later witnessed by the artist and pioneer John White in present-day North Carolina. As the official cartographer of the first English attempt to establish a military colony on Roanoke Island (1585), White also painted a series of stunning watercolors of the Algonquian peoples and their practices. Among his paintings is *The Broyling of Their Fish Over the Flame of Fier*, which captures a pair of fish roasting on a lofted wood-framed grill, enveloped in smoke, and lightly grazed by the flames of a log fire beneath. Either the fish are huge or the grill is small; in the corner of the frame, a second pair of fish are propped upright with sticks to receive the flame, but they look as if they are standing on their tail fins, keeping watch over the fire. Though White frequently painted indigenous Americans, his depiction of this early barbecue includes no people at all, as if to say that this cooking method was a character unto itself.

During White's initial sea voyage to Roanoke, under the guide of expedition captain Richard Grenville, the ship's cargo included an unknown number of hogs. From Columbus to the Spaniards Pizarro, de Soto, and Cortés, and on to Englishman Sir Walter Raleigh, just about every New World explorer had a historical hand in the dissemination of pigs to various parts of the Americas. And not one of these European men could have comprehended the culinary transformations each would spark. In 1493, during his second voyage across the ocean, Columbus brought eight hogs— hand-picked from Canary Islands' farm stock—to Hispaniola (the present-day island shared by the Dominican Republic and Haiti). This island soon became a port of breeding, shipping, and receiving hogs: exporting the animal—mobile meat—across the Caribbean and eventually to the Carolinas. Colonial policy dictated that swine remain unpenned to forage for themselves, meaning that within a century, feral hogs propagated and overran large swaths of the Spanish Caribbean and the British Eastern Seaboard. By 1855, a Virginian could complain that "hogs swarm like vermin upon the earth." To prepare them, colonists used readily attainable ingredients (wood, salt, spices) and sustainable techniques learned from the locals (lofted grill, smoke, and fire). From Haitian *griot* to the *lechón asado* of Puerto Rico and elsewhere, each locale would come to define its own roast pork culture.

It didn't take long for North Carolinians to develop an affinity for roasted hog meat. "Pork . . . is the Staple Commodity of North Carolina," the Virginian statesman William Byrd wrote in a March 1727 journal entry detailing a tour amongst his neighbors and their appetites. "The Truth of it is, these People live so much upon Swine's flesh, that it don't only encline them to the Yaws [a type of pox], & consequently to the downfall of their Noses [it was suspected at the time that the overconsumption of pork could cause one's proboscis to collapse in on itself to resemble a pig's snout], but makes them likewise extremely hoggish in their Temper, & many of them seem to Grunt rather than Speak in their ordinary conversation." Byrd feared the possible degeneration of his own body and soul from subsisting on a monotonous diet of swine, while warning his fellow Virginians not to do the same. He described his backcountry host, one Captain Willis Wilson, "a great Lover of Conversation," as plying him with "Pork upon Pork" while retelling "the same Story over & over."

Thankfully, North Carolinians didn't share Byrd's feelings. From his era up until the present day, hogs have continually outnumbered humans in the state. Today, North Carolina ranks tenth in hog population (just under ten million), but second only to Iowa in swine production (over ten million per year). Though no quantitative analysis has been undertaken, outside of my unscientific survey of North Carolinian eating habits and dining options, Tar Heels undoubtedly consume more pork at more pork-centric establishments than any other state. Iowa may produce more pigs, but in North Carolina there is more power in pork.

For instance, try driving anywhere south or east out of Raleigh without spotting one of the countless roadside billboards advertising "America's Largest Pork Display," found at the one-and-only Nahunta Pork Center. Within a twenty-mile span, I counted a dozen signs, each featuring a cartoon image of the Pork King, a jolly fat pig wearing a bejeweled crown. En route to my first Skylight visit, that peculiar phrase—"pork display"—rattled in my brain just long enough to force my morbid curiosity to detour deep into the swamps of east Carolina, swamps deep and boggy enough to swallow a hydrogen bomb accidentally ejected from a B-52 in January 1961, a ten-thousand-pound thermonuclear weapon that remains forever lost and buried alongside a farm highway named Big Daddy's Road.

At the Nahunta Pork Center I found what must be the nation's, perhaps the world's, only all-hog, whole-hog grocery. I sincerely doubt that any radioactivity from that atomic bomb leeched into the area water supply and food chain to create gargantuan mutant hogs, but I could be convinced, because this pork superstore carries every imaginable part of the pig and then some—"everything but the hair," according to its owner. In addition to the innumerable selection of bacons, sausages, and hams, there are both neck bones and "extra meaty neck bones," fresh pigs' feet both whole and sliced. In the half hour or so I spent perusing the wares of Nahunta, the metallic hum of numerous electric band saws never stopped buzzing as the butchers steadily worked to fill grocery baskets and ice chests with the fruits of the hog. Stuck somewhere between the shelf of stacked lard buckets and the rib aisle, I decided to escape before I too transformed into William Byrd's worst nightmare and began to grunt rather than speak.

By the 1930s, a few years into Pete Jones's boyhood and a century after Skilton Dennis launched a barbecue business that would establish a wood-cooked legacy, Ayden, North Carolina, was known for its whole-hog barbecue. Sometime between 1936 and 1942, WPA photographer Lee A. Wallace captured a local pitmaster at work in a portrait he captioned "Barbecue being prepaired [sic] at Ayden N.C." Wallace composed the shot in a simple wood-framed smokehouse—its walls open, from shoulder height on up, to provide ventilation. In the foreground is a knee-high brick-and-mortar open-top barbecue pit, where three hogs—each about a quarter of the size of today's factory-produced porkers—rest cavity side up on thin metal poles. A broom leans against the far back corner, brush side up, behind a man who stands between it and his barbecue. The simple grill setup, smoke, and animal flesh harken back over three and a half centuries to John White's watercolor of fish on the Algonquian barbecue, but only now there is a man present, a human face to the barbecue trade. After the photograph was recently unearthed from a WPA photo album, the Joneses identified the man as Emmett Dennis, the man who first taught his nephew Pete Jones all he knew about barbecue. Beneath a haze of smoke and light that flares across the negative, Emmett holds a cigarette in his right hand and wears a crooked fedora, overalls, and a look—directed right at the camera lens—of curiosity and exhaustion.

More than seventy-five years later, Jones-family barbecue is, from all accounts, much the same as Emmett's in preparation, taste, and texture. Back when I first visited the Skylight Inn in November 2011, in all honesty, I didn't much enjoy my serving of barbecue. To be sure, their hog is less an acquired taste than an acquired texture. The meat is too finely chopped for some eaters, including, at first bite, myself. Detractors decry the meat as mush, baby food, pulverized and pounded into submission. I've heard it said that you don't need teeth to eat it. Other critics, most hailing from the Piedmont region of central North Carolina, where coarsely chopped shoulder barbecue reigns supreme, turn up their noses at the very nose-to-tail nature of whole hog itself. In the late 1970s, a Piedmont-area newspaperman wrote that "the trouble with the Eastern North Carolinians is that they don't respect the integrity of a succulent hunk of pork. They shred it. They pull it apart in the same lazy, careless way that they pick cotton. Then they usually make their barbecue too moist and mushy. The only chewiness remaining is in the tough and indigestible gristle that somehow escapes the cook's eye." Despite his partisanship, the writer had a point: no matter how long the chopper dutifully scrapes, culls, and scraps the cartilage, bone, and other unpalatable pieces from the meat, some nasty bits will always end up in the barbecue pile, and thus in the sandwiches and on the paper trays of customers. But at the Skylight, it's not what you want to eat, it's how much of it, as the Joneses are fond of saying. So I kept on eating the family's barbecue, during a second and third visit to the area, right on up until I learned to love the stuff.

I just kept on eating until it tasted not only right, but perfect. I now count myself among the true believers.

When Pete Jones died on February 15, 2006, at the age of seventy-seven, not a small contingent of regular patrons thought Pete

Jones Barbecue was finished, unable to survive the passing of the great man. Jones had kept on working until he reached the age of seventy-five, and quit only then after being laid low by a heart attack. Some customers griped that it just didn't seem right without old Pete Jones standing behind his counter. Others said the barbecue tasted different, or insinuated that it was only a matter of time before the family would switch to gas-cooking their hogs, if they hadn't already done so. Many stopped showing up for their chopped barbecue altogether. But, in the years leading up to his death, Pete Jones often threatened that this would happen, that the Skylight would shut down within six months once he left this earth—a not-so-subtle warning and challenge to his family, the inheritors of the business.

Those inheritors have stuck to one rule since the Bar-B-Q King was forced to retire in 2004: Keep everything the same. Co-owners Bruce Jones, Pete's only son, and his cousin Jeff Jones, son of Pete's younger brother and business partner Robert, today preserve the Skylight Inn as if it were still that moment when Pete Jones first set eyes on his brand-new capitol dome, silvery and bright with promise. They still buy their pigs from the same farmer and slaughterhouse that Pete Jones first entered into a relationship with more than forty years ago. The cooking, chopping, and spicing processes remain wholly unchanged. The menu—except for the addition of barbecue chicken available twice a week and a banana pudding that has long been a staple of Jones family gatherings—remains a constant: the trifecta of chopped pork, slaw, and cornbread. In the documentarian Joe York's short film *Capitol Q*, Jeff Jones, without a hint of irony, tells the camera that "we still serve it the old-fashioned way, in paper trays, like our forefathers did." Sam Jones, the Skylight's public face since his grandfather's passing, tends to be the most emotionally expressive among the Joneses when it comes to illuminating the family business. "We want to make sure that we always keep up history's tradition and our family's tradition of whole-hog barbecue: the way it started, the way it's always been in our family. We will never change that," he told me. "Not long as the Lord will let me breathe air, we won't never change that."

Born into a whole-hog dynasty, Sam Jones's lot in life was little, but that little meant a whole lot. Sam's daddy still tells him that he used to put barbecue grease in his milk bottle to ensure that he'd mature to become a barbecue man just like his grandfather, Pete Jones, the Bar-B-Q King. Bruce Jones had begun working at the Skylight Inn when he was just ten years old, but the king had other plans for his grandson. Go to school and find a career you love, he'd tell Sam, and use the barbecue business to fall back on. But when he was four years old and no taller than the ordering counter, Sam was asked by a local newspaper reporter about what he wanted to be when he grew up. "I'm going to be the barbecue prince," he beamed, "and a trash man."

Sam's first experience in charming the media would not be his last. On May 5, 2003, in New York City, he accepted the James Beard Foundation's America's Classics Award presented by Coca-Cola, a tongue-twister of an honor signifying that the Skylight Inn was, in the words of the esteemed culinary awards organization, "a locally owned restaurant with timeless appeal, beloved for quality food that reflects the history and character of its community." Months before, a foundation representative called the Skylight to inform the Joneses that they would be presented with a bronze medallion etched with the famed fleshy visage of James Beard—an accolade most every chef, restaurateur, cookbook writer, and culinary journalist identifies as the Oscar of the food world. Bruce Jones notified his father that he had "just won a fifty-cent medallion and they're wanting to know if you want to go to New York and pick it up." In their stead, they decided to pass and send young Sam to retrieve what was sure to be a worthless gewgaw.

He received his family's prize at a gala reception held in a Times Square hotel. Twenty-two years old, he had never before been to New York and was "as green as a gourd," he likes to say. Standing before an assembled audience of a couple thousand, he looked just like his daddy and his daddy before him. But with the spotlights bouncing off the sheen of Sam's tuxedo jacket, and cameras recording the event for a national broadcast, Bruce and Pete Jones would never have stood for this. Sam thanked the Foundation for the award, and the crowd of culinary celebs, aspirants, and hangers-on blissfully laughed at his syrupy eastern North Carolina accent. Charismatic but never pretentious, and always quick with a local colloquialism, he quickly charmed the crowd. That night Sam Jones felt as tall as his family's capitol dome.

It was a quick and unexpected turn of events for the self-proclaimed prince of barbecue. Working at the Skylight throughout his teenage years, he grew to hate the place. When something went wrong—some unseasoned barbecue or dry cornbread, an unhappy customer or careless employee—Pete Jones's son and grandson inherited the blame. It wasn't the many things the Joneses did right, it was the few times things went wrong that would occupy Pete's attention. And at fifteen, after a blowup with his grandfather, Sam walked away from the barbecue business. He worked at the local gun shop, graduated from high school, and fell in love. There was life after barbecue. He went to the local community college, majoring in business administration. A composition professor assigned a fifteen-page research paper written on any subject of personal interest. "Well, shoot," Sam remembered thinking, "I'm writing it on the barbecue place. Plenty of history there to fill up fifteen pages' worth." There was fifteen pages and then some: Ayden and the Dennises, Pete Jones and Texas Pete, wood-cooked barbecue and hot hog-grease cornbread. And the longer Sam spent interviewing his grandfather, and the more pages he wrote, the more it became apparent that the Skylight Inn was once and would once again become his own history. Just when he thought he was out, barbecue pulled him back in. By 2000, Sam was back where he belonged. He looked at his role at the Skylight Inn, he told me, "through a different set of spectacles." The Skylight was not a job; this was a family enterprise, a piece in the larger jigsaw that is barbecue and the American South. And he could be, in his words, "one spoke in the wheel of making it roll another mile down the road." This is how Sam Jones learned to stop worrying and love the hog.

But in the past dozen years or so since he accepted the James Beard award, Sam has kept that wheel spinning faster and faster. Preceding my most recent visit, he was in the midst of a seemingly never-ending tour that would send him coast-to-coast spreading the Skylight's whole-hog gospel. Just the first half of his year-long itinerary sounded like an old Johnny Cash tune: I've cooked everywhere, man. Smoked hogs everywhere, man. He'd cooked in Murphysboro, Charleston, Raleigh, New Orleans, Greenville (NC), Kinston, Winston-Salem, Atlanta, New York. And to come: San Francisco, Napa Valley, Greenville (SC), Las Vegas, Charlotte. Back home, Sam's life was no less hectic. He recently celebrated, with his wife, Sarah, the birth of his first child and, in January, made his reality television debut on a competition cooking show called *BBQ Pitmasters*. He also started a two-year appointment as chief of the all-volunteer Ayden Fire and Rescue Department. Who better to promote fire safety and save lives than a guy who works with live flames for his day job?

But Sam's whole-hog junket has not been without stress and strain. He had to quit drumming and singing in his gospel group, Men of Faith. He missed his first Father's Day to smoke hogs at the hippie-meets-hipster Bonnaroo Music Festival, where he cooked alongside several chefs with high-end destination-restaurant empires. His travels have kept his father from devoting more time to his ministry, as the pastor has wanted to do, while imperiling one of the Skylight's foundational tenets. There should always be a Jones within the four walls of the Skylight, Bruce told me— people expect it and Pete Jones enforced it—and Sam's travels threaten to upend this rule. "He's a hard worker, but Samuel is more of a manager than worker," his father told me. Prior to first hitting the road in 2011, "Samuel had cooked probably three pigs in his life," Bruce Jones continued, finding it difficult to hide his disappointment.

Sam Jones, like whole-hog barbecue, has reached a critical juncture. His burgeoning career, intertwined with the storied history of the Skylight Inn, serves as a window into the modern-day popularization, dissemination, and gentrification of a large and varied swath of barbecue (and not just of the whole-hog kind), Southern, and idiomatic American cultures. At the moment, he owns a zero-percent stake in his family's restaurant yet manages it and promotes it as if it were his and his alone. (Talk had long circulated of Sam opening his own barbecue house.) He's taken an age-old culinary practice and a sixty-five-plus-year-old family business and carried them into the twenty-first century without changing a thing. Now he cooks more pigs away from home than in the home pits, where much of the cooking is done by employees and his uncle Jeff. Though his grandfather might not have supported his road trip rambles, Pete Jones would recognize the barbecue Sam cooks as his very own. Arguably the best barbecue in the nation can only be found in Ayden, North Carolina, but it might be found in your neighborhood, just down the street, this very weekend. Sam has been given a stage and takes every occasion to climb into the limelight. "That window of opportunity might not always be there, is the way I look at it," he told me. "So while you got a seat in that car, ride it."

Lately, he's been sharing that ride with a wider circle of friends and family. He sees the opportunities that have come his way as representing something bigger than the Skylight, greater even than Pete Jones. For him, the Skylight Inn is synonymous with Ayden and vice versa. Over the first weekend of June 2013, I followed Sam to New York, where he represented the family business and his hometown at the tenth annual Big Apple Barbecue Block Party, a two-day smoked meat bacchanalia that draws an estimated 150,000 barbecue lovers out to Madison Square Park. It would be the Skylight's first appearance at the event, which brings in heavy-hitter barbecue establishments—though few whole-hog pitmasters—from across the country.

On this ride, he brought along nine buddies—though he only needed half that number for the job—to help him smoke, chop, and serve hogs just like they do at the Skylight Inn. And on the Friday night before the event, Sam's group sought shelter from a downpour brought by the year's first named storm of the hurricane season, Tropical Storm Andrea. I half expected any number of these men to revolt. Soggy, grouchy, and obliged to cook ten hogs in a half-dozen untested pits along a Madison Avenue sidewalk, in the most unkind of elements.

Each passing hour brought new dilemmas. The crew reported to their cooking station to find their fuel source nothing more than a heap of water-soaked logs, the hogs too rain slicked to grip and lift onto the pits. The time needed to smoke the pigs was swiftly slipping away. The night was going full fathom five. But like a ship's captain, Sam steered his men through the storm: feeding them, urging them onward, boisterously crooning along to the country tunes playing on the group's stereo, singing louder than the rain.

By morning, those hogs were cooked, chopped, and spiced the Pete Jones way. The next day, under the most beautiful of sky-blue skies, thousands of people lined up for their first bite of Skylight Inn barbecue. "We all had been on the mountain together, and down in the creek bottom together," he told me weeks later, reflecting on that night while sounding just like his preacher father.

––––––

Back in Ayden, before finally taking leave of the Skylight Inn, I noticed a new face stationed at the butcher's block. With two cleavers in hand, James Henry Howell attacked the meat with a relaxed form, a bebop chop that immediately brought to mind the great jazz percussionist Max Roach, who was said to be the first drummer to not just keep rhythmic time but to make music. The heat lamp that hangs above the chopper's station illuminated Howell's features like a spotlight: a crooked nasal bridge winding up to a thick, pulsing temple vein; long, graying sideburns leading up to a short-cropped Afro. Howell is the only African American employee I'd seen up to that moment at the Skylight. Nearly seventy years old, he told me that he's only been at the Skylight for a dozen or so years but has been employed by the Joneses, working on the family farm, for much longer.

After he chopped a half side of pork, I trailed Howell out of the kitchen via a back door (where a sign warns in blood-red block letters NO BONES UNTIL 5PM) and down a covered concrete walkway that leads from the main building and into the pit house. There, he shook a cigarette from a pack of All Natural Native 100s, a discount menthol brand, inhaled deep and tired, and, with no place to sit, leaned against a doorframe—Pete Jones always insisted that there be no chairs in the pit house.

After his cigarette, Howell walked to the back corner of the room, through a heavy refrigerator door, and into a walk-in cooler, where a dozen or more pigs dangled from gambrels. Vertically stacked belly to back, with heads still attached, they hung like ghastly trophies in the muted orange glow of the fluorescent tubes. He took one hog down from its hooks and unloaded the animal into a bright blue wheelbarrow, which he then pushed, with some difficulty, into the next room. A few feet from the pit, he stopped and hefted the pig onto his right shoulder. He shuffled over to the pit, grunting under the burden of a carcass weight that must have exceeded his own by at least seventy pounds. He somersaulted the mass with a booming *ka-thunk* of a thunderclap to rest belly side down on the pit's grill.

James lit another cigarette and let the doorframe absorb his weight once again. I was exhausted from just watching Howell work and stood a few feet away, watching him smoke cigarette after cigarette in absolute silence.

CHAPTER 4

The Prometheus of Pigs

We can learn to be cooks, but we must be born knowing how to roast.
—JEAN ANTHELME BRILLAT-SAVARIN

I could feel the heat closing in, could hear the pitmaster cackling with a rebel yell of a laugh, deep devilish cachinnations that reverberated from the opposite side of the pit house through thick clouds of gray and white smoke, almost tangible. He was working not twenty feet away, by the hearth and chimney, in an increasingly dense, burning acridity generated by a fifty-fifty mix of smoldering oak and pecan coals. Squinting through the haze, I could just barely make out the pitmaster's shimmering figure. Despite his bulk, he seemed to move fluidly, serpentine, with the smoke. Wrapped in denim and camouflage, he carried a long-handled shovel in thick hands.

The pitmaster disappeared again into the invisibility of fog. I heard the squeal of wire rope worming through a long-rusted pulley, a set of corroded hinges opening the trapdoor of one of three barbecue pits that I counted when I first entered the building. I could just make out two pigs on the grill, blurry in the sooty opaqueness of the air. After a few silent moments, I heard the tinny rasp of the shovel's steel scraping brick. Then an echo that resembled hard snow falling with a soft crunch on frozen ground. I recognized the sound as a shovelful of fresh charcoal dropped on slowly extinguishing cinders and ash. The pair of sounds repeated—scrape, crunch, scrape, crunch, scrape, crunch, scrape, crunch, scrape, crunch—a half-dozen times in all.

The rope rewound through the pulley's wheel, the hinges reset, the barbecue pit had closed but hardly sealed tight. A cloud mushroomed my way, enveloping me in an immediate storm of smoke. Blinded, sinuses leaking, throat seared, I choked for breath, lunged toward the only ventilation: a five-by-three-foot hole punched into the cinder-block wall containing an old belt-driven fan that seemed to be blowing smoke back into the room. The pitmaster laughed again, at me this time. It hurt so much that I laughed along.

The plumes appeared to form both a halo and satanic beard around the man's fleshy face. "You've just about stayed in here longer than anybody else," he roared with amusement before his Cheshire grin faded back into the cloud. But my time logged in the pit house, ten minutes in this smoke-filled hell, was too ludicrously brief to deserve any sort of commendation. It took less than that same amount of time for me to learn an important lesson in whole-hog cooking: smoke matters, and without it there isn't any barbecue.

A different set of hinges croaked and the pit house's spring-wound door opened into a rush of clean Carolina air. We stumbled outside, spasmodically gasping like fish beside a neatly stacked woodpile, cord after cord of split logs piled man high. The smoke continued to bloom around us, escaping from cracks in the doorframe. Minutes later, it still hurt. But I recovered quicker than the pitmaster, who remained bent over at the waist, knees in hand, sputter-coughing smoke from his congested lungs.

When not doubled over from smoke inhalation, Larry Dennis stood six feet something and was linebacker big. After having given up bodybuilding several years ago to run his family's restaurant full-time, his body evolved to resemble the animals he just put on the grill: not fat, but solid. Slightly pink hued and doughy, but brick heavy. He looked like a man you want cooking your barbecue. I've met dozens of pitmasters, and most, if not all, are professed God-fearing Christian men and women, churchgoing followers of Jesus. Larry was the only one who confessed to being a heathen. After a round in his smokehouse, I might agree, but I'd also counter that he's a devil who makes angelic barbecue.

After clearing the remnants of smoke from his lungs and composing himself, Larry leaned against a stack of wood, winked at me with a grin, and lit a tiny cigar.

Like the Skylight Inn's Joneses, their second cousins and cross-town rivals, Larry and his father, Latham "Bum" Dennis, occupy another branch of Ayden's famed barbecue clan. Tracing their culinary lineage back to the family's original barbecue recipe that Skilton Dennis popularized back in 1830, they also stake a claim to being the ancestral inheritors of the nation's first commercial barbecue business. But unlike the Skylight Inn, their establishment, Bum's Restaurant, has never enjoyed the media attention often bestowed upon its cousins in 'cue, and Larry has candidly described the rivalry as "one's for locals, the other's for tourists." But where the Skylight Inn advertises their generational ties to barbecue's past with a single billboard, at Bum's Restaurant, history is the main selling point, written on the walls (both of the restaurant and the pit house), the menu, and the T-shirts worn by each employee. At Bum's, whole-hog barbecue is living history.

I joined Larry in the main dining room at Bum's to ask about his family's place in the chronicles of whole-hog barbecue. We sat in his preferred spot, a corner booth where he whiles away the quiet hours between the lunch and supper rushes, resting while his pigs sizzled on the pit, and often reflecting on why he is tethered to the whole hog.

He posed the first question before I could even open my notebook. "I wonder when barbecue was invented?" Then he proceeded to answer his own query. "That's like the first meal man ever ate. It's got to be," he said. "The first cooked meal a man ever made, it was barbecue." He removed his black railroad-conductor-style hat. Cropped close to the scalp, his hair was dappled ashen gray at the fringes, making a striking contrast to his baby-faced features. "And then whenever they'd come out with salt, pepper, and vinegar, I'm sure they start putting that on it. That's probably like the first seasonings they ever come out with: vinegar, salt, and pepper. I mean, you know salt and pepper been around a long time. Salt been here forever."

Larry shifted his posture and leaned back to support himself against the wall, better to survey his restaurant-sized kingdom. Sitting opposite him, I followed his lead and stretched my legs out across the booth's azure-hued nylon seat cushion, a pop of bright blue that here at Bum's, all white clapboard walls and brown laminate tabletops, has always to me seemed strikingly out of place. Hanging above and behind my head was a pair of framed photographic portraits: Ronald Reagan posing in the Oval Office and a close-up of a young Bum Dennis in his naval uniform. Larry called over a waitress and ordered a Diet Coke and a bowl of freshly fried pork skins. I took an iced tea, unsweetened, and settled in to hear the Dennis family history of barbecue.

"It's been around a long damn time," he proclaimed in his tobacco-twanged rattle of a voice. "In 1900, if any human being cooked a pig, they cooked it with wood and seasoned it with salt and pepper and vinegar. That's what everybody done, there weren't no other way to do it. That was it!" He grabbed a handful of pork skins and, excited now, shifted his weight to again sit upright in the booth facing me. "So, if you can trace your family back to the early nineteen hundreds, then you can take for granted that it goes back five hundred thousand years. Five hundred thousand years ago, men started cooking with wood, and we just didn't never stop."

I asked if he was joking as I shyly nibbled on a crackling. I'd recently heard rumors that he enjoyed a tipple or two of illegal moonshine, together with whispers that Bum's had been passing off gas-oven-roasted pig meat for the real pit-cooked stuff, an offense some Carolinians would agree should be punishable with jail time. Was Larry bullshitting me? Was he really tracing the roots of whole-hog barbecue that far back, to the Middle Pleistocene era, a period when a handful of archaic humans roamed the wide earth alongside several now extinct species of pigs?

"No, I'm serious. It's so easy that cavemen actually did it. That's the way they lived. So it can't be but so complicated. It ain't damn rocket science," he asserted. "If they didn't do it, what did they eat? They woulda starved to death. That's all they had." That's all he, and the authentic barbecue tradition he maintains, still has: the caveman's instincts to cook a whole animal over a few armfuls of wood. Convinced by his own argument, he leaned back contentedly against the wall and wrapped up the first chapter in his history of barbecue: "I think it's two billion people still cook with wood every day, that's the only means they've got to do it."

"Where'd you get that figure?" I asked.

"I googled it once."

Several months later I too googled this statistic. In 2010, the United Nations pegged the number of people who still rely on the traditional method of using biomass (scavenged wood, charcoal, animal and plant waste) for cooking at 2.7 billion, accounting for 40 percent of the global population. Adding fuel to Larry's speculative fire, recent archeological evidence seems to suggest that prehistoric humans did, in fact, cook meat over fire. In 2000 researchers discovered the Qesem Cave, located high in the Israeli mountains seven and a half miles east of Tel Aviv, where they unearthed a centrally located hearth, containing flint tools, wood ash, and charred bones dating back three hundred thousand years. The hearth contained, according to the archeological team's report, evidence of "spatial differentiation of activities" including animal slaughter and butchery, food processing, cooking, and consumption. The researchers further surmised that the hearth was repeatedly used for large social gatherings, thus making it perhaps the earliest identified barbecue pit and the Qesem Cave the oldest surviving pit house. Larry was right. He cooks just like a caveman, as do nearly half the people on earth.

As anthropologists and historians continue to uncover the beginnings of barbecue, everyone from the lowliest pitmaster to the most militant barbecue blogger has an opinion on the origins of smoked meat. Like the rest of humanity, we have a yen for fairy tales; carrying and passing down barbecue creation myths is the carnivore's habit. The ancient Romans believed that Lucius Laberius Maximus, a governor of the Egypt province in the first century AD, was the first man to eat a pig, and that before him the Egyptians were the first people to cook and consume boars. Around the same time, the Latin scholar Marcus Terentius Varro, in the second book of his *On Agriculture*, wrote that pigs were divinely gifted to mankind for their use in feasting rituals: "There is a saying that the race of pigs is expressly given by nature to set forth a banquet; and that accordingly life was given them just like salt, to preserve the flesh."

But my favorite legend belongs to Richard Hodge, owner of Richard's Bar-B-Que in Bolivar, Tennessee, and a pitmaster who long ago switched from cooking whole hogs to shoulders for reasons of price, convenience, and customer demand. In a 2008 interview, he shared the origin story he had grown up with: "People used to let their hogs run loose out in the yard. A house fire trapped some hogs underneath it, and when the fire was out, they decided to sample the meat. That's where I heard the origin of barbecue came from. It was in the South." Unbeknownst to him, Hodge was repeating a snippet of an absurdist folktale that dates back to at least the 1820s, when the English poet, essayist, and humorist Charles Lamb wrote a similar and, common for the times, Orientalist fable about an ancient Chinese swineherd named Ho-ti and his eldest son, Bo-bo. In "A Dissertation Upon Roast Pig," this swineherd father and son supposedly lived back when men ate their meat raw. According to Lamb, Bo-bo, a bumbling pyromaniac, burned down the family cottage and the litter of nine suckling pigs within. While fretting over how to explain this catastrophe to his father, a curious scent assailed Bo-bo's nose. "A premonitory moistening at the same time overflowed his nether lip," Lamb wrote. Searching for life amongst his charges, Bo-bo foolishly touched the burnt piglets, in effect scorching his hand. In bringing blistered fingers to mouth, the fortunate fool tasted, for the first time in human history, the fried flesh of swine. Crackling! "The truth at length broke into his slow understanding . . . and surrendering himself up to the new-born pleasure, he fell to tearing up whole handfuls of the scorched skin with the flesh next to it, and was cramming it down his throat in his beastly fashion." Bo-bo had accidentally created the whole-hog roast. The first pitmaster was born.

Origin stories are meant to explain the unexplainable, to give some meaning to the very fiber of the fabric that is humankind. It is simple. Barbecue's history is prehistory. Man cooks now as he did eons ago. The origins of meat and man are intertwined, reaching back into some nebulous dawn of space and time. Rocketing past the barbecuing caveman and into a more tangible beyond, the Dennis family odyssey takes us, in Larry's words, "right on back to the beginning," to the murky history surrounding the settlement of Ayden and a man they called Otter Dennis.

Dennis family lore describes Otter Dennis as a mean man, a ruthless fellow, a lawbreaker, and possibly even an outlaw. Today, he most certainly remains an enigma. Purportedly, Otter was the first Dennis and the founder of Ayden. The official history of the town's Collard Festival, a September event held annually since 1975, states that Otter was "a lot of things, but a gentleman he was not." Local custom says that he was a drifter who, sometime in the early 1800s, set up camp, along with his extended family, in a swampy morass about a mile and a half west of downtown Ayden and the present-day location of Bum's Restaurant. In one telling, he named his desperado outpost after himself, Otter Town. Another version of his legend reverses the narrative and recounts that otters flourished in the surrounding swampland, thus providing the pioneering Dennis with a nickname. Either way, the area surrounding modern Ayden did, in fact, bear this label. On a reproduction of a

Confederate military survey, dated July 1863, that hangs prominently displayed in the dining room of Bum's Restaurant, there lies Otter Town, located dead center in the map's middle, just west of Swift Creek and ringed by hardwood forests.

To avoid imprisonment at one point old Otter Dennis skipped town. Larry Dennis believes that "there was some meanness involved." But Otter left behind a reputation whose scandalous tendrils spread through the region that surrounded his eponymous village like so much oak and pecan smoke. Otter Town had earned an epithet, a curse that area denizens would only dare repeat with much venom and spite: "a den." This was a name earned for being, to quote Larry, "a den of thieves, a den of crooks, a den of criminals." It was a den of iniquity, a desperate, cutthroat town where the locals might make outsiders, trespassers, and transgressors squeal and bleed like a stuck pig. But when it came time to name the incorporated community in 1891, local residents embraced their moniker and chose "Ayden." If a den of anything was what people wanted to call them, that's what they would call their town, only with an added vowel for embellishment.

Naturally, this is not the sequence of events the town officially promotes. Instead, their more uplifting narrative states that an unnamed local resident chose the name after putting index finger to spinning globe. Aden, the Yemeni seaport city, as the story goes, became Ayden. A third, and even more unlikely, school of thought, and a scenario most surely popularized by the town's more devout citizenry, posits that Ayden was named for the Garden of Eden. Just, well, because.

After Otter's disappearance, local and family history skips forward a Dennis generation or two to Skilton Dennis (sometimes spelled Skilten or Skelton), the same man pegged with originating the Skylight Inn's famed 1830 barbecue, slaw, and cornbread trifecta. According to family lore, Skilton roamed the dusty back-roads and swamp-bogged trails of antebellum eastern North Carolina by horse-drawn covered wagon, feeding Baptist and Methodist congregations whole-hog barbecue. Like Otter Dennis, little else remains known about the man except that he passed the practice and enterprise on to his son, Skilton M. Dennis, and grandson, William Bryant "Bill" Dennis. This Bill Dennis, now the third-generation pitmaster in the family, eventually began to sell barbecue from a rented booth in downtown Ayden. By 1900, the Atlantic Coast Line Railroad, which connected the nation's capital with Miami, had transformed Otter's hamlet into a small market town, a distribution point for Pitt County's thriving tobacco and lumber trades. From his barbecue stall, Bill sold chopped whole hog prepared not by himself but by his wife, Susan (née Susan Mirina Garris). Presumably at the family farm, Susan Dennis would kill a hog, dress the carcass, and barbecue the meat and fat over wire grating that covered a shallow pit dug into the ground, into which she'd shovel oak-wood charcoal. The pitmistress turned pitmaster prepared the barbecue and drove it, via chuckwagon, into town for her husband to sell.

Bill's son John Bill Dennis eventually inherited the family business, heeding his calling to become a barbecue man. As written in "A Brief History of Bum's Restaurant and Its Dennis Barbecue," a trifold tourist-type pamphlet produced by the restaurant, John Bill "had inherited something that couldn't be explained except to say it was just there." Barbecue was not only a way of life but life itself, encoded into his DNA. "Born inside some of the Dennis men is a 'gift,'" the pamphlet continues, "a know-how about barbecue that no one else has." John Bill didn't have a choice. Barbecue was his birthright. Endowed by the barbecue gods with a talent borne by no one else, the Dennises may be seen as the modern inheritors of Prometheus, the Greek Titan who stole fire from the gods and gifted it to man, unbinding humanity from its lumpish Neanderthal state, thus enabling all of civilization's cultural and culinary twists, turns, and intricacies, including, of course, a smorgasbord of smoked meats. In their own telling, the Dennises took Prometheus's gift and, in turn, gifted whole-hog barbecue to mankind.

After John Bill Dennis came his cousin, Latham "Bum" Dennis, who had worked his teenage years as a pit hand under the tutelage of yet another pair of cousins, Pete and Robert Jones, at the Skylight Inn. Twenty-three years old and fresh out of a four-year tour of the Pacific courtesy of the United States Navy, Bum relearned the barbecue trade at the J. B. Dennis Cafe. John Bill taught him how to treat customers. He taught him how to make cornbread, fried chicken, and cabbage collard greens, a not-bitter-like-your-average-collards variety that grows tough like kudzu, but also sugary like sweet potatoes, in the soil surrounding Ayden.

John Bill, whose own son forwent the barbecue business to work in the nearby DuPont plant, soon realized that Bum was the one to carry on the Dennis legacy. Too busy to neglect the restaurant for long, Bum would take his future wife, Shirley, on dates to the café, where they'd sit in the first booth closest to the front door, the only one with a quartet of wooden columns like a four-poster bed. The pair looked perfectly picture framed. In April 1963, after nearly three years of working for John Bill, brimming with enough confidence to smoke his own hogs, and Shirley pregnant with their first child, Bum relocated to his own place down the road, the City Cafe. Less than two months later, Larry Dennis was born.

By the time his son was three years old, Bum was back at the original café, having, with his wife, purchased the restaurant for thirty thousand dollars from an elderly and ailing John Bill. Larry and his two sisters grew up in the new Bum's Restaurant. Here, they learned to crawl, walk, and ride a bicycle. But it was the eldest Dennis son, for whom the pit house could be a place of danger and wonder, who took to barbecuing. Though he had lots to learn, he was blessed with that Promethean gift, as if born with the knowledge of how to roast hogs. Bum taught his son as he had been taught. He told him that this was the first cookhouse built in Ayden proper, its cinder-block walls plumbed and mortared in 1941. He warned him that fire was dangerous and that pit houses often exploded; this one, in fact, had burnt down dozens of times. He taught him that whole pigs must be salted first, the coarse grains rubbed into the skin. He showed his son how to fire the pigs slowly at the start, skin side up, before quickening the pace, like a steam engine's stoker, adding heat and fire and smoke, faster and faster, six to eight hours, until the hogs were smoked through and it just felt right.

Larry was a good kid, growing up in the small-town South of the 1970s. He drove a gold '76 Cadillac Sedan de Ville while graduating from the newly integrated Ayden-Grifton High School. He was fascinated with guns, wanted to ride a Harley, and was raised on the era's southern-inflected rock. All this time, he worked at his family's restaurant, unable to escape the pull of his family's history and his own genetic destiny. More than three decades later, working at Bum's is the only job he has ever really had. The great-great-great-grandson of Skilton M. Dennis had become a pitmaster, the sixth-generation pit man in a lineage now stretching back well over a century.

But as for the seventh generation, Larry is skeptical that there will even be one. He has three college-age daughters, but for all the love he has for his children, they won't be Dennises forever, not the barbecuing kind, not ones imbued with that gift. To hear him describe it, "There ain't no more Dennises after this. After the generation I'm in, there ain't many boys left. In fact, on this branch of the tree, there ain't no sons." He sees the end of the Dennis family line, the end of the restaurant fast approaching. "I know nobody in my family wants it, and I can't imagine anybody else coming along wanting to do this"—he paused for several beats—"as a way of life." He expects that he has twenty more years in him of smoking hogs. He can't afford to retire, so "whenever I drop," he told me without any sort of morbidity, "that'll probably be the end." The end of a way of life.

I asked what if a son-a-law or, perhaps, another Dennis cousin wants to keep the family's fires burning. "Leave your children a note to come by here and check," he laughed, "and they can interview them then." For all he cares, he told me, after Bum's Restaurant is gone, everyone can go eat at Hardee's.

———

The next morning I met Larry for the start of the 4:30 AM opening of the restaurant. I arrived a bit early to find a pair of EMS responders, hungry for breakfast as their twilight shift winded down, patiently waiting at the locked door. Right on the half hour, Larry's white Ford Explorer peeled around the corner. Even in the predawn shadows of a small-town's darkness, he looked visibly exhausted climbing out of the vehicle.

"What you been doing all night, cooking a hog?" joked one paramedic.

"What else makes you tired?" Larry croaked back.

While the responders grabbed seats inside, I sat in silence, swaddled in the warm blanket of the early summer morning's seventy-seven-degree heat and humidity, and watched John Deere tractors and PepsiCo delivery trucks alternately roll by as downtown Ayden, much like myself, struggled to wake. Soon a string of gentlemen, arriving one by one and all well past retirement age, single-filed into Bum's and headed directly to the Bunn-O-Matic to serve themselves a steaming ceramic mugful. I followed them inside and, while anticipating a waitress to stop me, sleepily shuffled toward the coffeemaker, which yielded only a few splashes of brew. Disappointed and decaffeinated, I took a seat. On cue, a customer deliberately sauntered toward the coffeemaker and prepared a fresh pot. I'll later learn that his name, or nickname (I'm unsure which), is Junior, and that just days before he had suffered a heart attack and undergone coronary stenting. Junior took a seat, and, after the coffee had percolated, another customer rose to take the carafe and refill my cup, then that of every other man in the place.

Walk into Bum's any morning of the week and you'll see the faces of these same men taking their coffee and breakfast. They first fill the long center communal table before occupying the surrounding seats. They come to discuss politics and the Tar Heels and almost always agree on both. They talk about how no one farms tobacco anymore because the federal government subsidizes soy and cotton instead. They talk about how the bird and deer populations have disappeared, displaced by suburban sprawl, migrated farther afield, distressing the local hunters. They exchange tips on doctors, compare notes on surgeries and nurses. They flirt with the young waitresses, those still in high school, and they flirt with the older gals, who have been around long enough to have flirted back with three generations of these men. They see who can tell the biggest lie before finishing his plate of eggs, toast, sausage, and grits. Bum's serves sixteen total meals a week, and most of these customers, Larry assured me, will eat all sixteen. The statistic sounded far-fetched when we talked the day before, but looking out at this crowd of men that morning, I believed him.

This restaurant, I soon realized, was what the urban sociologist Ray Oldenburg popularly termed "third places," or "great good places," a rendezvous located outside the home and workplace that operates, for a certain segment of society, as the beating heart of American communities. Back in 1989, Oldenburg argued that the nation's recent urban and suburban development was hostile to the existence of these hangouts. Today, in an age when socializing, shopping, and even sex is done electronically, his book, *The Great Good Place*, reads as a quaint reminder of an era distantly past. But barbecue establishments, especially those of the whole-hog variety, where men often chat or warm themselves by the pit fire waiting for the pig to cook, remain some of our few surviving communal gathering spots. And here at Bum's this morning, every morning, it feels as if there is no greater great good place.

At 5:30 Bum Dennis himself, along with his wife, entered the building to cheers and handshakes. His birthday was yesterday. Thin and lively, he looked two decades younger than his seventy-six years. Larry chalks his father's vitality up to the collard greens that Bum eats every day, though, his son admits, "he might miss a Sunday sometimes." He grows each leaf himself on the family farm and in front of his restaurant, from the narrow strips of soil that lie between street and sidewalk. Most every time I've seen Bum, in person and in photographs, he's wearing all white: polo, slacks, baseball cap. He always looks good in the color, and this morning was no different. A faded navy-era tattoo of a Japanese lady, wearing a green dress and coyly turning toward her audience, runs the length of his Popeye-ish right forearm. (He and his son also share matching ink of the Fighting Cock bourbon logo on their calves. "So we can have a cock below our knees," the younger Dennis told me.) For the past forty years or so he's worn an impressively bushy set of whiskers that curl down his jaw and back up his cheekbones to end just below each ear. He grew the mustache on a dare, alongside twenty other members of his skeet-shooting club; he remains the only one to have kept the look. A proper mustache, he once told me, is one you can see from the back.

Several hours later, with the breakfast crowd winding down, I accompanied Larry for a quick tour of Ayden's downtown historic district. He needed a haircut and a cigarette, but in reverse order; though he'd made fifty the week before, he still hid his smoking habit from his mother.

We walked west, passing the town hall and police headquarters on our right, Guns Unlimited and the auto and tire shop on our left. Two- and three-story brick buildings, most dating from the railroad boom that ran through the postwar years, fill the eight square blocks of downtown Ayden. In 1979, the North Carolina Department of Transportation rerouted Highway 11, which once longitudinally shot straight through the town, a mile west of the historic district. Most of the old downtown businesses, all but Bum's, have long dried up. The downtown district didn't seem to offer much besides a preponderance of places to get one's hair shorn, permed, extended, and dyed. There was an antiques store (located in the former Bank of Ayden), a used book store (heavy on the romance novels), and a bakery surfing the third wave of the cupcake trend. Just down the road was the Vietnamese-owned gas station, where a kid, no older than thirteen, once solicited me to buy a barbecue pit from the back of a pickup truck. ("Brand new, cheap price.") But there was no billiards-filled barroom, no mom-and-pop corner grocery, no we-stock-it-all hardware store, no place to buy a pair of farm boots or a Sunday suit. Most surprisingly, there was no church. These ordinary signposts of small-town southern existence were, well, nonexistent. But there was also plenty of evidence of a greater effort to redevelop, reinvest, and redefine the town and its people. Hanging from light posts above vacant storefronts, banners fluttered with the branded, and ungrammatical, slogan "Welcome Downtown Ayden: Close to Home, Close to Your Heart."

At the City Barber Shop, Larry sat low in his barber's chair, chatting with Doug, who's been cutting hair here for nearly fifty years, about the past. It's a convention that does not bear repeating, a clichéd writerly fallback to describe the rural South, but most of the conversations I overheard in downtown Ayden really did involve some discussion of a slice of antiquity just out of reach. The presupposed good old days. The era of the Greatest Generation. Whether in the barbershop or Bum's Restaurant, the men reminisced about the old pickle plant (closed), the one-screen Princess Theatre (shuttered), the summer flood of '65 (thankfully long dried up).

After finishing his trim, Larry led me around back, behind the barbershop. There rested the remnants of an old brick pit and chimney; mortar crumbling, filled with old beer cans and potato-chip bags, these were the remainders of his father's original City Cafe. It was a reminder that there used to be more barbecue pits around the downtown area. The Ayden Fire Department once had its own pit-filled cookhouse, which they'd fire up for fund-raisers and special events, as did the Masonic Lodge and the Moose Lodge, until they all switched to drum-style briquette smokers. "When I was young, everybody knew how to cook pigs with wood," Larry told me. And whether you owned your own backyard cookhouse or you borrowed your neighbor's, "There was always a place to cook a pig."

Returning to Bum's, I found myself hungry for exactly that: cooked pig. Larry fixed me an overkill-sized spread that covered an entire plastic serving tray. There were sides of collards, smothered cabbage, and coleslaw. Porky black-eyed peas. Boiled potatoes that somehow contained more flavor than simply potatoes that had been boiled. Two kinds of cornbread: crunchy-fried corn sticks and sweet-potato-studded corn muffins. My favorite side item: rutabagas, boiled and mashed into fluffy peaks of neon orange; they were sweet and salty and, because of a generous stirring of lard, more than a little rich, a harmonious epiphany of flavors in every bite. And of course barbecue, a softball-sized scoop of the stuff, finely chopped and interlaced with bits of chewy skin. To finish: homemade banana pudding that had been whipped, Nilla-wafered, and meringued enough to satisfy just about every southern palate.

His father hadn't originally built his reputation on just barbecue, but all the fixins his full-service restaurant offered. "When they came out with that menu," Larry told me when we first met in December 2011, "that was everything that anybody knew how to cook." The goal remains as simple as providing indigenous southern home cooking when the home cook can't be bothered to provide: "This is what people eat and that's what we serve." Thus, he is hesitant to dish out any credit for recipes—there is no genius chef in the kitchen. "You can give anybody credit that you want to, but the barbecue, the vegetables—everything we cook was the same way that everybody cooked it." His father agreed: "The recipes at the Cafe," and thus continuing on to Bum's, are "just an extension from people's homes."

But this food is disappearing, Larry has told me on more than one occasion. The restaurant's only competition has been, in his words, "your mama," all mamas. And most everybody's mamas either stopped cooking long ago or hadn't convinced a new generation of mamas to keep at it. And with no southern-style home-cooking mamas left, "it's going to get harder and harder and harder to get the whole menu." He had a point. This food was time-consuming, becoming harder to source. It was unhealthy, to say the least, especially if eaten sixteen times a week. Though I did at times see multigenerational families sitting down for supper and the occasional grandpa stopping by with his grandson following a fishing trip, the customer base at Bum's, morning, noon, or night, skewed toward the AARP bracket. These collards, rutabagas, and cornbread could very well disappear alongside the whole-hog barbecue. Just in case, I ate every spoon- and forkful of food on that tray. I had outswined the swine.

Over lunch, Larry recommended that I visit one more place of historical value: his family's cemetery. I thought that, at the very least, I should honor the past generations of barbecue pitmasters who had fed me.

With that thought in mind I trudged into the noonday sun, headed toward the Dennis family cemetery, located a mile northwest of the restaurant. Within five minutes, sweat stung my eyes, and I wished that I had brought a bottle of water along for the walk. After a half hour of backtracking and weaving around road-construction projects, I spotted the graveyard of barbecuedom's founding fathers. It was located at a bend in the road, across from a swatch of bungalow-style housing projects, and down a gravel path. Surrounded on three sides by dense cornfields, six feet high and ripe to burst, the tiny cemetery was cordoned off by a simple steel fence. Checking for onlookers and brimming with the dreadful thrill that accompanies the act of trespassing, I unhinged the gate and walked onto the recently mowed lawn.

I soft-shoed past generations of departed Dennises and Joneses—the more recently deceased memorialized with tall concrete spires, their elders sanctified with unadorned stone markers. Circling the cemetery, I found, at its exact center, the burial plot of Skilton M. Dennis, born March 21, 1842, died November 2, 1900. Lying flat on the ground, the marker's inscription gave a rather prosaic but sweet remembrance to the man and his Christian soul. I stood in peaceful respite, belly full and sun sluggish, hovering over his final resting place for several moments. The tombstone was split right down its center, and through the crack in the masonry, a patch of dead brown grass poked through. I left the cemetery thinking that surely the founder of two barbecue dynasties deserved better.

———

The following morning we were seated again, but this time in the auxiliary dining room. This is where Larry Dennis occasionally escapes to, as an especially busy lunch shift winds down, to puff on an electronic cigar and do everything but think. I told him of my visit to the cemetery and again asked about the history of the Dennises of Ayden, about Otter Dennis and his den of thieves, about the Skiltons and their horse-drawn barbecue.

"I think it's all made up to be honest with you," he admitted without any hint of guilt.

"Made up?"

"I'm pretty sure it's all made up. They twisted it around and made up stories."

I felt the pangs of betrayal upon first hearing his confession. I'd been set up, made a fool, maybe even lied to. Just weeks before, I had graduated with a PhD in American history; for seven arduous years of graduate school I'd been trained to give the skeptic's treatment to any and all archival sources—memories dissolve and motivations change, documents misconstrue facts, people embellish or just flat-out lie. But you can almost always trust an expert, I learned. We all have to locate and give in to our expert sources, our witnesses to history. And what was Larry Dennis but the last in a line of nonpartisan experts? Over nearly two centuries, his family had possibly cooked more hogs than I had accumulated moments in my life. It wasn't just all smoke and mirrors; from the very beginning, I had been literally smoke-screened. Deceived by a surrogate for humanity's very first trickster himself: Prometheus.

But, after all, I quickly reconsidered, this is barbecue, the ultimate big-fish tale of American foods. The boasting and mythologizing, the sporting competition and reality show rhetoric that barbecue had recently become, the bigness of cooking a whole animal, the fire and smoke and explosions that could light up the sky like the Fourth of July: this was the very Americanness of it all. It all belonged here, right here, in tiny Ayden, North Carolina.

And who was I to judge Larry Dennis? He was one man, one Dennis, a participant in a bigger game. He didn't invent Otter Dennis. He wasn't present when the first Skilton, whoever he was, salted his first side of hog's flesh. These stories had been passed down for who knows how long. But he had been there to witness the Joneses and their Skylight Inn, his familial and friendly competition, lauded with praise (and they were Dennises by blood, even if not by name!). He had seen the area's farms dry up, the avian and four-legged wild fauna disappear, and, following these two losses, much of his customer base evaporate. He could look out the front windows of his restaurant and watch business after business shutter. And then he would look at his own business, now the anchor of downtown Ayden, and realize that there was likely no one to take over once he was gone. Over the past forty years he had experienced all that is solid about his small southern town melt into air. But he kept cooking the only barbecue he knew.

I had one more question to ask, the one I'd been holding back, wanting to ask since that first day in the pit house, until now. "D-d-do you think . . . ," I stuttered. The question was difficult for me to form. I finally spat out the words. "Do you ever think all that smoke is unhealthy?"

His response was rapid-fire: "Hell yeah, I know it is, you know it's got to be. There ain't no doubt." He rapped his electronic cigar—peach flavored—on the table, knocking three times.

"Does it bother you?"

"It bothers me thinking about it, and then, like some days, I get real congested. Not real often, but, like right now, I'm . . ." He stopped, reconsidered, and looked down at the table, looked at his hands. "Last week was even worse. But I j-j-just . . ." He had trouble speaking the words, exactly as I had earlier: "I just can't hardly breathe, and I know that's what it is." He again knocked his e-cigar three times against the tabletop. After a long, uncomfortable pause he looked up at me. "When I was a teenager, I could lay right down in there and go to sleep, got smoke all over, wouldn't even bother me." He took a last long pull from his cigar and, murmuring softly through the inhalation of vapor and the hazy fog of the past, said, "Funny what you do when you're young."

He stopped for one final outstretched exhale of faux smoke, sat his cigar down, and, pushing the table away, rising from his chair, announced, "Let's go spread some coals."

CHAPTER 5

A Pitmaster's History of Barbecue

**In this world, pigs, as well as men,
Must dance to fortune's fiddlings.**

—THOMAS HOOD

*L*eaving Ayden, I moved west to eastern North Carolina's more populated and industrialized west-central region—bisected by the Interstate 95 corridor that connects Miami with Washington, D.C., New York City, and beyond—where the whole-hog barbecue restaurants often come warehouse sized.

In the town of Wilson, a step inside the doors of Parker's Barbecue reveals a troop of attentive young men standing in formation, all wearing white-paper caps and starch-white uniforms, ready to usher patrons to their tables. They feed twenty thousand customers a week. That's about as big as barbecue gets, but still peanuts compared to Bill Ellis Barbecue, just across town. Ellis's website promotes his operation as the "Microsoft of Barbecue" and boasts an 850-seat restaurant, his own pig farm (stocked with five hundred sows spread among twenty-six lucky boars), enough space to cook one hundred hogs at a time, a ten-thousand-square-foot convention center, and a fleet of forty long-haul trucks—each outfitted with a mobile kitchen—to cater from coast to coast.

Bill Ellis, Parker's, and other little inland empires dedicated to barbecue don't need capitol domes or creation myths to attract customers, just a steady supply of pigs to keep them fed. In the farm community of Tar Heel, Smithfield Foods, the global food conglomerate recently purchased by the Chinese company Shuanghui International, operates the world's largest slaughterhouse and meat-packing plant. Though the population of Tar Heel hovers just over a hundred persons, a mass of 2,500 Smithfield employees arrive in two rotating shifts to kill, prep, pack, and ship more than thirty thousand hogs each day. Seen through the eyes of Google Earth, the one-million-square-foot behemoth of a meat-making factory resembles an aircraft carrier lost in a sea of loblolly pines.

In 1924, "Uncle" Bob Melton became the first to transform this region's hog culture into a whole-hog movement when he opened the state's first sit-down barbecue restaurant in Rocky Mount, less than a half-hour's drive north of Wilson. But Melton's Barbecue was no more. Hurricane floodwaters destroyed the business in 1999, long after Bill Ellis and Parker's had switched to the convenience, safety, and economizing of gas cookers in order to feed their flocks. Only a single local establishment stayed true to wood and flame: Wilber's Barbecue, the smoked pride and sauced joy of Goldsboro, North Carolina.

My visit to Wilber's coincided with the eighty-third birthday of the restaurant's namesake and owner, Wilberdean Shirley. He still works every day, I would later find out, from opening to close, six in the morning until nine at night, a schedule he's kept since starting the business back in 1962. But tonight he was taking a rare day off. A hostess seated me along a back wall in one of several dining rooms. I scanned the golden pine-paneled walls, a shrine to the life and career of Shirley, giving the place a clubhouse feel. There was his Korean War uniform, framed photographs of him posing with Presidents Bush Sr. and Clinton, as well as items testifying to his rabid support for the athletic abilities of the North Carolina State University Wolfpack. A section of one wall was dedicated to Franklin Delano Roosevelt, a shrine within a shrine to a time when this region's voters overwhelmingly polled Democrat.

Though it was late into the suppertime hour, customers still packed the restaurant's many seats. At a neighboring table, an elderly couple sat side-by-side, slowly chewing bites of barbecue, fried chicken, and hushpuppies in church-like silence. Two tables over, a trio of middle-aged women quietly enjoyed this Friday night in their best Sunday dress. Most every table held hands and bowed their heads to pray before eating, a scene being simultaneously repeated in dozens of barbecue restaurants within an hour's drive.

Perhaps most indicative of the regional import of barbecue is the fact that Wilber's, as well as Parker's and Bill Ellis, are open all seven days of the week, a line in the sand of Sunday sacrilege that less capitalist-minded areas of the South dare not cross. Wilber Shirley's mother went to her grave hoping and praying that her son would close on the Sabbath. He ignored his mama's wishes. It's not that Shirley and the others are hell-bound heathens. It speaks more to the fact that their customers demand barbecue every day, even the Lord's Day—following church service, of course.

After finishing my meal, I walked out back behind the restaurant, where I witnessed a scene most assuredly not duplicated at any area pit houses that night. There I found a middle-to-late-aged man standing on the sloped shoulder of a vast midden of split oak logs. He tossed the thick wood pieces into a wheelbarrow—once colored red but now faded to pink. He then scrambled down the wood heap and squeakily wheeled his bounty to rest alongside a smoldering trench-dug fire that burned adjacent to the pit house.

I introduced myself as a writer from New Orleans, explained my interest in whole-hog barbecue, and asked if I could watch him smoke some pigs. Looking me over and without missing a beat, he said, "If I met a man down in Louisiana with some money, we could open up a barbecue place down there." Admiring his moxie, I immediately liked the man and asked for his name. "Keith Ward," he said. "But everybody calls me Pop." I agreed to come back in four nights. Wilber Shirley's singular dedication to slow, wood-cooked barbecue only works, I would soon discover, because of men like Pop.

Returning to my car, on the far side of the four-lane divided highway that runs in front of the restaurant, I noted a tall billboard that shone like a spotlight at nightfall. "WHAT'S IN A NAME?" it shouted in big, bold letters. "Choose a new motto for Goldsboro." Mayor Al King was sponsoring a contest to rebrand his city. With its downtown strip filled with shuttered storefronts and a sprawling manufacturing corridor that sits entirely deserted, the mayor undoubtedly hoped to reenergize his tax base, capture some much-needed tourist dollars, and add a bit of luster to this once-vibrant cultural and industrial gateway to eastern Carolina. Nowadays, it seemed that every business in town relied on the support of Seymour Johnson Air Force Base, which houses and/or employs more than 40 percent of the town's 37,000 citizens while sending jets sonically ripping overhead most hours of the day. The base's own motto—"Dominant Strike Eagle Airpower . . .

Anytime, Anyplace"—hardly jived with Mayor King's vision of economic revival and feel-good boosterism.

If the good people of Goldsboro wanted a new motto they should look to their own barbecue history.

The city is home to arguably the most compelling and largely ignored storylines in the chronicles of the nation's barbecue culture. Before Wilber Shirley, predating Pete Jones and even Bob Melton, Goldsboro once nurtured a whole-hog pitmaster who put North Carolina barbecue culture on the map. This man spawned a barbecue lineage that survives a century later, cooked at the White House, and is the only pitmaster to have a biographer publish the story of his life in book form. The sum total of this man's life becomes even more striking when his race is added to the equation. Unlike the business owners mentioned above, he was black, a person of color who built a business and legacy while coming up in the fiercely segregated South, a man fittingly named Adam.

Born in 1890, Adam Scott grew up in a relatively progressive community, especially considering the time and place. The county seat of Wayne County, turn-of-the-century Goldsboro enjoyed an active railroad yard, a large and dynamic Jewish population, and an African American population empowered by the one hundred thousand Union soldiers who camped out in the area under the command of General William Tecumseh Sherman during the Civil War and the subsequent Reconstruction reform that, at least for a short time, successfully improved black suffrage and education. Thomas Dixon, the famed racist reactionary and novelist, preached in a local Baptist church just a few years before Scott's birth. Dixon's experience witnessing Goldsboro's creeping struggle toward racial equality, a movement he detested, provoked him to pen *The Clansman*, the novel that would in turn influence D. W. Griffith's fanatically bigoted Hollywood bonanza *The Birth of a Nation*.

After quitting school before reaching the eighth grade, Scott lived as an itinerant laborer for the next twenty-five or so years, pursuing those jobs available to a young black man living in the Jim Crow South. He worked in a local sawmill and later apprenticed for an uncle, altering suits at a downtown men's store, before moving to Georgia to labor in a turpentine still. A large man, he thought about becoming a boxer but gave up after his first split lip. He might not have become a pugilist, but he remained tough, a fighter. He worked as a waiter and cook in Atlantic City before returning home once again to marry his childhood sweetheart, Bessie Bright, who bore him seven children in quick succession. Eventually he signed on as an elevator operator and custodian for the exclusive and exclusively white Algonquin Club in downtown Goldsboro.

According to his authorized biography, *Adam's Ribs*, published six years before his death in 1983, sometime in the mid-1910s Scott prepared and served barbecue for the patrons of a club dance, filling in for a man named Arnold Sasser, who had taken ill. Little is known about Sasser's barbecue career except for the fact that Scott credited him with cultivating his whole-hog expertise. To feed two hundred partygoers, Scott barbecued seven small pigs, none weighing over fifty-five pounds, in a trench-dug pit. "Everybody said it was the best 'cue they ever ate," he told his biographer. He continued to cater parties while taking on odd jobs (tailor, suit presser, janitor, bank messenger, Pentecostal pastor) but would have to wait more than a decade to own his own barbecue business.

By the early 1930s, Scott smoked a single hog every Saturday in an earthen pit dug in the floor of the garage that stood behind his house on Brazil Street, delivering the barbecue to the surrounding neighborhoods. It did not take long for people to start buying barbecue from his back door. He quit his other jobs—except the church—to focus on the barbecue trade. Customers could eat Scott's chopped pork off tin plates, sold at a quarter a plate or ninety cents per pound, from the pitmaster's back porch. Corn pone and coleslaw rounded out the menu. He continued to tinker with his barbecue sauce recipe, eventually settling on a combination of vinegar, pepper, and eight secret herbs. The formula, he claimed, came to him in a dream.

After decades of struggling with job security, Scott must certainly have felt like his rising popularity was a dream. People kept coming for his barbecue, forcing Scott to expand his operation. A pair of brick-lined pits soon replaced the trench in the garage. He borrowed money from the bank to build three separate additions to the back porch. Eventually the porch would be torn down to make way for a dining room that could accommodate 150 people. During tobacco season, Scott often fed 2,000 workers a day. This brought the attention of the IRS, which billed him for back taxes owed. But the first man of barbecue kept on smoking. His fans unofficially renamed Brazil Street after Scott's business, calling it Barbecue Alley. Four North Carolina governors visited the alley, as did Hollywood idols Mickey Rooney and Ava Gardner, who was born in nearby Smithfield. And in March 1933, Scott was invited to cater a White House Rose Garden party to celebrate Franklin D. Roosevelt's first inauguration. The event must have stood as the highlight of his career.

The people of Goldsboro soon began calling Scott "the Barbecue King."

I returned to Wilber's under the soft glow of dusk, as black clouds ominously gathered in the distance, and located Pop stepping out of a walk-in cooler behind the restaurant. With half a hog, split down the spine, crooked under his left arm, he signaled me over with his right before plopping the carcass into that same shabby and rusted wheelbarrow. "How was your weekend?" I asked. "Not good," he answered, disappearing back into the cooler. His voice was scratchy with smoke and punctuated with a persistent cough. I waited until he reappeared with another half hog in hand. "Why's that?" I asked. The half dropped from his palms, landing with a slap against the first. "Well, I worked, and that's good, but I've had problems on my mind. And I've just worked on." A single rivulet of blood, like a tear, ran down this last side of chilled meat. Pop stepped out fully into

the warm air. Blood stained the palms of his hands and covered his left boot. He had big bloodshot eyes and wore long sideburns and a short goatee, both salt and peppered, that covered his lined and weary face. His arms were thin and ropey but swelled with sinewy tissue each time he took a hog into his hands and heaved it into the wheelbarrow. He resembled nothing so much as a knot. Maybe worn and slightly frayed, but a firmly tied knot nonetheless: tight, taut, and ballasted.

I decided it best to leave him alone, to watch him work from afar. As Pop pushed the wheelbarrow and its haul of four hog halves into the pit house, I found a squat and knobby oak log on which to sit and survey the scene. I noted the trenched fire pit that roared with a dozen or so burning logs, their heat blistering the air. The pitmaster's tools of the trade leaned against the exterior of the pit house's long-defunct brick chimney (abandoned, Pop later told me, because it made the building's cramped interior too hot to bear): a plastic rake and another heavy-duty metal one; three square-bladed shovels of various sizes and lengths; a ten-tined pitchfork.

As Pop scooted his wheelbarrow out from the pit house, I noticed that stretching back behind the mammoth oak wood pile, a garden overflowed with the summer's best: squash, bell pepper, and okra; trellised tomatoes; and creeping cantaloupe and watermelon vines. The garden flowed into rows upon rows of corn, which disappeared with the horizon into a thicket of pine trees. Overhead, a three-quarters moon began to take shape in the impending twilight. It was all very peaceful and pastoral, and I stared deep into the fire, rooted to my oak log seat, lost in daydreams and enjoying the breeze, which blew cool across the cornfields, heralding the approaching storm.

Suddenly a trio of fighter jets returning to land at the air force base shook me from my reverie. I looked up to see Pop back on the woodpile's slope, gathering fuel for the fire, while thick bands of vapor trails from the jets evaporated overhead. He smoked a cigarette while he worked and waved to me with a smile. Pop grabbed the arms of the wheelbarrow, which by now overflowed with several hundred pounds of wood, and lifted up. The cart tipped over, spilling its contents along the bottom of the woodpile. Pop threw his arms to the sky, grumbling inaudibly. I looked away, embarrassed to have witnessed Pop's misfortune and quietly hoping that I could turn back around to discover that I had dreamt the whole thing: there would be the wheelbarrow, upright and neatly stacked with wood, with Pop still smiling. But looking back, there he stood, stooping to pick up logs he had already gathered. I stood up, ashamed, unable to decide between lending a hand and running away, when, on the opposite side of the woodpile from Pop, the storm finally and with a cataclysmic fury whooshed sideways across the cornfield. The sky turned black. Wind bowed stalks, lightning split ozone, and rain turned dust to mud. Pop and his wheelbarrow of wood were instantly inundated. I ran into the pit house, seeking shelter.

The pit's interior was oppressive, low-ceilinged and dark, swallowed up in the impenetrable blackness. A fluorescent bulb burned a pale golden pallor across the pits, barely illuminating the room. Charred wood crunched underfoot. I ran my fingers along the cement walls and across the edges of the brick pits; a black lacquer—residue from an untold number of wood and grease fires—covered every surface with a film that was both sticky and slick. The unused fireplace at one end of the pit looked like the stuff of children's nightmares: a huge gaping maw, open and empty and

old, dressed in a newsboy cap, baggy work shirt, heavy boots, and overalls. He was likely one of the thousand or so tenant farmers, most all of whom were black, who lived and labored, for most if not all of their lives, on the Braswell Plantation.

In the first photograph, with sleeves rolled to his elbows, he gingerly mops sauce onto a row of hogs that rest on sticks above a shallow ditch. The hogs, which look to be a quarter size smaller than the specimens I'm used to seeing, lay skin side down, their meat and fat and ribs exposed and ready to welcome the vinegar and spice bath. In the next, Hemmer steps back to capture the pitmaster mopping a different set of hogs on the opposite end of the pit. Back and to the left of the pit, two men stand just within the frame's reach but remain out of focus and partially obscured by the pitmaster's shadow. One, we can tell by his dress, is another pit hand. The second is a white man who wears a panama hat. A cigarette dangles limp from his lips.

In the final shot, taken from the far end of the pit, the photographer steps back once again to reveal the full span of the pit, complete with nine whole hogs on sticks. The pitmaster and the man in the panama hat now stand opposite each other at the pit's center. Right hand on hip, the latter casually regards the former, who, head bowed, shovel replacing mop, continues tending to his hogs. The pitmaster never looks directly at the camera. He is not credited in the captions. He remains forever anonymous, in name and body.

"Photographs objectify," Susan Sontag writes in an essay on the human capacity to empathize with others. "They turn an event or a person into something that can be possessed." Or, I would like to add, consumed.

Together, Hemmer's pitmaster series becomes the perfect

study in contrasts: beginning with sauce and meat before exposing divergences between black and white, labor and leisure. The
story written between the lines of these three photos unfolds
like an onion—a reporter's camera gazes upon a supervisor, who
monitors a worker, who attends to a task—divulging the layers
upon layers of observation and inspection that occurred around
the barbecue pit in 1944, that repeated itself when I stepped
inside the pit house behind Wilber's seventy years later, and that
will occur each time someone asks a pitmaster if he can watch him
cook some barbecue.

———

As the rain abated, I offered to buy Pop dinner. "Something different would be nice," he conceded. "I eat the same thing every night."
He did not have to clarify that supper was customarily the day's
remaining and reheated barbecue. The pitmaster wanted a Subway
sandwich, ham and turkey with American cheese, dressed plainly
except for yellow mustard.

Returning a half hour later with our supper, I found Pop shoveling the first round of coals under the night's allotment: nine hog
halves in addition to sixteen shoulders, which Wilber's chops fine
and mixes in as a meat-and-fat supplement to their whole-hog barbecue. Coals in place, he led me through a swinging screen door to
an adjoining room, like a doctor's waiting room but smaller, where
he had set up a pair of elementary-school-sized wooden chairs,
rickety and carbonized. With his white apron, he wiped the seat
of one chair clean and motioned for me to sit. He demonstrated
that we would now have to watch for the possibility of flare-ups.
"Just a little flame of fire" he called it, making the symbol for leap-
ing flames in the palm of his hand, a pit fire, fueled by dripping

hog grease, that could spread from the briefest flicker to a full-on inferno in a matter of minutes. "We burnt this motherfucker down so many times," he laughed, slapping the paint-blistered walls. "The grease gets out of control. You just can't help it."

Pop switched off the single overhead light and the bulbs in the pit. It was just past nine PM. We sat in the dark, eating our cold-cut sandwiches, watching for flare-ups through the screen door. The preparation of whole-hog barbecue had entered its most crucial phase: waiting. It's what separates Wilber's and others from the two Ayden barbecue houses: here a pitmaster is on duty almost around the clock, most certainly throughout the night, replenishing the coals in the pits about every half hour while keeping the hogs safe from recurrent fires and the occasional sticky-fingered marauder (a room full of smoked meat makes for enticing and easily pilfered booty). "All I can do is sit here and wait," Pop told me. "Read the paper, if I got one. Nothing else to do but put wood on the fire in the meantime." Another whole-hog pitmaster, Rodney Scott in Hemingway, South Carolina, calls this the pitmaster's capacity to "hurry up and wait," his ability to hastily build a fire, put hogs on the grill, and heat the pits with coals before settling in to experience the lonely and ponderous passing of the midnight hours. "Most of the night is waiting," Pop explained. "Most of the night is waiting."

Sitting side-by-side in the room adjacent to the pit house, I watched Pop as he watched for fire and told me his story. Keith Ward originally came from La Grange, just southeast from Goldsboro; "a little, small place" is all he would say to describe the town. His father originally nicknamed him Popeye. "When I was born, once my eyes came open, my dad said he never saw such big eyes in his life, like they were gonna pop out. I guess when I came into the world, I saw everything and wanted to go back in my mama." He smiled and nodded.

"It's a funny nickname," he continued, "'cuz I'm nobody's pop." He raised his wife's three children, though, before and after she passed away fourteen years ago, earning his paycheck at Wilber's. He first began working there at the age of thirteen, maybe twelve, he doesn't recall exactly when. He hauled and cut wood alongside his father, Eddie Lee Ward, one of the original Wilber's pitmasters, hired circa 1964. Eventually Pop legally worked there as a busboy before becoming the dishwasher while he finished high school and later taking part-time work helping his father around the pit. Though officially retired, Eddie Lee still keeps a sporadic schedule, returning occasionally to cook a night of hogs, while his son, Pop, takes the week's four busiest shifts.

Later that evening, Pop's brother Anthony stopped by the pit house on his nightly rounds working for the local power company. Seeing the siblings together reminded me that I had brought with me a recently published book on regional barbecue, the cover of which featured a quarter-length profile of Eddie Lee's hands folded across his aproned chest. It was the first time either of them had seen the book. They stared at the cover in disbelief and recognition. "That's him," one son shouted. "That's Daddy's hands," the other proclaimed with pride. The photograph showed a big left bear paw, cratered and calloused, weathered and worn, softly cradling his right hand. These were the hands of a pitmaster. Hands that intimately resembled, I glanced over to discover, those of Pop.

Besides handing down his genetic code, Eddie Lee, like other pitmasters, taught his son what he knew about cooking hogs. But, Pop told me, so much of being a pitmaster is discovering one's own method, finding one's own path around the pit house. "Even though we all doing the same as far as cooking the pigs, we have different ways of doing things," Pop stressed in regards to his student-teacher relationship with his father. "At the end of the day, I feel that his is sometimes better than mine, and sometimes mine is better than his. We both do good cooking. He does excellent cooking. He taught me how to do it and I learned my own style."

I openly questioned what Pop was telling me. Style? With a toolkit containing just wood, smoke, and fire, I wondered, could a pitmaster determine how good, or bad, the barbecue really is? Can a pitmaster have style, individuality, character? Can smoked meat have a personality? Or does the magic happen in the kitchen, with the addition of spices, sauces, cleavers, and cornbread? Could a pitmaster really account for a distinctive flavor profile readily distinguishable in the final product? Yes, Pop confirmed, qualities of not just taste but texture—ratios of smoke to char and fat to muscle—should be noticeably distinctive when fashioned by different hands. And it's because those very hands inherit, embrace, and explore all of the idiosyncratic variables that come with the job. "Everybody that cook don't cook the same, so you form your own style. You form your own style," he emphasized.

Despite the fact that, at first glance, a whole-hog pitmaster cooks the same pigs day in and day out, it did not take Pop long to convince me that nothing remains the same day to day. If one hog is lean, the next porker might be all fat. Fire is unpredictable, with the potentiality for serious consequences, while the weather can fluctuate just as dramatically as flames. Like Ricky Parker, Pop could identity drafts and air pockets, hot and cold spots. He knew how to account for seasonal changes and was able to detect the slightest atmospheric shifts and execute accordingly. Confronted with a late start, as Pop was because of this evening's downpour, he could speed up, or, conversely, slow down, the cooking process. Simply stated: everything can and will affect barbecue, and it is the pitmaster's task to make sure that the barbecue is always ready on schedule. Pitmasters could adopt the unofficial creed of the United States Postal Service: they are delayed "neither by snow nor rain nor heat nor darkness from accomplishing their appointed course with all speed." To this, Pop might emend the phrase's ending to read, "with all speed and style."

A pitmaster's style comes down to the pitmaster's tricks of the trade, and that individual savvy comes down to expertise, instinct, and just plain habit. One pitmaster's favorite shovel could be another's accursed tool. Pop told me, for example, that other pitmasters here at Wilber's often arranged their pigs in distinct patterns on the pit. Some crowded them on the far or near ends, while others jammed them tightly en masse at the pit's center. Pop fired his hogs at thirty-minute intervals, while another pitmaster might spread his coals every twenty or forty minutes. Additionally, pitmasters might spread precise amounts of coals under distinct regions of the hog's anatomy: a heavy shovelful under the hams, say, or a lighter load underneath the shoulders. In whole-hog barbecue, the pitmaster's personality shines through.

But while "the boss man," as Pop calls him, poses with presidents, the pitmaster's contribution remains unheralded, his name unknown to the great majority of customers who eat his barbecue night after night. As is not uncommon in the South—nor limited to the region—Wilber Shirley and the whole front of the house staff at his restaurant, minus a busboy, are white. The clientele I saw eating in the dining rooms several nights before had also been almost entirely white. Pop and the rest of the back house staff, encompassing the kitchen and the pit, are black. It goes without saying that Wilber's waitresses don't inform their customers that "tonight's barbecue was prepared by Keith Ward." Despite a half century of service, Eddie Lee Ward's portrait is not enshrined on the restaurant's walls. Most frustratingly, both father and son get paid for the day's work. Their pay does not increase when they cook more hogs or work longer hours. "It's the same thing if I cook one pig," Pop confided, "and the same thing if I cook twenty-five pigs," as he did this past Father's Day. "It's not what it should be, truly not what it should be."

Not what it should be, but most assuredly what it is. Call it exploitation; blame it on the enduringly dismal state of race relations in America; or chalk it up to fate, to the dance all men and pigs must perform while fortune plays her fiddle—but it didn't seem so far off from the documentation left behind from Hemmer's visit to the Braswell barbecue, some seventy years ago.

I stepped outside to stretch and yawn and think. I watched as great gray pillows of smoke rose from the pit house to crest over the restaurant's parking lot and called my girlfriend, Susie, to tell her what Pop had just told me. "Do you think the disappearance of this form of cooking is progress?" she asked.

"Yes," I said. "Yes, I'm afraid it may be."

Peering into the distance, I could just make out the billboard, its message now blurred in a smoky fog: WHAT'S IN A NAME?

———

Innumerable thousands, rich and poor, came to dine on barbecue at the back door of Adam Scott's house. And every single one of them, each and every customer, was white. Such was the social and political state of affairs during Scott's reign as king. He could cook and smoke pigs at the home of the president of the United States but he could not legally sell a tin plate of barbecue to many of his own neighbors. For black patrons, takeout was the only available option.

Matters of race and barbecue have been eternally and inseparably linked. In *Savage Barbecue: Race, Culture, and the Invention of America's First Food*, literary scholar Andrew Warnes explores his theory that the indigenous Caribbean word "barbacòa" was adopted by colonial English settlers who equated the American Indian cooking practice they found in the New World—whole animals smoked over fire, as viewed in the paintings of John White—with a sort of primitive or savage "barbarism." America's barbecue culture, Warnes argues, has never shed its intrinsically xenophobic and radicalized roots.

Though Warnes's thesis might seem a touch eggheaded to some, it remains true that the pit house has indelibly remained, both real and symbolically, contested ground. Historians of the antebellum South have uncovered plentiful evidence of barbecue used as a paternalistic device between a master and the enslaved. In 1897 the freedman Louis Hughes described the realities and contradictory forces behind the plantation barbecue in his memoir, *Thirty Years a Slave*:

> *Barbecue originally meant to dress and roast a hog whole, but has come to mean the cooking of a food animal in this manner for the feeding of a great company. A feast of this kind was always given to us, by Boss, on the 4th of July. The anticipation of it acted as a stimulant through the entire year. . . . About noon everything was ready to serve. The table was set in a grove near the quarters, a place set aside for these occasions. The tableware was not fine, being of*

tin, but it served the purpose, and did not detract from the slaves' relish for the feast. . . . Some of the nicest portions of the meat were sliced off and put on a platter to send to the great house for Boss and his family. It was a pleasure for the slaves to do this, for Boss always enjoyed it. It was said that the slaves could barbecue meats best, and when the whites had barbecues slaves always did the cooking. When dinner was all on the table, the invitation was given for all to come; and when all were in a good way eating, Boss and the madam would go out to witness the progress of the feast, and seemed pleased to see the servants so happy. Everything was in abundance, so all could have plenty—Boss always insisted on this. The slaves had the whole day off, and could do as they liked.

For Mrs. M. E. Abrams of Whitmire, South Carolina, barbecue could act as a form of celebration without the master's benefit. "We n'used to steal our hog ever' Sa'day night and take off to de gully whar us'd git him dressed and barbecued," she told a WPA interviewer in 1937. "[We] has de mos'es fun at a barbecue dat dare is to be had."

During the long civil rights era, barbecue houses across the country often acted as the site of protest and change. Soon after President Lyndon Johnson signed the Civil Rights Act of 1964, which, along with enforcing the constitutional right to vote, outlawed segregation in "public accommodations" such as restaurants, four African American men attempted to integrate Ollie's Barbecue in Birmingham, Alabama. In a civil case that would eventually reach the Supreme Court, Ollie McClung insisted that the government had no right to impose regulations on privately owned businesses. *Katzenbach v. McClung* became one of two simultaneous Supreme

Court decisions that compelled private businesses to abide by the Civil Rights Act. McClung integrated his dining room.

The same could not be said for Leonidas John Moore, proprietor of Moore's Barbecue in the coastal town of New Bern, North Carolina. He litigated to keep his restaurant segregated for three years before padlocking the door and bulldozing the building when finally forced to integrate. He relocated down the road and pigheadedly built a restaurant without a dining room, serving barbecue on his terms from a walk-up window.

It's no wonder that two decades later, Bobby Seale, cofounder of the Black Panther Party, titled his cookbook *Barbeque'n with Bobby*, purposefully spelled with a "que" because that is how, he wrote, African Americans pronounced and spelled "barbecue." Though some members of the black power movement have since deemed Seale a sellout for hawking a cookbook, he continues to defend barbecue as a unique form of resistance.

Barbecue King Adam Scott's entrepreneurial achievements should also be considered revolutionary. Two decades before the Civil Rights Act, he decided to parlay his success into a real, full-seating restaurant to be owned and operated by his eldest son, Martel. Scott's Bar-B-Q, located one block south of Barbecue Alley, opened with separate dining rooms for white and black customers. In 1946, Martel obtained a patent on his father's sauce recipe. It remains a gold mine for the Scotts. Sold under a bright yellow label, Scott's Family Barbecue Sauce ("It's the best ye ever tasted," the slogan reads) is a regionally iconic condiment, with more than one million bottles sold annually.

In a regrettable twist of events, a fire damaged Adam Scott's house in 1946, closing the chapter on the original Barbecue Alley location. Scott would go on to become a favored caterer among the elite class of North Carolina businessmen, especially R. J. Reynolds,

Jr., heir to the tobacco fortune. He continued catering well into his late eighties and never stopped preaching, finally passing away at the age of ninety-three.

Scott's Bar-B-Q, renamed Scott's Famous Barbecue, remains intermittently open under the care of Martel Scott, Jr. But his grandfather, the first king of barbecue, would hardly recognize the barbecue served there, as the family long ago switched to cooking their whole hogs with gas.

———

At an hour past midnight the smell of roasted pig meat wafted from the pit house into our screened-in porch of a seating area, stirring us awake with hunger. Pop kicked off his shoes and lit cigarette after cigarette. I tried my best to get comfortable in my tiny chair. And every half hour he excused himself to fire his hogs. And I'd follow behind. As the night's hours wore on, both he and I moved progressively slower. With each scoop of coals, every heavy step into the pit house, time seemed to be slowly calcifying.

At some point in the night, I asked Pop if the late hours and low pay made the pitmaster's profession worth it in the end.

Offering a list, he made it abundantly clear that he had long considered his own value to the Wilber's name. "I think in the end, what makes it worth it is I gotta job, for one. I'm happy to feed the public, for two. I enjoy cooking for people, three. Number four: I'm more or less an independent worker while I'm here alone. And maybe number five, sometimes I go up front and people look at me and say, 'The barbecue was good.' And just those few words can make my day, just to hear them say that. To me it's a good thing to know I'm satisfying somebody's taste. Maybe not everybody, but somebody. So, that makes it worth it to me."

Though Wilber Shirley may own the business, Pop the pitmaster takes ownership of the barbecue. His own unique pitmaster style is Pop's resistance.

As the hours drifted past and the rest of Goldsboro slept, we talked about what men talk about when gathered around a fire, argued issues humanity has debated for thousands of years: politics versus the betterment of society, God versus organized religion, Larry Bird versus the rest of the NBA. It felt good to discuss anything and everything but barbecue.

I watched as Pop occasionally dozed off, often with a lit cigarette in his mouth. But each half hour, his internal clock buzzing, he sprang up to fire his hogs. At 3:27 AM, an undercover cop stopped by to beg him for a single rib. The last words I remember Pop saying to me were, "The night gets kind of long sometimes around here." And I silently nodded away in agreement as the white noise of pig grease softly sizzling over hot coals lulled me to sleep.

I awoke with dawn still rooted to my chair, punch-drunk and aching all over. From the pit house, I could feel the radiant heat echo off the still-smoldering coals. Next to me, Pop's seat sat empty. His shovel stood by the door, cool to the touch. He was gone. But the air remained thick with the scent of barbecue he had spent all night cooking.

The smell of crisped hog meat followed me as I sleepily shuffled to my car. Before driving off I took one final look across Wilber's parking lot. "WHAT'S IN A NAME?" asked the same billboard. "Choose a new motto for Goldsboro." And I recalled something Pop had said earlier in the night while reminiscing over the barbecue houses of Adam and Martel Scott: "I knew those people. They were just ordinary people," he told me. "There have been some great barbecue places in Goldsboro over the years that I remember, but here at Wilber's we are still standing. We are still standing."

We are still standing. Goldsboro, you have found your new motto.

———————

Before taking leave of Goldsboro, I drove toward my final scheduled stop in the city, to track down one of the last surviving links to the Adam Scott dynasty. I parked downtown and walked the two blocks to my appointment at 319 South George Street. The cute pale-yellow building sat perched on a corner lot along the fringes of a residential neighborhood. Above the building, a sign reading GUY PARKER BARBECUE, the letters stained to rust from dripping water, creaked back and forth in a gentle breeze. Grass sprouted from several cracks in the empty parking lot. Finding the front door locked, I peered into the restaurant's windows and waited for a response. The lights were on, the tables tidy and set. At ten minutes before noon, it looked like Guy Parker's was ready to welcome a stream of hungry lunchtime patrons but just waiting until the clock struck twelve to officially open for business.

The door swung open to reveal Yvonne Parker, who ushered me inside with a hug and a smile, a smile that was full and grandmotherly and rarely if ever left her face. She wore librarian glasses that hung on a chain, a zebra-striped blouse, and floral-stamped pants that existed on some higher plane of harmonious design with the fruit-patterned curtains that hung in the windows. As at many barbecue restaurants I've visited, pig tchotchkes, among other swine-centric iconography, adorned much of the dining room. There were ceramic pig ornaments, plastic pig totems, and numerous paintings of pigs. The hands of a pig-shaped wall clock remained stuck at four minutes to four.

Near the register, Christmas cards still hung taped to the wall, though it was mid-June. A calendar remained pegged to a date seven and a half years in the past: January 2006. Where the dining room had before looked clean and ready for service, I now realized that the paper napkin dispensers that sat on every table all held napkins that had turned yellow and brittle. Like a scene straight out of a postapocalyptic film, this was a restaurant frozen in time.

Parker motioned for me to join her in a booth, its plush brown vinyl seat cool and inviting. I faced a large hand-painted wooden sign hanging from a transom that fed into a second dining room.

7 DAYS WITHOUT

GUY PARKER'S B•B•Q

MAKES ONE WEAK . . .

Adding to the clever pun, the letters in "weak" gradually shrank in size to resemble Lilliputian characters starved for barbecue. "Mr. Jim Walton had that sign printed and he brought it in here himself," she said after noticing me grinning at the restaurant's slogan. "He was eating in here all the time. So he saw that Guy never had a sign, so one day he had one made. He says, 'Since Guy didn't get the sign done, I got it done.'"

Guy Parker and Yvonne, his wife of fifty-seven years, never liked signs. "Sometimes at two or three o'clock in the day, we had a sign made where it says, 'Sold Out of Barbecue,'" she told me. It hurt her to put that sign in the window, to make customers weak for want of Parker's meat. "We probably lost money like that, but we felt a lot better whenever our food came out here to this table, and you could enjoy it, and you ate it, and it would taste . . ." And at this recollection of the ghosts of tastes past, Yvonne Parker's words drifted off into memories of life with her husband.

"You see, I'm a country girl," she began by way of introduction.

"My mother and father owned a big farm in Dublin, North Carolina. And I grew up in the country and, of course, my mother had eight children. We had such a good mother but she died so young." Yvonne moved to Goldsboro her senior year of high school and took a job waitressing at Scott's Bar-B-Q. There she met Guy Clifton Parker, Jr., a strikingly handsome young man from the seaside town of Beaufort, North Carolina, who worked the pits alongside Martel Scott. Parker was also a marine veteran, recently returned from the Pacific theater, where he had fought at Iwo Jima. He was also a talented painter and draftsman, passing up an opportunity to attend art school in California to stay close to home and cook barbecue. Guy and Yvonne married and as newlyweds lived in Adam Scott's old home on Brazil Street. The couple struck out on their own, eventually opening their restaurant on South George Street in 1965.

There was another sign that the Parkers didn't want to put up in their restaurant's window. "We never had a sign telling who to come in here," Yvonne told me. Meaning, conversely, the Parkers also never posted a sign refusing service to others. Though the Civil Rights Act of 1964 outlawed racial segregation in public accommodations, such as restaurants, the mostly white-owned businesses of Goldsboro remained defiantly segregated for some time. By 1965, with Adam Scott's barbecue house long shuttered and Martel Scott's restaurant operating with racially divided dining rooms, Guy and Yvonne Parker decided to open their doors to everyone. Yvonne remembers her adolescent daughter, Annette, confused by the race rules the Parkers chose to ignore. "She run and say, 'Mama, there is some white people out here and they want to know if they can come in and eat.' I said, 'Yeah, baby, tell them they're welcomed to just come right on in.' She was making so many trips to the kitchen until I finally told them like this, I said, 'Listen, anyone that wants to come in and eat are welcomed. You all seat them, and make them welcomed.'" By choosing to set a welcome table for all, Guy Parker's Barbecue became the first integrated restaurant in Wayne County, and certainly one of the earliest in North Carolina.

Throughout our conversation, Yvonne occasionally mixed up the past and present tenses, causing me to hope that the hands of that pig clock would magically start to tick, tick, tick, and Guy Parker himself would walk out of the kitchen with a couple of chopped barbecue sandwiches in hand. We would eat and share stories.

But Guy Parker, I knew, had passed away in 2006, a victim of lung cancer. Diagnosed on a Monday, he died five days later. He was eighty years old. Not only was the man a lifelong smoker, but had spent nearly six decades working in confined quarters, enveloped by smoke. Yvonne and her children chose not to keep Guy Parker's

Barbecue open without its namesake. The restaurant remains a private shrine to a husband and father who embraced a different path, a new way to serve barbecue.

Back in the present moment, Yvonne Parker smiled and said, "Well, young man, I don't know whether I have given you any facts or not." She handed me an original bottle of Guy Parker's Old Fashioned Barbecue Sauce and sent me on my way. Of all the barbecue sauces I have collected along my journey, it resides not in the kitchen but near my desk, the only bottle I will never open.

CHAPTER 6

My Own Private Barbecue

This day is the last this day. You won't see this one no more.

—STEPHEN GRADY

Every food writer and culinary fanatic dreams of finding that one undiscovered restaurant. We all aim to be pioneers of uncharted territory, the first to set foot into a backcountry or outer borough dining room, hear the wooden floorboards—or linoleum—squeak beneath our giant steps, and secure lifelong bragging rights to being the first to write up the best bagel found outside of New York. We aspire to be the Columbus who firmly plants the foodie flag at the only authentic Szechuanese restaurant in Kansas. Or finding the Kerala-born short order cook working at a Waffle House outside of Denver who shared a bite of his wife's malabar matthi curry, the best anyone has ever tasted. We are on the hunt for spots with a good backstory and sense of place. A kitchen that serves up implausibly perfect food from a location that is unimaginably remote. And most importantly, whether the dishes skew trendy or provincial, the name must not yet have appeared in print, the chef or pitmaster on no one's radar, the regular customers not on subscription lists to *Bon Appétit* and *Saveur*. We hunger for the thrill of the hunt as much as we hunger for the food we might find when we arrive.

Barbecue enthusiasts have been known to take this search to new heights. We all want to go down in history as the one who found the Atlantis of fire and smoke, the barbecue joint at the end of the world. I've scoured Internet message boards searching for a mention of any hidden gems, asked gas station attendants directions to their favorite smoked pork shacks, and driven through dead-end towns hunting for a fix. On the road, I scan the horizon for dark clouds of smoke, often driving with the windows down, my nose exposed to the open air, doglike, seeking the faintest sniff of burning meat.

On the interstate out of Goldsboro I spied a thin column of gray-black smoke in the distance, about three miles ahead. I rolled down my windows and exited the highway, looking for some 'cue in the heart of the country. I drove on and on, passing harvested fields of grain, twenty minutes into the middle of nowhere, knowing that somewhere up ahead stood my undiscovered barbecue shack. As the chase deepened, I could smell the barbecue. Closer now, the smoke grew into a tornado of porky goodness, reaching high up into the sky. I imagined other barbecue hounds, men with bigger bylines, on my tail. I had missed out on an opportunity to eat at Guy Parker's by seven years, but I would find this place, wherever and whatever it was. Half of the taste is in the chase.

Of course I arrived at the source of all that smoke to find not a barbecue pit but a field of wheat straw being slowly devoured by fire. Laughed at by the barbecue gods. I had let my belly get ahead of my brain. For the time being, I would stay hungry.

I proceeded to my last stop in North Carolina, the state's newest whole-hog establishment. The United States Postal Service locates Grady's Barbecue in the townless town of Dudley, just ten miles south of Goldsboro. But in reality, Grady's is nowhere. The restaurant rests on a triangular spit of land at the crossroads of two rural highways, one of which is named Sleepy Creek Road. It's a well-chosen name, because this is among the sleepiest places I've ever been.

On my first visit to Grady's, back in 2011, I pulled into the small gravel lot late in the evening in hopes of procuring the hours and days of operation, which I located on a handwritten notice tacked to the front door. With my headlights illuminating the paper sign, I saw that the vital information I sought had long been washed into an inky blur. This little Bermuda Triangle of barbecue swallows up cell phone reception, not that I've ever had any success in getting the owners to answer the restaurant's listed phone number. But I knew they had been open—I could smell the scent of recently smoked hogs lightly coloring the air.

As I pulled back onto the highway, a man materialized from the piney woods that blanket the road, shouted something wild and indistinguishable, and, like a ghost, dissipated into the thicket. For a moment, I considered not ever returning, not just because of the crazed woodsman, but it was as if the Grady's owners did not want to be found. Unlike the state's other whole-hog joints, which have crawled into the digital age, Grady's not only does not have a website but, until recently, did not have much of an Internet presence at all, besides Google Maps, which describes the business as simply "Hushpuppies, good people."

A week later, I found my way into Grady's Barbecue. The owners,

Gerri and Stephen Grady, were both shy, soft-spoken, and well past retirement age. Mrs. Grady (rhymes with "caddy") warmly greeted me from the front steps of her modest white cinder-blocked barbecue house at seven in the morning. She led me to the smokehouse, a tiny whitewashed structure with a sloped roof and a single chimney that rose into the sky like a church's steeple. In fact, the building's exterior looked so much like a rustic chapel that I half expected to walk in and see three pews and an altar. But instead, I found her husband shoveling coals under a single hog, a specimen several times smaller than I had been used to seeing. Grown accustomed to pit houses where the jumbo-sized hogs always outnumbered the pitmaster, I could not help but experience a sense of disappointment. This lonely pig felt anticlimactic, no different from thousands of marginally amplified backyard grill-outs that take place during football tailgates, bachelor parties, and imitation Hawaiian luaus.

After swatting through the clouds of smoke, I realized that the pig was cleaved completely down the backbone. Like the whole hogs I had seen in Goldsboro, this one was halved. Stephen Grady had arranged these two halves so that the belly and front and hind legs of the first curved around the back of the other, as if, like a couple in bed, they were hugging, or, to use the postcoital parlance, spooning. I pointed at the pig with what must have been a baffled expression. Grady nodded with a sheepish grin, revealing a single gold front tooth, and explained the setup. Often working alone in the smokehouse, he could not securely lift the entire pig's weight on and off the pit, despite its meager stature. He was, at the time, nearly seventy-seven years old. His wife, nine years younger.

For the Gradys, choosing to open a barbecue shop was more afterthought than calculated business plan. It was Stephen's brother who remodeled the ramshackle service station at the cross-roads. He opened his doors on a Friday, July the Fourth to be exact, the busiest possible day to leap headlong into the barbecue business. The next morning he refused to endure a second day. "He said it was the smoke," Stephen Grady told me. "He said, 'No, that's not for me.' And he was serious. So here we are."

So here they were: new owners of a barbecue business, and they didn't even have to change the name on the door—Grady's Barbecue. But their sum restaurant experience numbered exactly one afternoon, when Gerri helped her brother-in-law on that first chaotic Independence Day. She had recently been forcibly retired from her position as a nursing assistant, while Stephen was winding down from a long career at the local sawmill, alongside raising hogs, cattle, and crops on his own farm. Spring chickens they were not. They were also newlyweds, both recent divorcees with plenty of grown children, who had forged a marriage from a rekindled childhood friendship.

Sitting side-by-side across from me in a dining-room booth, Stephen and Gerri outlined the story of their romance and head-long foray into the whole-hog life while wearing matching navy blue shirts and holding each other's hand. He spoke in a singsong whisper that invariably sounded like poetry. Her voice was bright and silvery and ringing with laughter. I asked them for details of how long they had known each other. "We rode the same school bus," he said stoically. She filled in the details: "I tell everybody [that] he ended up plucking me. He watched me grow up and plucked me." They passed sidelong glances between each other and would not divulge further on the subject of their youthful or more recent dalliances.

But they would talk about their passion for food. "I've always cooked, about all my life," she told me. "My mama run me in the kitchen ever since I was about eight or nine years old. I used to go in with big, long lips, but she taught me how to cook. So from that day to this one I try to cook like my mama, my grandmama, and my mother-in-law. I enjoy it. Thoroughly enjoy it."

That joy shines bright each time I sit to eat from Gerri Grady's kitchen. It starts with the homemade ice tea, which she meticulously brews in a stovetop pot. She pours me a Styrofoam cupful of unsweetened tea from a recycled gallon-sized glass jar that bears a faded label for Mt. Olive brand pickle relish. This tea has legs. It rolls across my tongue, tasting leafy and natural. She knows I love vegetables, her vegetables especially, some of which are farmed by her green-thumbed husband. The steamed cabbage tossed with black pepper and apple cider vinegar. The garden-grown squash, stewed with long strands of onion, punched up with spice, and bursting with mouth-tickling umami. It's not without reason that a sign, hanging in the dining room, reads, "Welcome. Highly Seasoned Foods." My favorite, the collards, chopped fine and smothered, taste as green as they look, dark and vegetal and still growing, as if just unrooted from the soil. They taste best in the spring and summer, when the restaurant serves the bounty from Mr. Grady's annual harvest of four hundred heads of collards. I try to save room for a few bites of coleslaw, potato salad, and butter beans before finishing with a piece of Mr. Grady's sweet potato pie, its filling dense and creamy. He bakes a few each morning, before the sun rises, while waiting for a bonfire of hickory and oak wood to convert into charcoal. I always leave regretting that I hadn't ordered a second slice.

At no other barbecue house do the side dishes so gracefully complement and possibly even enrich the smoked meat than at Grady's. But it is for the barbecue that I keep returning. The meat is a perfect blend of coarsely chopped white meat, dark meat, and crisp-fried pork skin. I've watched as Mr. Grady, wearing industrial-strength rubber gloves that extended well past his wrists, mixed the still-scalding-hot chopped meat by hand to ensure that each impending bite would incorporate that ideal ratio of fat, flesh, and crackling. There's sauce—eastern Carolina's canonical recipe of salt, pepper, vinegar—mixed into the meat and cruets of more on each dining-room table, but I'd gracefully eat this barbecue without a condiment. A customer once told Stephen Grady that he was blessed with the ability to "season food the way peoples want it without putting anything on it." The fact is, the man knows just how to cook a pig.

"I have always known how to cook a pig," he told me. "I can't even remember when I learned how." But he did remember helping his grandfather, Walter Matthew Grady, and later his father around the pit. "When I was a boy, my grandfather had his own little grate. He was the barbecue cook of the neighborhood," a poor African American community with the impossibly idyllic name of Buckleberry, located outside the farm town of Seven Springs, North Carolina. Grandpa Grady was the local pitmaster for hire, bartering expertise for goods at a time when there "weren't a whole lot of money going around," the grandson recalled. "It was kind of like a favor here and a favor back later." He'd cook small hogs, just large enough to feed a family affair: fifty, sixty pounds at the most. No one dared attempt to barbecue a pig much larger than that. So when it came time to forge his own fires, Stephen Grady acquired a pig, dredged up those long-lapsed memories of assisting his grandfather, and went to work.

Though he is a big man, rangy and conditioned to a rigorous farm life, Grady has over the years made several modest concessions to his age. He built a modified brick and mortar pit, shorter than most, so that he can arrange, turn, and gather the pig's meat from his knees, with his body's mass comfortably centered on solid ground, rather than stooped over at the waist. This also explains why he cuts his hogs in half before smoking: convenience dictated by necessity. Each evening, just before midnight, he starts firing his hogs over a layer of standard charcoal briquettes. This establishes a controlled burn, reduces the risk of flare-ups, and allows Grady a few hours of—he admits—fitful sleep, before returning to finish the hogs with hardwood coals before dawn. He described his work routine as "get 'em hot, go home, take a nap, and back at four o'clock."

Other whole-hog pitmasters have condemned charcoal as a corner too closely cut, a charlatan's shortcut, tantamount to cooking with gas. I might ordinarily agree, but I would also wager that Stephen Grady can fly circles around pitmasters a quarter of his age. "People nowadays just are not going to work this hard," he told me. Besides running the pit house, he still farmed, in addition to the collard patch, more than three dozen acres of hay and soybeans. He also, until recently, raised a herd of beef cattle. "That's farming," he said, "hard to get out of your blood." Conceding: "Although you lose money, you keep doing it." He let loose a long laugh, the first and perhaps only I'd ever seen from the otherwise stoic man.

I found myself falling hard for the Gradys, and not just their food. I love the barbecue house they have built for themselves. The dormer windows framed by frilly white and pastel curtains. The plastic plants in the corner, the plastic flowers on each table. The faux wood paneling on the walls, the chipped Formica tables, the bright red booth seats rubbed raw from years of happy eaters. The dining-room air freshener—the kind more commonly located in restrooms—that like clockwork, with a mechanical whirl and splurt, spritzes a deodorized chemical mist over the heads of diners. Never mind the hushpuppies—the common North Carolina variety of fried corn meal that I seldom, if ever, hold dear—the Gradys were good people.

In June 2012, six months after first meeting the Gradys, I helped lead a tour through the whole-hog hotbed of eastern North Carolina sponsored by the Southern Foodways Alliance, the University of Mississippi–based organization that first put me on the road to track down and document the region's varied barbecue cultures. During the trip's planning stages I insisted that the Gradys be included. Whether or not my vetting swayed the SFA's lead coordinators, they hired Gerri and Stephen to cater Saturday's big-ticket barbecue picnic, complete with fried chicken and sides. That afternoon 120 well-traveled culinary sophisticates— food tourists, journalists, and chefs—from across the nation descended on Grainger baseball stadium in the nearby town of Kinston to get high on Carolina smoked hog. In the hours leading up to the lunch, I felt uncontrollably protective of the pair. Could the Gradys even feed this many people at once? The crowd lined up buffet style before sitting down to eat at a scattering of picnic tables, while I nervously observed from afar. Would that Top Chef finalist in attendance think their barbecue any good? I couldn't eat and instead stood at a distance watching Gerri and Stephen greet every tour attendee as if they were on a first-name basis with each. Fried chicken? Who talked them into that? I forgot they even sold fried chicken. I needed to take a walk and resolved to locate the Gradys' staging kitchen, which I found just beyond the baseball stadium's front gates. There sat parked a white van and towable cargo trailer with "Grady's Barbecue" stenciled in fancy red script along the side of both. I peeked inside. It was a behemoth, a military-like operation: outfitted with a full kitchen and, reminding me of my favorite *Simpsons* quote, enough deep-fat fryers "for every part of the chicken." An employee I had never seen before coated and fried batch after batch of yardbirds, while another chopped and mixed barbecue. Both kept their heads down and worked as I gawked in amazement. The Gradys were evidently not new to the catering game.

Though I had previously grasped the fact that I was not the first barbecue junkie to fall in love with Gerri and Stephen Grady, I had fooled myself into expecting that I would introduce them to the world. Between their professionalism, the big-rig catering truck, and the fact that they had sated the passions of a hundred-plus barbecue devotees, the very idea of the Gradys needing to be found, by me or anyone else, was absurd. The Gradys were not in want of discovering.

But I have rediscovered Grady's almost annually, on my return drive down Sleepy Creek Road. I return here with ulterior motives, grander designs, driven by impulses much more complex than the pleasure of filling up on a plate of barbecue. I journey to Grady's for the food, yes, but I come here to lose myself, find myself, and renew myself. And though I was not the first to discover Grady's—it has been on the barbecue tourist trail for well over a decade—each time I walk through the front doors I feel like this place was built just for me to discover. This is my place, a space that provides me with a sense of direction, my own private barbecue.

But time is running out, the opportunity to rediscover Grady's will soon draw to a close. As far back as 2000, Stephen Grady told GQ food writer Alan Richman, who declared Grady's to be North Carolina's best barbecue, that he only had a half decade of smoking pigs in him. Grady of course did not stick to his five-year plan. Nearly a dozen years later, he was still in business. I raised this issue in December 2011, on my first visit to Grady's. He assured me that sometime in the new year he would take a vacation, his first since 1982. For one month, two months, maybe even three—he wanted to drive.

Three decades ago he drove west, passing through the Great

Plains and Hill Country of Texas, stopping at the Grand Canyon and Las Vegas, cruising all the way to California, like Sal and Dean, before turning back. Now he desired to head north, to Canada. "You can get lost in Canada," he confided. With his wife by his side, he'd drive until sleep and discomfort forced him off the road and stay "right here," he told me, wherever here was, "for a few days or a few weeks or maybe a month, and then move on." Though it might annoy their customers, Grady's would remain closed; their children from previous marriages didn't want any part of the business. He would put a sign on the door, "Gone on Vacation," Stephen Grady said. And "I ain't gonna say nothing about coming back." And when he and Gerri returned, if they returned, they might reopen and "go back to work," he said plainly, honestly, "maybe till we die."

Though he normally acceded the conversational tide to his wife, Grady finally opened up while talking of the possibilities of a future vacation and did not hesitate to impart his seven decades' worth of wisdom on a greenhorn such as myself. I ate up every word. "The human body was not made to stay still. It was made to move," he answered when asked why he doesn't retire sooner. He would keep moving, by foot or car, until his body failed him. Almost eighty years old and stubbornly shaking off retirement, Grady lived and cooked hog by hog, hour by hour, day by day. "I try to enjoy every day as I go along," he said before sharing his life's motto. "This day is the last this day. You won't see this one no more." At this I turned off my tape recorder, not because I had run out of questions, but because I felt tears in my eyes.

I feel them now.

I've returned to Grady's twice since. I arrive not knowing if I'll find their smokehouse closed, but I'm always happy—shamefully, selfishly happy—to discover them open, to order a plate of barbecue with all the available sides, to know that the Gradys have delayed their eternal road trip just one more summer. Next time, I think to myself. Next summer there will be a sign on the door. It'll read "Gone on Vacation" in a faint and faded script. And I'll leave wishing that I would have taken the earlier opportunity to have ordered an entire sweet potato pie.

CHAPTER 7

Ricky Parker Builds a Legacy

I often questioned what attracted me to Ricky Parker, what compelled me to return year after year, summer after summer to Lexington, Tennessee.

There was the barbecue, of course, which I felt myself hunger for, my belly aching with emptiness, each spring when the weather warmed, the outdoors blossomed with fresh possibilities, and the open road beckoned. The cravings rumbled awake in early April, when the hardware stores stacked bags of charcoal high enough to resemble a monolithic shrine to the backyard gods. When meat-scented smoke perfumed the air in public parks and, especially in my home city of New Orleans, outside of bars, where enterprising grillmasters cooked from the back of their curbside pickups. This is when the world, my world, began to smell of barbecue.

By May, when I began counting down the days until the semester's end, I'd start planning a road trip. Could I wait until July, or would I hit the road as soon as I turned in my final paper? Would

I drive up to Memphis and stay with friends for a night or take the straight shot to Lexington, shaving fifty miles off the total distance and ensuring that I would make Scott's by nightfall? But Ricky would have always sold out of barbecue by then. He usually extinguished his pits, locked the doors, and hung the SOLD OUT sign from the window by four PM, sometimes hours earlier. I often stayed at the Econo Lodge, a shabby motel that sat directly across the highway from Scott's, with an ancient blue-haired lady behind the counter who rented rooms at fifty-five dollars per night. In the mornings I could wake up with the sun, walk outside, and smell fresh barbecue. Before heading over, I'd pick up coffees and a sack of biscuits and hash browns from McDonald's to share with Ricky and his sons—a bribe of sorts to cajole them into letting me hang around the pit house until the hogs were done. I'd stick around until lunch, then order a pound of barbecue: a heaping of chopped shoulder mixed with a handful of its crusty, exterior bark and with a pull of middlin' on top.

So I traveled up to Lexington each year to sate my hunger for another plate of barbecue, but I also went to satisfy my curiosity about Ricky Parker. What info could I glean this visit? Would he, as usual, be too busy to talk? Was he still shooting for one hundred hogs? How in the hell did he continue to do what he did? Knowing Ricky's work ethic, the hours he put in, his obsession bordering on pathological: I recognized that Ricky wouldn't be cooking hogs forever. He was nearing fifty years old. He said he was slowing down, that he used to run but now walked. Men didn't live to work much longer if they worked like Ricky did, though to me, it still looked like running.

I turned friends and family on to Scott's so they could share in my love for the barbecue, but also so that they might update me on the status of its pitmaster. He still cooking? How'd his barbecue taste? Like me, my stepfather, Danny, took time to make the stop each year. He remember me? Ask about me? I'd question other barbecue enthusiasts, many of them longtime fans of Ricky, who'd just returned from their own road trips to West Tennessee. How's his health? How'd he look?

Whispers spread by friends and Scott's devotees, facts or fictions—it was hard to distinguish between the two when it came to Ricky. Ricky had cornered the local swine market to ensure that only he could get his hands on a fresh hog. Ricky was in jail. These were the updates I needed to hear—Ricky had his obsession, and I had mine. Ricky had curbed his drinking. Ricky was drinking again. Ricky had switched from Jack Daniel's to vodka because it sat better in his stomach. But I often couldn't bear to listen; it seemed his life was spiraling downward. It wasn't alcohol but something else. Ricky didn't look right, didn't sound right, didn't act right. That barbecue ain't shit.

But no matter the talk while I was away, each summer I'd return to Lexington and Scott's and find Ricky just where I had left him. In the pit house, holding his shovel, or behind the counter, sliding the glass window aside to shake my hand before taking my order and shouting it over to Zach or Matt: "Pound of barbecue, hot!" There he was.

There was Ricky Parker.

———

If every spectacle includes and concludes with an explosive ending, the climax of Ricky's whole-hog cooking was the "flip," that final moment, after twelve or more hours of cooking, when with a heave and heft he flipped each hog so that the outer, or skin side, of the whole beast was rotated upward to earthward revealing what had long remained hidden: what was once a fleshy pink corpus transformed into a beautiful mess of slightly charred rib bones protruding from a ruddy-gold mass of roast meat.

Whether by hand-cranked spit or engine-spun rotisserie, the heat source for roast meats needs to be distributed evenly to ensure a well-cooked pig, side of beef, whole fish, or what have you. Think of the perfectly toasted marshmallow, its caramelized surface achieved by twisting it over the campfire; without motion, the marshmallow will burn unevenly, blacken, and might even combust.

But a whole hog is not a marshmallow. Two-hundred-pound pigs are much too heavy, too bulky to reliably turn on a spit. Conceivably, a pitmaster could rotate a hog every hour or two, but the energy involved in hefting the carcass up and over, anywhere between four and twelve times in a cooking cycle, within arm's reach of fiery coals, as the meat becomes hotter to handle and increasingly grease slicked with rendered fat, would make the endeavor unbearable. Multiply that by twenty hogs all cooking at once, and even the most vigorous of pitmasters is faced with an impossible task.

For anyone who's turned even a spit full of chickens over a roaring fire, the work becomes quickly monotonous and tiresome. Before the modern-day mechanization of the rotisserie, turnspit dogs kept meats slowly rotating over the open fire. In the sixteenth to mid-eighteenth centuries, throughout Britain and its colonies, including America, households might have owned a *Canis vertigus*, Latin for "dizzy dog," a specific breed raised to run in a wheel—like those favored by hamsters—which spun a chain connected to a fireplace spit. Also called kitchen dogs, cooking dogs, underdogs, and the vernepator cur, or "the dog that turns the wheel," these short-legged, long-bodied Sisyphean pups also worked in early New England sculleries. The cruel treatment of the turnspit dogs eventually fell out of favor, and helped lead to the formation of the

American Society for the Prevention of Cruelty to Animals, and the *Canis vertigus* became extinct.

Luckily, for the sake of mutt and man, pitmasters long ago figured out that whole hogs did not need constant turning if they remain belly, or meat side, down. Well-insulated pits, hardwood coals shoveled at timed intervals and deposited consciously around the carcass's perimeter, and vigilance against flame and flare-ups will keep a pig evenly heated, its meat uniformly browned. But eventually all hogs need to be rotated, flipped upward so that the meat can meet its maker and greet the world as barbecue.

Ricky Parker, naturally, had his flip technique systematically diagrammed, a series of steps by which the pitmaster and his pit hands would never deviate. First, he needed to determine that a hog had been cooked through to doneness. Tenderly squeezing its thick, round hams, like a doctor probing for foreign bodies, he could feel if the skin had separated from the flesh underneath. It felt, to me, like handling a slightly deflated basketball: applying a bit of pressure formed an indention that would snap back into shape when released. He then enveloped the hog's outer upturned skin with a single layer of tinfoil. A steel grate, the exact same lattice-type framework that held the pig on the pit, was placed atop the now foil-topped hog. Ricky then tightly fastened these two grates together with strands of wire, sandwiching the hog in between. With a great inhale and flexing of biceps, he hoisted this massive hog sandwich up and toward his chest, using the bars of the pit's grill to guide and glide the bottom-most grate, before pushing out and, releasing his weight to gravity's fortunes, upending the hog to land belly up.

One by one, day by day, across thirty-five years, Ricky Parker flipped hog after whole hog. I attempt to total the numbers but my head spins dizzily just thinking of Ricky: our *vernepator pitmasterus*, the man who spun the wheel.

Ricky Parker had met the enemy and it was a stainless steel box, the size and shape of a pool table, a closed-lid oven big enough to fit a whole hog, with four legs on wheels for added mobility, in case one needed to roll it closer to your standard 240 volt electrical outlet. A product of nearby Jackson, Tennessee, this contraption went by the generic name Hickory Creek Bar-B-Q Cooker—though there is no Hickory Creek anywhere on this side of the state. This was the very latest in smoking technology, a modern marvel that promised to take the work out of barbecue, and it was everything Ricky hated.

Within a half-hour's drive of Lexington, I had met several pitmasters—though you could hardly still call them that—who switched from wood-fired pits to these metal monsters. One demonstrated that his Hickory Creek took just two sticks of hickory, one inch square by ten to twelve inches long, incinerated in something called "smoke tubes," to cook an entire hog overnight. Another lifted the hood to his cooker like we were going to inspect the horsepower of his car's engine—there were streaks of grease here and there, but it still looked sterile, antiseptically clean. He boasted that his cooking process now consisted of loading his meat into the oven, setting the time and temperature controls, and pushing a button before going home to laze around, sleep through the night, and never have to worry about a pit fire again. Fourteen hours later, his barbecue would be ready for serving. He assured me that his customers still supported the business, and he now made more money doing less work since converting to electric power. He closed the hood, and in the metal's mirrored shine I recognized my reflection and the look of gloom that shaded my face.

I asked Ricky if the Hickory Creek salesman had visited him. "He calls me quite often. And he tells me I need one of these things, where I can go home and get some rest. And I told him, 'What am I going to do? I'll be bored.' But he always calls me."

Ricky, like his fellow whole-hog traditionalists, might stick to doing the same thing—cooking with the same wood and spicing with the same sauce—that the men who trained him did, but he would never be bored. He might remain unchanged, a diehard, a pig-headed classicist, an adherent to his swinish orthodoxy, but Ricky did not do boring. "This place ain't never changed," he told me, and he planned to run his business that way until the day he died or was forced into retirement.

"If they made me quit cooking with wood, and I couldn't buy whole hogs," Ricky liked to tell anyone who questioned his future in the business, "I would totally quit." He, like many whole-hog proprietors, took pride in the grandfather clauses that protected their pit houses from ever being shut down by the local fire chief. But few acknowledged that the whole whole-hog business model is one big grandfather clause, an accumulation of provisional exemptions frozen in history despite the passing of time. Whole-hog stalwarts must keep their menu short and simple; operate in a rural area, which helps in keeping labor costs and menu prices low; and, perhaps most fundamentally, have the good fortune of inheriting the establishment, customer base, and several lifetimes of experience from a family member.

But Ricky was a smart man. He wanted to leave a legacy behind, something for his five children, two of whom, Matthew and Zach, had been helping him at Scott's Barbecue since about the time they could walk. He understood that the vast majority of his sweat and toil went up in smoke each day. He recognized the need to be remembered, the desire to be great.

In November 2005, he accepted an invitation to smoke two hogs at the Culinary Institute of America's eighth annual Worlds of Flavor event held on their Napa Valley campus. His barbecue would be featured alongside the traditional cuisine of cooks and chefs as far-flung as Oaxaca, Istanbul, and Bangalore. Though he needed a whole lot of Wild Turkey to calm his jitters, his barbecue and easy charm impressed the palates and spirits of the culinary jet set.

The next year, he traveled up to New York for the Big Apple Barbecue Block Party, an affair on its way to becoming the nation's premier smoked-meat showcase. It was here, at a documentary short film screening that featured the pitmaster, where I first met Ricky, a full two years before I would travel to Lexington for his barbecue. That afternoon, I watched as he smiled at his own face projected on the pull-down screen and laughed as the audience laughed along with his countrified turns of phrase. At the Q&A that followed, someone asked Ricky about his first impressions of the big city. "Well," he said, "this morning I was standing on the street outside my hotel, smoking a cigar and drinking a coffee, when someone tossed a quarter into my cup. They thought I was homeless." Nerves soothed from his earlier experience in the culinary spotlight, he was ready to bring Tennessee whole hog to the masses. But the barbecue was not to be. The fire chief patrolling the event quashed Ricky's plan to cook over an open fire.

When I made my first pilgrimage to Scott's Barbecue in the summer of 2008, Ricky had renounced any ambitions of making it big on the national barbecue circuit in order to focus on his business at home. Contrary to his dedication to never changing a thing, he had recently completed construction on a new pit house—a great temple of a building—to replace the outdated and cramped shanty of a smokehouse that Early Scott had built decades before. Ricky's pit house remains the grandest in size and scope that I've ever seen, with cathedral-tall ceilings, twin rows of brick pits spanning the length of the room (about forty by ten feet), a built-in meat locker, and, something I've never since come across, an entire side room dedicated to sauce production.

The following year, he would make an even more momentous change by adding his name to the marquee out front. Twenty years after purchasing the business from his adopted pitmaster of a father, Mr. Early, Scott's would now be known as Scott's-Parker's Barbecue. It was a tongue-twister of a name, sure, but one befitting the two men who had worked to keep whole hog alive in West Tennessee.

With these changes, the new pit house and new name, Ricky was more than cementing his legacy; he was building a birthright for his children, especially his two eldest sons. Born just over a year apart, Matt and Zach were both skinny, quiet high-schoolers when I first met them in 2008. Matt gravitated toward the service counter, while his younger brother shadowed his father in the pit house. Ricky hoped his second-oldest would succeed him as the head pitmaster at Scott's-Parker's but also feared what this would entail for the boy. "I want Zach to do this, but then again I think I'm going to deprive him out of his life. But he's got to understand, you got to give up a lot to do this," he told me, before listing the events that a dedicated pitmaster, in his estimation, must skip out on. "Vacations, going to ball games and seeing your girl play softball or watching boys play football." As Ricky wound down his list, it became quite clear to me that he was atoning, in his own way, for the moments and milestones that he had missed throughout his own life and the lives of his children. For Ricky Parker, barbecue came before all else: "If you got family that's died, you can't even go to a funeral because you got hogs cooking. There's a lot of things you got to sacrifice."

Ricky Parker would sacrifice them all.

CHAPTER 8

South Carolina: The Battleground State

I knew that what could be true of my
pig could be true also of the rest of my tidy world.

—E. B. WHITE

$\mathcal{S}$ix months after my last fact-finding mission, I was back on the road for the Southern Foodways Alliance to document the faces and places behind the barbecue in the other Carolina. Denny again joined me on the RV, which now sported a decal on the back that officially branded us as the Barbecue Bus. The logo was a surprise gift courtesy of my parents, who, bless their hearts, thought we could use some interstate publicity along our journey. I was too embarrassed to tell them that an additional decal they had made that read "Oink if you love BBQ" maybe went a little too far.

For our swing through South Carolina, I expected to find much of the same: idyllic backdrops for leisurely drives, food that made me feel a part of a place and a people, cordial folks eager to share their stories, a receding whole-hog culture. Nothing separates the Carolinas, I thought to myself while packing my bag, but a direction. But like all good assumptions, it was both half right and more than half wrong.

For a century before the Carolinas became distinct halves, they constituted the Province of Carolina. This was a proprietary territory ruled by an impressively influential roll call of English nobles and politicians looking to make a quick buck through colonization and agricultural development. By 1729, the British Crown bought back their shares and carved two Carolina colonies from the province. Soon after, a survey team, hired by colony commissioners to set a fixed boundary between the colonies, slogged along a diagonal line traced upon a map of the Eastern Seaboard toward their rendezvous with the 35th parallel, the northern latitudinal border that would eventually delineate the South from the Deep South. But the exhausted and often unpaid surveyors abandoned their project twelve miles short of their destination, unintentionally framing the Carolinas' misshapen, and still disputed, boundary. South Carolina bore the brunt of the survey snafu. Whereas North Carolina's outline looks bold, majestic—an outstretched arm (or gun, unfortunately) muscularly pointing toward the destiny that would ultimately manifest in the heartland of the United States—I always thought South Carolina looked like a child's interpretation of a gnarled and battered heart, a crooked little place looking for love.

Despite their shared heritage and history, crossing the border from North Carolina into South Carolina can feel like undertaking an interplanetary hop and skip to the next world over. The Mason-Dixon line, the cultural frontier that once split the northern and southern states, is, of course, the more famous American boundary, but it's along the serpentine borderline that cleave the Carolina sisters where our nation's cultural shifts are now most noticeably deep and abiding.

South Carolina revels in its own southernness, as if accepting fate over choice. The identity of the state is fixed, embraced, pushed front and center, determined as much by an adjectival modifier as by history. South Carolinians are born doubly southern.

The dueling Carolinas become apparent as soon as you cross that blundered border down Interstate 95 and, like a mirage shimmering into view along a desert horizon, a sombrero-topped tower, rising sixteen stories high, gently looms into view. Zigzagged in pink neon tubing and looking big enough to comfortably crown the head of any one of the four Mount Rushmore presidents, the audaciously tacky hat welcomes travelers to South of the Border, an awful pun and a way station for carloads of families scrambling farther south and east for sand, sun, and Disney World. South of the Border is the proto-Epcot, a campy novelty minus the futuristic utopianism. It is a theme park with just a single theme, a world showcase of one, an amusement park without the fun, a roadside attraction built at a time when Mexican culture was more digestibly stereotyped (one of the many dozens of billboards that line the highway on both sides of the Carolinas' shared border advertises the weather forecast: "Chili today, hot tamale!"). Only Pedro, South of the Border's mustachioed mascot, venerated in a hundred-foot-tall neon-lit statue that from afar, driving from the north, seems to straddle the road, stands between this Carolina border crossing and more barbecue. But though I always want to pass Pedro with a hearty adios, I cannot help but stop each time for a healthy dose of kitsch.

I set the Bus's controls for the heartland of South Carolina, the Midlands, the state's geographic center, nestled midway between the Appalachian Upcountry and the Lowcountry of the Atlantic coast. I swung around the outskirts of Columbia and piloted toward Batesburg-Leesville, a town in the southwesterly orbit of the capital city. Long before Batesburg and Leesville were municipally merged in 1992, an imposing railroad line bisected the middle of both, uniting the two small towns while dividing each into separate halves. Driving through Leesville to Batesburg and back again, I got the impression that this was less an example of the iconic whistle-stop American town, but rather a residentially zoned railway depot, a place where everybody lived on the wrong side of the tracks. In Leesville, Jackie Hite's Bar-B-Q, one of the state's three remaining wood-fired whole-hog barbecues, abuts one side of those tracks.

James Lee "Jackie" Hite is big, a physically and mentally imposing presence, a man who walks and talks with the shit-kicking demeanor—though stereotype it may be—of a small-town southern sheriff. In fact, he has held most every local political position but parish police chief. Back in 1966 he graduated from fireman to Leesville's fire chief, before serving as a water commissioner, a city councilman, and magistrate. He ran for sheriff and lost, then ran for mayor and lost by six votes. He recovered, rebounded, and ran for mayor again, winning that election and the next two. After two decades of the political life he retired to focus on his barbecue business. Twenty-five years later, supporters were still dogging him, despite his being seventy-two years old and slowed by open-heart surgery, to run for office again. "Messing with politics is one of my favorite games," he told me, winking. "I'm not saying I ain't gonna run for mayor again either." Today, Hite continues to serve his people through the politics of pork.

"Most people ain't even know where my place is," Jackie Hite told me, waving toward an empty morning-hour dining room. "The local people don't want a lot of people here because they said it would be too crowded. It's people in here, but it's not a whole pile of people."

Returning for lunch, I counted up the customers: by my amateur estimation, the dining room looked to be filled with about a quarter pile of people or so, all silently munching through plates of barbecue. Another dozen or so individuals stood clutching Styrofoam plates, quietly queued up, like pilgrims waiting to touch a holy shrine, before a buffet-style steam table. I paid for a plate, took my place behind an elderly woman whose royal blue blouse neatly matched her bouffant, and inched my way up the line. We waited as preceding customers swarmed the first station of the buffet table: barbecue.

Heat lamps threw a string of pale-orange halos upon a four-foot-long chafing dish that contained an unholy mess of barbecue pork. With the meat chunked and pulled, and fried pork skins scattered about, it looked as if a pig had exploded. I rummaged through the meat with a pair of kitchen tongs, piling my plate with some dark, a couple pinches of white, and a triangular jib of crisped skin. I moved on down the line feeling more than a bit bewildered. A barbecue buffet? Just as I was beginning to find my barbecue bearings, I felt I'd crash-landed, a man fallen to earth, Piggy Stardust.

The table's far end opened up on to the usual blanket of southern sides: collards and cabbage and limas, green beans with boiled potatoes, macaroni swamped in neon-yellow cheese, potato salad, fried okra, squarish lumps of yeast rolls, and mayonnaise-whipped coleslaw. There was fried chicken, banana pudding, and an untouched salad bar. In the thick of the sides was a deep-troughed warming pan brimming and burbling with a brown-gravied stew called barbecue hash, or simply hash, in this part of the state. Though from the way customers ladled thick globs of the stuff onto their plates, it looked like an embarrassing kissing cousin to chili that had fortunately been consigned to oblivion long ago. This mysterious meat soup evidently played the sidekick role to barbecue here. Following the lead of my blue-haired guide, I poured a dipperful over a bed of white rice. I smiled at her with a knowing nod, to tell her that I knew just what I was doing.

Seated at a table, plastic fork in hand, I studied my plateful of spoils with the analytical intent of a scientist sifting through a Martian soil sample. First, I poked around the pile of barbecue. The meat was tinted an unnatural shade of bronzed-yellow—like the hog had fallen asleep in a tanning bed—the telltale sign of South Carolina's

THE ONE TRUE BARBECUE

famed mustard sauce. To be sure, the sauce contained the classic hints of vinegar and spice, but I knew, from the mildly pungent scent that wafted up from the plate, that I was eating mustard-covered barbecue. Similar to but different from America's tried-and-true ballpark-style yellow mustards, this sauce triggered slightly sharper rattles across several surfaces of the tongue, minor earthquakes that those bland French's varieties can never touch. I've always been a bit of a mustard freak; the shelves of my refrigerator door, like those of most artisan-label-hoarding foodists, fill with Dijon-zipped this and chipotle-zapped that, but for the first time I understood how mustard got its name. From the Latin *mustum* (young wine) and *ardens* (hot), mustard is a paste made from the spicy mustard seed with an acidic liquid, like vinegar. I dove in for a few more fork loads. But I still wasn't completely convinced; mustard felt all too alien. Wasn't North Carolina–style vinegar and spice enough to accent barbecued pork?

My buffet spoils turned downright peculiar when I guardedly turned my fork toward the hash, a runny mound of ground-meat gravy that just taunted me to take a bite. Hash is basically whole-hog soup, a curious culinary invention that can only be fully appreciated by those who are committed to consuming an entire animal in one sitting. Hashmasters combine everything edible (the meaty muscle tissue) and semi-edible (skin, fat, cuts from the head, and other offal) from a hog, boil these piggy parts in gargantuan black iron cauldrons (repurposed wash pots and molasses kettles), grind or pull the meat, and add liquid, before rounding out the stew with a filler (potatoes, onion, and sometimes even beef) and spices to cook a second time through. Along the hash corridor that runs through South Carolina's midsection, the stew is flavored with either ketchup or mustard, while in the Upcountry hash is often and quite quizzically—because this is still hog country—made solely with beef.

Jackie Hite spices his hash, like his barbecue, with the same yellow mustard, shading the ground meat a dull earthy tone. It looked like cafeteria food, which, served on a buffet line, made sense. It was stringy and thick enough to eat with a fork, but, like the hashes I tasted elsewhere throughout the state, the taste and texture put me off from eating more than two or three forkfuls. I passed my plate to Denny. That boy will eat anything.

I had no desire to try hash again, but I would not pass up an opportunity to watch it being made. We returned to Jackie Hite's two weeks later for a behind-the-scenes tour. Arriving half an hour early for our scheduled appointment, I let myself in through an unlocked gate. The hash house sat in a corner between the kitchen and the barbecue pits. Inside, Hite's pitmaster, Tim Hyman, stirred a hot-tub-sized stew pot with a wooden paddle. Traditionally, the hash kettle was fired, like barbecue, with hardwood coals. Though Hite switched to propane to boil his stew following his heart attack, he insistently tosses a few shovelfuls of hickory embers alongside the pot to impart barbecue's classic smokiness to the stew.

I peered over the cauldron's edge, where gelatinous chunks of pork and slivers of yellow onion boiled and bubbled in the gurgling hell broth. One hash hound has described the dish as "liquid meat," and, boy, was he right. I had always thought that I would not mind a visit to a sausage factory, but the old adage about never wanting to see the stuff being made finally rang true. The stench of boiled meat—seventy-eight gallons of boiled meat to be exact—filled my nostrils, my stomach, my head. Woozy and feverish, I felt as if I had swallowed a whole hog whole.

Just at that moment, as I wobbled in my hash-induced haze, Jackie Hite burst through the kitchen door. "I thought I told you to be here at nine," he hollered in his best bad-cop imitation. Hands raised in surrender, I apologized and slowly backed away from the hash pot while pulling on Denny's shirtsleeve. Red faced and roaring mad, he pointed to the exit, grumbled something about "keeping a man's time," and demanded that we immediately remove ourselves from the premises.

Was Hite a stickler for punctuality? A vigilant guardian of a classified hash recipe? Was he tired of me hanging around his place? Or maybe something else was at work. Too afraid to ask, Denny and I stepped double quick to our vehicle and, like Bo and Luke Duke evading Sheriff Rosco P. Coltrane of Hazzard County, sped away in a cloud of gravel dust. Laughing off our escapade, while cautiously glancing in the rearview mirror, I vowed to never again come between a man and his hash.

———

Most barbecue proprietors carry few secrets. Their pits are open source. Ain't nobody gonna put in these hours, work this kinda work, sweat this sorta sweat, many have told me. So look around, take notes, but just don't ask about the sauce. A sauce's ingredients, instructions for assembly, thoughts on tasting notes: all inquiries are off-limits. Sauces, like bloodlines, harbor secrets. Sauce recipes are handed down but rarely, if ever, written down. Sauce is the one rule of barbecue: you do not talk about sauce.

I've been met with dead-eyed stares and been threatened for asking about sauces. Sauces are grave business. Literally. Pitmasters like to tell stories about men dying with their sauce recipes locked away in their heads.

When I asked Curt Blankenship, a Tennessee whole-hog pitmaster who has since closed up shop, about sauce, he eulogized local barbecue man Priest Ellis's fabled creation, a recipe, legend says, he carried to his grave. Ellis's wife claimed to possess her husband's knowledge, but no one believed the poor widow.

No telling why Mr. Ellis didn't sell his recipe before drifting away to that great pit house in the sky. Because though good barbecue brings people in to eat, great barbecue sauces make money. Wherever there is barbecue, stories circulate about sauce recipes stored in bank vaults, sauce techniques carried by immigrants to the New World, ingredient lists as classified as the recipe for Coca-Cola or the president's nuclear launch codes. Barbecue sauces annually account for two billion dollars in sales, and most every barbecue-shop proprietor wants a piece of the action or, at the very least, a few inches of space on the shelves of a regional grocery store chain. It's the American dream dipped in vinegar and ketchup (and, more often than not, with these national shelf brands, high fructose corn syrup, caramel coloring, "natural" smoke flavor, and preservatives). Anybody can become the next Stubb's, the next Sweet Baby Ray's.

Jon Ivory, pitmaster at Sam's Barbeque in Humboldt, Tennessee, told me of a customer who paid two hundred dollars for a gallon of Mr. Sam's famous sauce. Richard Hodge, owner of Richard's Bar-B-Que in Bolivar, Tennessee, admitted to cleverly scheming his way to the perfect barbecue blend. "Well, that deer up there on the wall," he said, pointing to one specimen among many in his trophy-filled office. "A friend of mine traded me three ducks and a gallon of barbecue sauce for the hindquarter of that deer. And the next time I saw him I wanted to know how to make that sauce. And he said, 'I'll tell you what I put in it but I'm not going to tell you how to make it.'" Hodge finally re-created his buddy's sauce after five years and five hundred gallons of attempts, all for a recipe that contains just, he begrudgingly told me, half vinegar, half ketchup, and three different spices.

Several pitmasters have maintained that their sauce recipes emerged from dreams. Adam Scott of Goldsboro admitted as much. Like Jacob, Joseph, or any of the other Old Testament dreamers, divine inspiration has guided men in their search for the perfect vinegar-to-spice ratio. John "Big Daddy" Bishop swore that God provided him with the recipe that allowed him to open the original Dreamland Café in 1958, just south of Tuscaloosa, Alabama, in the appropriately named neighborhood of Jerusalem Heights. His commercial relationship with the Almighty was "kind of hard for me to talk about," he told one reporter. But not too hard to sell. Dreamland Bar-B-Que is the nation's most famous rib joint: a fledgling franchise with seven locations across the Southeast and a line of sauces and seasonings.

Big Daddy Bishop's recipe, like most brand-name sauces found coast-to-coast, belongs to the sugar + spice + salt + tomato + vinegar vernacular popular in Memphis and Kansas City, a sort of kicked-up ketchup that hits all five basic taste notes, from sweet to umami. But, of course, each region of the country has its own sauce variation. North Carolinians in the western part of the state add a touch of ketchup to the east's traditional vinegar, salt, and pepper blend to form a sauce they call dip. In north Alabama, they use a mayonnaise-heavy white sauce that mixes beautifully with smoked or grilled chicken. In my hometown of New Orleans, McClure's Barbecue gives a shout-out to the city's Vietnamese population by combining hoisin and soy for a rich, spicy brine bomb of a sauce.

South Carolina, the nation's smallest and most diverse barbecue-centric state, has five distinct sauce varieties and regions. In the eastern Lowlands of South Carolina, they eat their pork with the same vinegar-pepper combination that is popular up the coast in eastern North Carolina. On the opposite end of the state, a pair of sauce regions are embodied by South Carolinians who add tomato ketchup to their dressing—lighter in the north and west, heavier along the Georgia borderlands to the south. A third ketchup variety defines the fourth region in the state's sauce pastiche. In the dozen or so Dukes family barbecue shops located throughout the state, the sauce comes thicker than other Heinz-fortified variations and stained a burnt-orange hue, due to an additional hint of mustard. In Orangeburg, the medium-sized city located halfway between Charleston and Columbia that spawned this little quirk, one barbecue shop owner told me that he calls his sauce "rust gravy."

Among its patchwork quilt of sauces, it is South Carolina's mustard sauce that stands out. An oddity ostensibly descended from another planet, it is the David Bowie of sauces: blond, beautiful, and, though it is way beyond weird, always inexplicably appealing. Despite the fact that only a small swath of South Carolina barbecue establishments serve the yellow stuff, it has become recognized as the state's unofficial sauce, with its success owed to the state's unofficial first family of barbecue.

South Carolina's most storied, and it would be right to add infamous, version of mustard sauce is aptly nicknamed the Golden Secret. The original brand of the Bessinger clan, the life and times of the Golden Secret is thickened with mystique, family squabbles, and broad, public battles involving the politics of race, war, and southern history, making many South Carolinians wish that the secrets behind the Secret had remained, well, secret.

According to family lore, the Golden Secret emerged from Orangeburg County, an inland area settled by German and Swiss immigrants beginning in the 1730s. In the waning years of the Depression, Joseph Jacob Bessinger, a cotton farmer in the town of Cope, struggled to do exactly that: cope. He was a churchgoing man and a fine home cook, raising eleven children. But he desperately needed hope. And in 1939, hope came in the form of a newspaper article that alerted his saintly wife, Genora, to an area restaurant in need of a new owner. Bessinger sold off the family's only viable asset, a milk cow named Betsy that kept the family fed during those hungry years. With that seventy-five dollars in milk money (other versions of the story add a mule to the equation), Bessinger purchased the Holly Hill Café in a nearby town of the same name. Though he hadn't a day of restaurant work behind him, money could be made here. On Saturdays, Holly Hill absorbed thousands of outlanders from the neighboring farm communities, field hands and overseers in need of food, beer, and trouble. Unlike in the cotton fields, a better life could be grown here. Seven years later, Bessinger reopened in a new location across town, under a new name:

Joe's Grill. Big Joe, as he was called, served lunch-counter food: hamburgers, blue-plate specials, and, on the weekends, barbecue.

At some point, Big Joe began saucing his smoked pork with a mixture of mustard and vinegar and spice. It made sense: mustard and Germans, Germans and pork, mustard and pork. Maybe the idea belonged to Big Joe. Maybe he inherited the recipe from his father, or his father's father, or some other sauce-souled prophet with deep Germanic roots. Maybe that first pot of mustard sauce was carried over by the inaugural ship full of Germans in 1735. Maybe it was not German at all. The exact moment of inspiration has been lost to time, but that brief flashpoint of genius, to whomever the credit is due, lives on.

Like all great barbecue sauce cultures, there is a distinct uniformity to the range of mustard sauces found throughout South Carolina restaurants and groceries today: mustard bold and vinegar tanged, a little salty, and stippled with black pepper. The best-tasting, and most aesthetically pleasing, varieties are always, always, the color of goldenrod, a deep, muted glow that warms the senses as it gilds the pork. South Carolinians defend this dash of culinary esoterica against skeptics, barbecue know-it-alls, and the whole damn state of North Carolina. They prize their golden-hued sauces like gold. And as Shakespeare wrote regarding humanity's abiding and often blind devotion to that soft, sometimes priceless metal, there is no "worse poison to men's souls." If gold corrupts and barbecue sauces brim with secrets, we might expect a golden sauce to be the most soul poisoning of all.

Throughout the 1940s, Maurice Bessinger, the eighth-born among Big Joe's brood, acted as his father's right-hand man. During the early breakfast rush, each morning from five to eight AM, Maurice ran the Holly Hill Café as a one-man operation. Just eleven years old, he'd have to stand on a stool to reach the stovetop. After a midday break to attend school, Maurice returned to work the afternoon and evening shifts alongside his dad. Maurice knew that he would inherit the family business one day; in his autobiography, self-published in 2001, he writes that his father told him as much. But there were other Bessinger boys, including Melvin, a World War II veteran, D-Day survivor, prison-camp escapee, and GI Bill college student, who was seven years Maurice's elder. When a sudden heart attack left Joe's Grill without a Joe in 1949, the war-hero son stepped in to replace his father. Mirroring the best of Shakespeare's tragic characters, the spurned heir, Maurice, rather than fight the battle at home, chose self-exile, joined the army, and, one year later, found himself at the front in Korea.

Following Big Joe's death, the arrival of a new Bessinger-owned barbecue shop became a seemingly annual event throughout South Carolina. Each opening, and inevitable closing, portended another soap-operatic schism between brothers. Just before his father's passing, Melvin opened Eat at Joe's across town from Joe's Grill. In 1953, Maurice returned to South Carolina and with another older brother, Joe David "J. D." Bessinger, opened Piggie Park in Charleston. Within five months, they split; the elder brother kept the restaurant, bringing in brother Woodrow, while Maurice decamped to Winston-Salem to open another, now nonaffiliated, Piggie Park. North Carolina didn't take to barbecue from the other side of the state line, so Maurice hightailed it back to South Carolina, relocating to Columbia, to launch the second coming of Piggie Park. Soon after, Melvin, together with another brother, Thomas, opened their own drive-in barbecue restaurant to compete with J. D.'s original Charleston location. Naturally, they named their operation Piggie Park. Back in Columbia, Maurice had hit the barbecue jackpot, opening six additional Piggie Parks across the state capital by 1963. Finally, at some nebulous point in time, Robert, the Zeppo Marx of the Bessinger brothers, operated two barbecue storefronts in North Charleston. Thankfully, these locations were never named Piggie Park.

If you're confused, so am I. For reasons I have not been able to figure, South Carolinians have always been partial to a handful of barbecue dynasties, mini fiefdoms that operate under the same name. Are they set in their ways? Untrusting of outsiders? Is this a remnant from the time South Carolina was a royal colony?

A distant cousin of Jackie Hite operates the similarly named and older Hite's Bar-B-Que in West Columbia, while another cousin operated the since closed Porky D's in Lexington. Then there are a dozen establishments—maybe more, no one seems able to agree on an accurate headcount—covering two-thirds of South Carolina that operate under the Dukes name. Some Dukes locations are owned by Dukes family members; other Dukes locations have been purchased by non-Dukes; while others do not carry the Dukes name and are not owned by Dukes, but still serve what they advertise as Dukes-style barbecue (more on that in a minute). The point is, Bessinger barbecue, in all its familial iterations, spread Big Joe's mustard sauce across the map of South Carolina like an invading virus, with each brother serving his own version. Nowadays, this mustard-sopped sauce is a nationally known condiment. The Golden Secret produces gold like Joe Bessinger's cow—poor Betsy—once produced milk. In fact, if he were alive today, Big Joe could trade back his original recipe for millions upon millions of dairy cattle. But once money could be made elsewhere, the Bessinger's hometown was forgotten. The quiet closings of Joe's Grill and Eat at Joe's yanked little Holly Hill from the limelight, reducing the town to a mere footnote in barbecue's history.

Though Melvin Bessinger registered the copyrighted use of the Golden Secret name, it was his scrappy younger brother Maurice who became the king of South Carolina's mustard barbecue. Trotting into the twenty-first century, his empire had expanded in directions no other Bessinger dare stride. He had built his very own Willy Wonka–styled barbecue factory, pumping out bottles of his Carolina Gold brand sauce for grocery store shelves stretching from New York City to Tampa Bay. His white-mustachioed face beamed proudly from the packaging of Maurice's Gourmet BBQ dinners, frozen and microwavable barbecue and hash for those devotees who could not make the drive to any one of his eleven locations scattered throughout South Carolina. He smoked hams to feed the masses—estimated at twenty-thousand-plus customers each week, an impossible number to supply with whole-hog barbecue—but steadfastly refused to alter his cooking process (twenty-four hours over hickory coals), though every other large-scale barbecue entrepreneur in the nation had switched to gas-fired cookers. Maurice Bessinger was on top of the world.

But then he hit his moment of hubris. On July 1, 2000, after years of debate, protests, and boycotts, the state legislature finally removed the Confederate flag from atop South Carolina's capitol dome. Bessinger was incensed.

Since returning from the Korean War, the barbecue mogul had fancied himself a southern patriot, an ardent defender of states' rights and American freedom, and a proud citizen of the state that fired the first shots in the Civil War. He supported conservative politicians, locally managing the four presidential campaigns of Alabama governor and arch-segregationist George Wallace. A sometimes political gadfly himself, Bessinger ran for state congress in 1964, blaming his defeat on "out-of-staters, college professors, government officials and other liberals." A decade later he competed in a crowded field of gubernatorial candidates as a recently born-again Christian, barbecue entrepreneur, and gentleman farmer (running a cattle ranch nicknamed Tara, after the plantation in *Gone with the Wind*, naturally), who appeared at rallies in an all-white suit and tie, straddling a pure-white horse. Strangest of all, and perhaps most indicative of the intertwining of politics and pork in South Carolina, another successful barbecue restaurateur, Milton Jefferson Dukes, joined the race to challenge Bessinger for the governor's seat. Safe to say, both barbecue men lost that election.

So as two students from the Citadel—one black, the other white—lowered the Confederate flag from the State House (and placed it, not so inconspicuously, at a monument honoring the Confederate dead on the capitol's front lawn), Bessinger removed the Stars and Stripes. In its place he hoisted the Confederate flag, the battle flag of General Robert E. Lee's Army of Northern Virginia, the rebel flag, the Dixie flag, the old Southern Cross, high above each of his nine restaurants. He opened a religious mission in the parking lot of his flagship Piggie Park and distributed literature covering, among other far-right-wing topics, a biblical defense of slavery.

The reaction was swift: several major grocery and wholesale chains pulled Maurice's Carolina Gold and mug-stamped TV dinners from their shelves, the NAACP called for a boycott of his restaurants, and the national news media pounced on the unreformed barbecue baron. On *The Daily Show*, Bessinger bumbled through a Martin Luther King, Jr., Day interview with Stephen Colbert, telling the satirist that he believed the reverend would have joined him in supporting Confederate Memorial Day, a holiday officially observed in eleven states of the former Confederacy. His wholesale sauce and frozen dinner business nose-dived by a staggering 98 percent. Yet Bes-

THE ONE TRUE BARBECUE

singer's restaurant business gradually ticked upward. Anticipating future battlefields like Chick-fil-A and Paula Deen that would herald the coming culinary culture wars, South Carolina again became the site of the first shots fired. Unrepentant and bolstered by the support of his customers, Bessinger took aim at those retail chains that dared to purge his sauce and sued those bastards.

This was, of course, not Bessinger's first race-baiting, reactionary standoff. In late 1964, three black plaintiffs—Anne P. Newman, Sharon W. Neal, and John Mungin—sued the barbecue mogul for violating the newly enacted Civil Rights Act. In his autobiography, Bessinger remembers the afternoon when Mungin, a Baptist minister, appeared at the door of his downtown sandwich shop. "Mr. Bessinger," the minister challenged, "we want to integrate your restaurant." "Like Hell you will," Bessinger cracked back. He was, at the time, president of the National Association for the Preservation of White People. In his first lawsuit, Bessinger argued that the far-reaching act, which desegregated "public accommodations," in turn infringed upon his constitutional rights because "his religious beliefs compel him to oppose any integration of the races whatever." The plaintiffs lost their state district court bid before the United States Supreme Court unanimously overturned that vile decision two years later. By then, Bessinger had not only closed six of his seven restaurants to pay his lawyer fees but had long before integrated that last remaining Piggie Park location.

More than three decades later, Bessinger's song remained the same. My copy of *The Little Book of BBQ Law*—yes, such a title, compiled by the American Bar Association, exists—outlines the details of his case, *Bessinger v. Bi-Lo, Inc.* (2005). Bessinger sued nine retail grocers, including the Bi-Lo chain and Walmart, and even several individual store managers, "alleging that discontinuation of his products constituted violations of the South Carolina Unfair Trade Practices Act." Two courts disagreed that Bessinger's lawyers had sufficiently proved that the grocery chains had violated the Trade Act by acting in an "immoral, unethical, or oppressive" fashion in removing Maurice's barbecue sauce from their shelves. "Moreover," the Honorable William P. Keesley wrote in his judicial opinion, "as free market participants, the defendant grocery store chains and their respective managers have the right to choose with whom they conduct their business," a sly inference that the court might have found Maurice's flag-waving to be immoral, unethical, and oppressive.

The pages of *Defending My Heritage: The Maurice Bessinger Story*, his incendiary autobiography, or "manual of action for survival," as he called it, spill open with blatant bigotry, misplaced resentment, and far-right-wing paranoia. It is very difficult to read. Like so many racists, Bessinger steadfastly insists in these pages that the barring of black customers from his establishments, the bloody flag waving, and the lawsuits were "not about race."

In my South Carolina summertime travels of 2012, the Maurice Bessinger brand evidently rated as popular as ever, with fourteen of his own Piggie Parks now dotting the state. The architects behind Maurice's West Columbia headquarters might have taken a cue from the South of the Border theme park. A towering BAR-B-Q sign, its neon glow reminiscent of Vegas and likely visible a mile or more up and down this frequently gridlocked stretch of four-lane blacktop, welcomed patrons. An anthropomorphic pig stood upright and cocksure atop the sign; dressed in a red shirt and cap, the porker appeared to be smirking. Nearby, perched above what looked to be the corporate offices, big block letters spelled out CHRIST IS THE ANSWER. In an opposite corner of the property—which, end to end, stretched, in my guesstimation, over a small Bible college–sized plot of land—a tall redbrick chimney issued a thin thread of smoke into the afternoon's glorious firmament. I scanned the sky but couldn't locate the infamous Confederate flag. Instead, a jumbo-sized American flag waved peaceably in the breeze. Two years prior, I would come to discover, Bessinger had removed the battle flags from his Columbia-area restaurants, blaming the rising cost of dry-cleaning bills.

Because I am a half-Catholic, half-Jewish nonbeliever who subscribes to the basic tenets of racial equality and human kindness, I strangled the steering wheel while taking several deep, serenity-granting breaths before heading inside for a taste of Carolina Gold.

I have eaten plenty of bad barbecue in my life: microwaved mystery meat; pork doused with vegetable oil to remoisten stale grub; pork the taste and color of cigarette ash. Maurice Bessinger's barbecue was not the worst bite I've ever chewed, but it ranks mighty low.

Ironically, ambiance is key in a barbecue joint, certainly not to the extent of a five-star restaurant reviewed in *The New York Times*, but atmosphere does matter. One of my favorite pieces of barbecue prose comes from *Searching for the Dixie Barbecue*, in which Wilber W. Caldwell explains his "funk factor" evaluation technique, "the name given to a system for rating exactly how well a barbecue place conforms to the myth of the seedy 'joint.' It is a simple scale of one to ten, which can be used to rank any establishment. The higher the score, the worse the place, which is to say the better." Dirt floors, plastic flowers, firearms, and flies add to the appeal. Carpet, stainless steel utensils, and designated handicapped parking spaces deduct points from the total funk factor score. This is all sounds like a bunch of hogwash, hyperbole written for a laugh, but, of course, all barbecue writing is hyperbole.

So maybe my Piggie Park visit started rolling downhill before I took my first bite of barbecue. Maybe it began with the table full of stomach-churning right-wing propaganda that welcomed patrons in through the front door. Or the painted portrait of South Carolina's barbecue tycoon himself, clad in a white suit, holding a bottle of Carolina Gold, and posed smiling in front of the rebel flag. Or perhaps it came down to the barbecue: bland, dull, forgettable. Every table was packed. Hundreds of customers, white and black, appeared to be enjoying their lunches. But I could hardly lift fork to mouth. I left hungry.

———

A pilgrimage to Holly Hill was in order. If the Mississippi Delta gave the world the blues, and New Orleans the gift of jazz, Holly Hill serves as the cradle of South Carolina's mustard-sauce culture. Commenters lurking in barbecue-centric corners of the Internet maintained that Holly Hill was no longer worth the drive. In 2010, Thomas Bessinger, with his sons Michael and Tommy Jr., remodeled and reopened the old Joe's Grill, a location long abandoned by the family. But despite the warm feelings this homecoming brought, a restoration to the throne if there ever was one, the family's financial stab at nostalgia dried up quick and closed within two years. It was doubtful the Bessingers would ever return to Holly Hill.

In an even bigger blow, the town's last surviving whole-hog barbecue restaurant had recently been sold, part and parcel, to new owners. Sweatman's Bar-B-Que was a South Carolina landmark,

a family-owned institution dating back over half a century. Operating out of an old farmhouse, Sweatman's was the kind of place
that eschewed modernity a decade into the twenty-first century:
no listed phone number, no advertising, no credit cards, no menu.
Only open on Fridays and Saturdays, lunch and supper. Just grab a
plate, belly up to the buffet, and help yourself to as much barbecue
and sides as you can eat. Owners Bub and Margie Sweatman had
made a dining destination out of Holly Hill. After he passed away
in 2005, the couple's daughters took over, vowing not to change a
thing. But less than six years later, they had sold the family business.
Rumors circulated that the new owners, a local couple by the name
of Behr, would be making some changes: raising prices, eliminat-
ing the all-you-can-eat buffet, perhaps even tossing out the whole
hog for cheaper cuts of meat. The Behrs hadn't ever run a barbecue
shop, people said. Sweatman's wouldn't survive. No way. No how.
The sale became big news in a town long struggling to crawl out
from under the burden of southern history. "Pray for Sweatman's
Bar-B-Que," wrote one columnist. "Lord, help them not to mess up
Sweatman's."

It didn't take more than a glance to realize that these were not
the brightest days in the history of Holly Hill. A walk up the main
avenue that runs through the crumbling downtown district revealed
a small-scale Detroit-style streetscape alternating between burnt-
out gaps where buildings once stood and long-abandoned storefronts. Blight was an afterthought; nature had returned. Vines
burst through plate-glass windows to overtake shuttered offices.
The basin of a centrally located fountain sat parched and choked
with leaves. Along the sidewalks, pink and white crape myrtles
thrived, blooming proudly. The town pulsed with death and life. I
withered in the summer heat.

I could have been walking in any of the small southern towns that I've passed through in search of barbecue. Empty streets and shops. A new generation of businesses, symbols of the New New South, anchored themselves on the fringes of the old downtown: Subway, Hardee's, and CVS. Check cashing counters and tax rebate centers. Family Dollar, Dollar Plus, and Dollar General lined one side of the street, one after the next, like discount dominoes. Stopping by Holly Hill's visitor center, housed in an old railway depot, I learned that this was another railroad town, though a train hadn't stopped here in years. Which economic collapse killed this town, I thought: 2007, 2001, 1979, 1973? Which of these locally owned business will be the last to vanish: the secondhand store where I browsed through shelves of densely foxed books? The corner diner where I ate rubbery pancakes delivered fresh from the microwave? Sweatman's Bar-B-Que?

A century earlier, Eli Alston Wilkes, a traveling Methodist preacher, had the same first impression of the town: "The only difference between Holly Hill and Chicago is that Chicago is bigger—Chicago is immense; Holly Hill is insignificant," he wrote. "Chicago has pork packers; Holly Hill has pork eaters and producers. The same sort of human nature prevails in both towns—the same sort of sins and sinners, and the real good people of both places have the same characteristics."

I read Wilkes's words in a slim history of the town found among the local public library's meager stacks. I was looking for words of encouragement, enticement to stay and explore Holly Hill, and "pork eaters" and "real good people" were all the convincing I needed.

I drove northeast from Holly Hill, past a small wooden sign painted with the town's roseate motto ("Proud Past, Progressive Future"), past rows of cotton and corn and soy, down the two-lane highway that connects the town to the state's lake district resort area, its asphalt worn and ribbon cracked, in the direction of Sweatman's.

If not for the pig-shaped sign and American flag that welcomes visitors down a gravel-lined driveway, Sweatman's Bar-B-Que might remain hopelessly unfindable. Bordering a thin band of woodlands, sandwiched between neatly plowed fields, and shaded by a grove of pecan trees, the restaurant is enveloped by a hundred different shades of green. In 1977, Bub and Margie Sweatman purchased this abandoned turn-of-the-century farmhouse. Looking like a plantation in miniature, the building was modestly sized but with room enough for plenty of tables, handsome but humble enough to build a pit house out back. I have still found no finer setting to enjoy a plate of barbecue.

Walking out back, I found a man busily stoking a fire.

"Still got whole hog?" I asked.

"Tomorrow," the pitmaster answered. "Tomorrow and the day after that." He introduced himself as Douglas Oliver, a Sweatman's employee for more than three decades. Over the evening's ebb and morning's arrival, I would discover that here was one of Preacher Wilkes's "good people" I was searching for, an individual who imbued this most trivial of towns with a weighty significance.

As Oliver worked the fire, I walked the grounds. I took in the restaurant's picturesque front porch; chased a pair of kittens around a precarious ziggurat of hickory, oak, and pecan firewood; sat under a broad-limbed pecan tree and just breathed, happy to be out of Columbia. I snuck inside, where the golden hour's soft burst of sunlight shot through red gingham curtains, flooding the interior with a pink haze. I crept across the hardwood floors that creaked with each step and found a mantel-hung painting that depicts the founders as an updated American Gothic: Bub Sweatman's left arm cradles his wife's waist, his right nestles a baby pig. Together they stand in front of their paradisiacal farmhouse turned barbecue house.

With dusk's approach, and eight pigs on the pit in the first of their ten hours of roasting, Oliver sat down to talk. He brought me to a spot just outside one of the pit house's doorways, facing west, so he could watch the sun fall away, beyond the highway and distant fields. "Peace and quiet," he said, nodding to the early evening, the temperate climate, the beauty of our surroundings, a place to "think about the past and the future, whatever." A place to "keep your head on straight, you know. You got a job to do and just keep on doing it. Time will go by."

Douglas Oliver was born within an arm's reach from where we sat, on Connor Station Farm. His father sharecropped that land, raised thirteen children (Douglas the youngest) amid 2,500 acres of corn and soy. Mom nurtured and fed the family, sustaining them on bowls of herring and rice, butter beans and okra picked fresh from her garden, and meat when there was money enough. "You gotta have worker ants," Oliver told me to summarize his years on the farm. "You got the queen and you got all the workers." On Connor Station Farm, the ant in chief, overseer of the estate, was one Bub Sweatman.

Like most barbecue men, Harold Odell Sweatman was first and foremost a farmer. Raising plenty enough pigs, with an abundance of acreage to dig a barbecuing hole or two on his land, whole hog came naturally to the man everyone called Bub. For several years, he smoked and sold barbecue out of an empty farm building, steps from his own home, that he and his wife nicknamed "the old dairy." Bub barbecued on weekends after farming throughout the week and stuck to this schedule even after he and Margie renovated the farmhouse. Sweatman's was a success from the start, and the couple's three daughters and six grandchildren joined in helping feed the barbecue-hungry crowds. Within its first year of operation, the coauthors of the first-ever barbecue guidebook, *Hog Heaven: A Guide to South Carolina Barbecue* (1979), ranked Sweatman's as among the best in the state.

Around that same time, Douglas Oliver, newly graduated from high school, began working for old man Bub as a meat cutter. For Oliver and others, the meat cutter position served as an apprentice role to becoming a pit cook. To prep their meat for service, instead of a rough chop, Sweatman's hand-trims their smoked hogs, removing gristle, bone, and skin, before cutting and dividing the roasted flesh into fork-sized pieces of white and dark meat bound for the buffet table. This is the only barbecue establishment I've seen perform this arduous task, an act that requires delicate finger work from a quartet of employees armed with sharp, curved fillet knives.

Eventually, Oliver moved into the pit house, working under the legendary pitmaster Chalmon Smalls. Born to a sharecropping family like Oliver, Smalls came up and worked alongside Bub Sweatman on Connor Station Farm. He would become Bub's right-hand barbecuing man. Smalls was a genius of a cook, a man whose instincts for smoking hogs have remained unsurpassed. According to Oliver, his mentor could tell the doneness of a hog just by sniffing the air. "That's how good he was," Oliver told me. "He was a pitmaster," he said. "He still is." In 2005, Smalls retired at the age of seventy-seven. "I stepped in when he stepped out," Oliver said, "and I been doing it ever since." Whether to honor his teacher's legacy or to suggest that he isn't done mastering the barbecue trade, Douglas Oliver has since refused the title "pitmaster." He is "just a cook," he told me. "That's it. Just a cook trying to do the right thing, trying to cook something good."

But by now, Oliver might have cooked more hogs than his predecessor. I asked him to guesstimate a number. He did the math in his head: 22 hogs a week on average, multiplied by 50 weeks of barbecue per year, over 30 years, equals 33,000 total hogs cooked. On second thought, this sum sounded much too low, so he rounded up to 45,000 to 50,000 hogs. I did not doubt him for one second. Oliver's life and labor were built right into the restaurant's name, he laughed, poking fun at Bub's surname. "The sign says, Sweat . . . a . . . Man." Each and every man sweats, but Oliver has perspired longer and harder than most.

Back when Oliver started working for the Sweatman's, they used to serve thirty-five whole hogs over a weekend (though now they rarely cook half that number). In those days, the Sweatman's crew felled their own trees to warm the pits, using lumber from the woodlands back beyond the old farmhouse. Oliver remembered the mosquitoes swarming so savagely that the men had to drag the newly felled timber out whole from the thicket before chopping it into manageable sections or risk being eaten alive.

He told me about the night Holly Hill was visited by Hurricane Hugo, the most powerful and devastating storm on record to strike South Carolina. There were eight hogs on the pits the evening of September 21, 1989. Oliver remembered looking over the neighboring fields—just as he has done every night before and since—and watching the hurricane steadily descend, as if in slow motion, upon the pit house. Its hundred-mile-per-hour wind gusts cut a scythe through most of the pecan orchard, toppling the trees like statues of deposed dictators. As the storm washed over, for what felt like hours, Oliver, Bub Sweatman, and the other men on duty huddled in a corner of the pit house, praying that its cinder-blocked walls would hold strong. The next morning they stumbled out into the apocalyptic landscape Hugo had left behind. Miraculously, one pecan tree, planted just steps from the pit house, fell the opposite way that the winds came, sparing the building, the hogs, and the men. In isolated Holly Hill, immediate relief was nonexistent and power would not be restored for weeks, so Bub fed the community on fire-cooked hash and hogs.

After hours of talking with Douglas Oliver, between breaks of watching him toss shovelfuls of coals into the pits every half hour, I wandered off to my berth in the Barbecue Bus. It was a breezy June night, and I fell asleep to the scent of charred wood and roast pork.

Oliver woke me with a few slaps on the side of the Bus: he had a treat for me. Back in the pit house, the hogs rested skin side down on the grill, their cavities singing skyward the praises of their perfectly smoked meat. The pitmaster—he was a master and not a mere cook—dipped a plastic pitcher into a five-gallon bucket full of yellow liquid, Sweatman's mustard sauce, before pouring this golden nectar, in a deep, syrupy steam, across the flesh-exposed side of a whole hog. I was reminded of my ninth-grade reading of Ovid's *Metamorphoses*: Zeus showering gold upon unsuspecting Danaë in order to seduce the fair princess. The meat's black-charred exterior drew out the sauce's rich pigment, which caught the room's harsh fluorescence and, like a diamond, reflected the light into an oozy, plasmatic prism of not a spectrum of colors, but just one: gold. Call me seduced.

Then Oliver reached inside the hog and, with thumb and forefinger, pinched a morsel of meat from beneath the lower rib bones. He held this piece upward, like a mother bird feeding her nestlings, like a prospector examining his discovery in the light, this pure golden nugget glowing in the dark pit house, and handed it over to me. Meat fresh from the pit, barbecue straight from the pig, now steaming in my mouth; I juggled the flesh with my tongue to keep my insides from burning. Tastes of wood and smoke and mustard—yes mustard!—mingling with the fat and flesh to form the best single bite of barbecue I have ever eaten.

A PAIR OF SOUTH CAROLINA CODAS

I revisited Holly Hill a year later, in July 2013, not expecting much to have changed. A drive past Joe Bessinger's Grill proved me wrong. Through the curtained windows that face the highway, I could see lights, customers sitting at the diner's lunch counter, steam rising from the griddle. It was all very Edward Hopper's *Nighthawks* travels down south. Hanging above the door, a freshly printed plastic banner advertised Kenny's Kitchen.

A high-school-aged waitress greeted me with a menu and went

back to diddling with her phone. I scanned the list of appetizers and stopped short: fried wontons, fried tofu balls, shrimp pancake. I called to the waitress, who noticed my hesitation. "The owner's Chinese," she said while cud-chewing a wad of gum, before adding an "or something," at the end, her intonation rising to a question as if to exhibit the extent of her teenage ignorance.

Minutes later, Kenny stepped out of the kitchen with my order of wontons (his signature pancake had been eighty-sixed that afternoon). Kenny was Kenny Do, a Saigon-born ethnic Chinese who immigrated to the United States in 1979. Since then, he had cooked his way across the nation, in restaurants big and small. He found his way here after authorities in the Charleston suburbs where he lived told him he could no longer legally farm chickens, even for his own use. After moving into a log cabin perched on a hill above downtown Holly Hill four years earlier, he purchased the former Joe's Grill from Thomas Bessinger and opened his kitchen just days before my visit. Though barbecue was not on the menu, he hoped locals would try any one of his dinner specials, including lemongrass pork with fresh basil, pork with black pepper sauce, and fish-sauce braised pork.

As I ate, my only thought was a wish that I could have forcibly dragged Maurice Bessinger along for the ride. Who knows what Bessinger would have said to Kenny Do, a perfect illustration of the twenty-first-century South, with all its racial and ethnic complexities and diversities, but I think even he would have enjoyed Kenny's wontons.

Leaving Holly Hill, I drove toward Orangeburg. For the past year, my attempts to track down Chalmon Smalls had proved fruitless. I needed to meet the man, wanted to ask him if there was truth to the legend: Could he really sense when a hog was done and ready using only his sniffer? With the help of Douglas Oliver, who had recently reunited with his mentor, I finally located the legend behind the legend.

I met Smalls and his wife, Daisy, at the Orangeburg home of their daughter, Thelma, with whom they were now living. Walking into her living room, it became immediately evident that the retired pitmaster was not in the best of health. His movement alternated between the tremors and rigidity that accompany Parkinson's disease. His speech wavered between soft and slurred, lucid and powerful.

For the next hour, the two of us sat at his daughter's dining-room table. I asked questions. Chalmon Smalls told stories. Some I understood, much I did not. He filled in some historical gaps. His ties to the Sweatman family stretched into the distant past: his father worked under Bub Sweatman's father on Connor Station Farm. He remembered when Bub died and recalled how the Sweatman children buried their father with a bottle of Coca-Cola and a bag of peanuts, his favorite snack combination.

I asked Smalls if he still thought about cooking hogs. "I had a dream about it," nodding as if a secret had been passed between close friends. "I never told my family that I dream about it." He told me that he never used the term "pitmaster" to refer to himself; instead, he was known throughout Holly Hill as the Barbecue Man. But Bub gave him another nickname. "He always called me Captain," Smalls said, his voice rising to a shout, stronger and clearer than it had been all that afternoon. "He never did call me Chalmon; he called me captain." The Captain of Barbecue, who steered Bub Sweatman's ship for four decades.

CHAPTER 9

Will Success Spoil Rodney Scott?

**Perhaps say some, the hog artfully mirrors the pathos
of the country itself: huge, maladroit, and always straining
toward some elusive dream beneath yet another clod of dirt.**

—WILLIAM B. HEDGEPETH

*R*odney Scott is in his element. Humming along to Booker T. & the
MGs' swinging-sixties deep-organ hit "Green Onions" as he starts in
with the salt. Arm extended high, shaking grains on down over the
charred pigs in rhythm to Al Jackson, Jr.'s hi-hat beat. In comes the
bassist's caveman stomp—*thump-thump, thump-thump, thump*—and
now he's bobbing his head while dashing red pepper flakes with his
right hand, cayenne from his left. The music, the pitmaster are heat-
ing up now. He's dancing around the pit, the pig his partner, as the
capsicum ignites, exploding invisible tendrils of spice across the room.
"Yeah!" Booker signals another chord progression and Steve Cropper's
guitar solo winds its way through the smoke. On cue, the pitmaster
reaches for black pepper and a second, unmarked container. Shaking.
Now Rodney grabs a mop and painter's bucket full of sauce. He swabs
the pig once, twice, again; calls this "spreading the love around." The
taste of vinegar shimmies into the air, while the sauce simmers in the

hog's cavity, staining the meat a bright curried orange. The original drum thump and organ bounce shift back in, and he's working the flesh with a serving spoon, scooping the tender meat in on itself to let the sauce soak down to the skin. Booker cools down. As the next track starts to play, the pitmaster moves on to the next hog.

———

On my most recent visit to Scott's Bar-B-Que, the South Carolina interstate touted a brand-new breed of billboard advertisements: a slick, tourism-department-sponsored branding of the state's patchwork barbecue culture. "So Close You Can Taste It," read one. "Family Friendly. Foodie Approved," ran another. Others made feeble attempts at e-coolness: "BBQ You'll Blog About" and "#SCBBQ." Many of the billboards featured smiling faces—a carefully selected show of racial and generational diversity—gazing adoringly at barbecue sandwiches or a mess of chopped pork. All of the billboards encouraged viewers to visit a website that offered a South Carolina BBQ Trail Map, which featured more than two hundred restaurants scattered throughout all three corners of the isosceles-shaped state and incited eaters to "bite into the birthplace of BBQ."

Maurice Bessinger, the grand wizard of South Carolina barbecue, had passed away two months earlier, on February 22, 2014, at the age of eighty-three. The billboards appeared to be reckoning with the man's legacy, the state's sad racial history, and the complex state of affairs concerning anything and everything barbecue. They welcomed eaters to a new era in South Carolina barbecue, encouraged visitors to sit at a table that could be inclusive, peaceful, and fun.

The state tourism board probably could have simplified their ad campaign, while saving a bit of money in the process and still hitting all those sweet notes of heterogeneity and trend-surfing, by posting images of Rodney Scott, the modern face of not only South Carolina barbecue, not just whole-hog barbecue, but, arguably, an entire nation of barbecue-obsessed citizens. Owner and pitmaster of Scott's Bar-B-Que, Rodney makes South Carolina barbecue enjoyable again.

It starts with the music, blasted full volume through the graveyard shift and into the next afternoon. Rodney's mixtapes stream from a grease-cloaked stereo and speakers linked to an iPod that lies safely tucked inside a Styrofoam takeout container. His musical wanderings take him from Motown to Nashville via the Bronx with a stop at every Chitlin' Circuit juke joint in between.

In most every pit house and restaurant kitchen I've stepped foot into the stereo acts as so much white noise, thankfully present but omnipresent and often forgotten. But Rodney's pit-house-curated playlists fuel the pitmaster and his crew of helpers and hangers-on during the relentless hours of strength-sapping work; like fire and smoke, they are just another ingredient in the hog-cooking process. James Brown keeps them awake. KC and the Sunshine Band, another favorite, makes them dance and sing along. The voices and rhythmic pulses of Hall and Oates, the Notorious B.I.G., and hundreds of others seem to somehow seep into the barbecue, marinate the meat. I imagine that this is the epitome of soul food. Soul + food.

But Rodney's stereo also acts as a beacon of sorts, a welcome sign or clarion call to anyone within earshot. And here in Hemingway, the quietest of whole-hog towns (population 444), sound travels far and wide. Dot, the lady who lives across and down the highway from Scott's, once told Rodney she can "hear y'all partying from the pit." But she never calls to complain about the volume, the cops never show to shut the place down. Everybody around these parts knows that anyone and everyone is invited to his party.

He is young, gifted, and, to complete the Nina Simone lyric and civil rights anthem, black. And in the culture of southern barbecue, post-Bessinger barbecue, South Carolina might just need a hero who looks and acts like Rodney Scott.

If cooking whole hogs was an Olympic sport—and there is no reason it shouldn't be—Rodney Scott would be our gold medalist. In tiny Hemingway he stands as a barbecue giant. Rodney has the larger-than-life aura of a man who could be famous for doing something other than cooking hogs, combined with the modest attitude of a guy with whom you'd actually like to eat barbecue.

The first time I met Rodney, two years earlier, he was chatting up a pair of fashionably arranged women who had driven the two hours from Charleston just to taste his barbecue. Besides putting up with the groupies (myself included), Rodney juggled a pair of cell phones, an older model and a new number that rang with Hollywood producers anxious to build a reality and/or travel show around him and his extended circle (he eventually demurred with a polite no, objecting that his life lacked the necessary drama to make interesting television). Rodney represents the future of barbecue and projected the air of a superstar just waiting to be discovered—everybody knows it, and everybody wants a piece.

As the women admired Rodney's forearms—brawny and fire scarred—he autographed for them a pair of Scott's Bar-B-Que T-shirts, the backs of which bear the pitmaster's barbecuing motto: "It's All Wood."

Wood is the secret ingredient at Scott's. The secret is not in the lumber itself—all real whole-hog pitmasters use hardwoods to heat their pits—but in the act of sourcing the fuel. If Rodney Scott ever found it necessary to carry a business card, his occupation should read: "Scott's Bar-B-Que Owner, Professional Pitmaster, and Amateur Arborist." Rodney rarely purchases wood, instead procuring it from the backyards and forested byways in and surrounding Hemingway. Area home and business owners know: if you have a tree that has fallen or needs help felling, call Scott's.

Rodney, like most tradition-sticking pitmasters, outlaws charcoal from his premises, but unlike most, he considers cutting down a tree the first step in the whole-hog process. "Cut, chop, cook," he likes to repeat as a Zen-like mantra, mirroring the language of modern, conscious food consumers (local, organic, sustainable) who might not only be on a first-name basis with their farmers, but can recite the name—and breed, health status, etc.—of the chicken that delivered their morning egg. "You know exactly what's going on," Rodney told me. "You cut it down. You cut it up. You burned it. You know that that's a tree that came from the road by the big oak tree. You know what you got, what you're using, and it's no question of what's in it." This is wood as food, and the workweek starts with the chainsaw's snarl.

One early July morning I joined Rodney and his father, Rosie (short for Roosevelt), for this first part of the cooking process. A pair of employees had called asking their boss for some tree-cutting support. This was the first clear day after three weeks of constant rain—accompanying storms had toppled trees across the region—and a soggy patch of ground was proving problematic in tackling some timber that needed help coming down.

"How many barbecue places you seen sharpen their own chainsaws?" he laughed while honing the teeth of his stump cutter. We piled into his father's battered and dust-washed white pickup truck—its inspection sticker long expired—and drove west toward the town of Stuckey.

"Wealthy folk around here," Rodney said as we pulled into the driveway of your typical suburban brick-faced home (it actually belonged to the Stuckey family for which this town was named). His workers stood, arms akimbo, sizing up a rangy live oak, its limbs twisting in several directions to span as wide as the tree stood tall. He introduced the men as Sonny Boy and Bo Diddley—yes, like the blues musicians—and asked if they had been drinking. Sonny Boy said no and sheepishly explained that he had split the tree's base halfway before it tilted forward a few inches to rest against another tree.

"Two-dollar tree cutters," Rodney griped back while yanking on a neon orange hard hat with attached ear mufflers. He cartwheeled his arms like a baseball pitcher warming up, yanked the rope to jumpstart his chainsaw, and disappeared into the overgrowth that surrounded the oak. We could hear him buzz-cut the tree's low-hanging branches, clearing space to maneuver around the trunk. He started sawing opposite of Sonny's wedge cut, throwing an arc of wood chips and sawdust high into the air until his own segment grew to just barely meet the first. The tree teetered on a pencil-thin lip of wood. Rodney pushed against the lean until the oak creaked on its axis in the reverse direction to rest, absurdly, against another tree. The two bluesmen and I did our best to suppress our laughter, while Rosie guffawed loudly.

Suddenly, with a scream and crash, Rodney scrambled from the bramble. A chicken snake, harmless but terrifying at more than five feet in length and thicker than my forearm, slithered from a hole near the newly stumped tree. Now we all followed Rosie's lead, doubled over and cackling. Rodney said, "I don't like this one bit," and sent Sonny Boy in to finish the tree. Rodney, Rosie, and I drove to our next destination, a wind-fallen pecan tree limb on a property several miles away.

Three hours after first setting out, we returned with a trailer and truck load of wood, a week's worth of barbecuing fuel. Sonny Boy and Bo Diddley unceremoniously tossed the logs into a sprawling junkyard of oak, hickory, and pecan that spread in seven different directions. Blood-smeared ID tags, once pinned to the trotters of hogs, littered the dirt. One read 137 in black ink, others 147, 144, 146: the weights of hogs, slaughtered, dressed, and delivered from a nearby abattoir.

Despite the salvage-yard aesthetic, there was order to the woodpile's chaos, an intent and purpose in the preparation of coals. "The pecan gets hot quicker," Rodney explained. "The hickory wood stays hot a little longer. And the oak stays chunkier, thicker—nice smoke flavor to it. So out of those three, you got your instant heat, your steady heat, and then your big flavorful coals." Here, there is an art to the science of fire making.

Rodney's son Dominic, a lanky teenager, sat on a wide stump dividing chunks of wood with the aid of a hydraulic log splitter. Off to the side, an older gentleman with time-wrinkled cheeks and a grizzled beard cut timber with an ax. After a few more strokes, noting my interest, he pointed to a broad piece of wood and handed me the ax. This was not like the handy branch splitter I used in Cub Scouts. This ax must have weighed thirty pounds. Its handle measured a good four inches around, its head a solid wedge of black steel. It looked and felt like a weapon straight out of *Game of Thrones*. The axman wasn't much bigger than myself: I could do this. I squared my feet, hips, and shoulders, aimed for the log's centermost growth ring, and gave the ax my mightiest swing.

Sproing! The ax bounced off the wood's surface like Elmer Fudd striking a rubber tree, setting off a vibration that rumbled through my hands before tremoring through my entire body. The man was nice enough not to laugh.

This was Rodney's uncle Sam, whom everyone, blood relations or not, calls Uncle Sam. Though he's retired and doesn't keep regular hours at Scott's, Uncle Sam is Rodney's right-hand man; he often lingers behind the scenes and almost always accompanies his nephew to cook at out-of-state events. Sweet and good-humored, he speaks, like his sister Ella, Rodney's mother, in a soft lilt that sounds vaguely Jamaican, a singsong accent that manifested, somewhere down the family line, from the Gullah language spoken by, until recently, isolated African American communities that populate the coast and sea islands of the Carolinas and Georgia. Rodney teases that Sam just "swings an ax for a living" but privately and pridefully relates tales of his uncle wowing crowds at carnivals while driving the hammer at the strongman game. Last time they visited the state fair together, Rodney, no ax-swinging slouch himself, left after winning two teddy bears for his girlfriend, while his uncle kept on swinging—a modern-day John Henry, ringing the bell over and over again.

Uncle Sam retrieved the ax from my still-aching hands and sliced

James Henry Howell

The Skylight Inn's trifecta of barbecue, cornbread, and coleslaw.

Rodney Scott's burn barrel awakens.

Terry Blow shovels hardwood coals into the pits at Scott's Bar-B-Que.

The storefront of Scott's Bar-B-Que, Hemingway, South Carolina.

Keith "Pop" Ward rests after a night of cooking hogs at Wilber's Barbecue.

The spread at Grady's Barbecue.

Douglas Oliver pours some liquid gold.

Larry Dennis carries fire at Bum's Restaurant.

Robert Dixon presents a tray of fresh barbecued chicken.

through a few more logs while offering pointers. Use your entire body for power to build momentum in your chop. Follow through with your wrists to drive through the wood. Don't miss. I gave it another swing. I missed. I tried again. And again. I tried until I could not raise my arms overhead. Frustrated and tired, I felt emasculated, unmanly. I quit and handed the weapon back to Sam. Dented and bruised from my meager blows, the log seemed to mock me just by sitting there, intact and whole. This time Uncle Sam laughed.

Ax in hand, Sam lined up for the kill and smashed the log squarely on its head. The ax ricocheted back. "Save you for later," he whispered to the log while stroking its bark. "Throw you in just like that later on." For a moment I felt redeemed, but returning to the woodpile later that night, and later that weekend, and the year following, and the year after, I have yet to get that ax to work properly.

Whether split, chopped, or thrown into the fire whole, each scrap of oak, hickory, and pecan ends up in one of Scott's three imposing burn barrels. The barrels are salvaged from abandoned gas tanks that Rodney unearths—typically while hauling away donated lumber—from local family farms that have gone belly-up over the past couple generations. The barrels are a brilliant but simple feat of engineering. The cylindrical drums stand upright, six feet tall, their tops lopped open to receive chunks of wood. Just below their midsections, a misshapen ring of fist-sized holes puncture the sides of each barrel. Truck axles poke out from these openings, like toothpicks in a potato, five in all, which trap the logs, keeping them suspended. Once set ablaze, the wood smolders slowly, forcing the resulting embers to drop between the axles to fall to the barrel's base. There, a square hole has been cut from which the freshly formed charcoal is ready to be shoveled out and into the nearby pits. Above this fire door, three larger holes are carved into the side to resemble a face.

Throughout the night, with the aid of a long metal pole, the fire is stoked by violently driving this shaft up and down, like using a water pump, causing more coals—redder, hotter coals—to fall to the floor.

The genius of the burn barrel's design has been recently replicated by businesses and backyard pitmasters nationwide, while its image has become an iconic facet of the Scott's experience. Over time, the repurposed gas tanks warp and melt under the intense heat. Aglow and burning with flame, the barrel looks very much alive: a creature vomiting fire and ash, its head emitting sparks that loft ten feet high to singe the leaves of overhanging trees. At night, and especially during those evenings when the mercury drops to lows that make holding a cold brew a bitter and unwelcome act, Scott's pit workers huddle around the barrel, often joined by other men from the community who sometimes arrive full of drink stronger, warmer than beer. These men lend a helping hand—splitting wood, shoveling coals, telling good stories and great lies. They sit circling the barrel as if worshipping an angry three-eyed god who stands waiting, waiting, waiting for its sacrificial offering.

For Rodney Scott, these fireside gatherings define barbecue more than meat and sauce. For him, barbecue is a place, a space for people to commune. When asked for his definition of barbecue, instead of repeating the dogmatic "barbecue is a whole hog cooked over wood coals," Rodney offered a twist. Barbecue is "a gathering," he told me, "because you rarely find an event without a grill or somebody who is barbecuing or grilling. And, of course, for us it's been a business as well, but we still try to interact with our people in the community to kind of remind them that it's just a laid-back type of thing."

This was barbecue as social theory, barbecue as something deeper than barbecue. This was a pitmaster moving toward the development of a philosophy of barbecue.

A barbecue is "a reunion," he emphasized, "a party for everybody to come and join in and enjoy each other's company." He's right. Nobody grills alone, no publishing houses are rushing to release a cookbook titled *Going Solo at the Pit* or *The Pleasures of Barbecuing for One*.

And at Scott's, unlike most pit houses, no one ever works alone. There are always at least two men on the clock. Oftentimes, I've noticed over the years, I cannot distinguish the employees—an amorphous network of relatives and neighbors—from those gathered here just to be here, to join the circle around the burn barrel, to enjoy one another's company.

That unseen but understood welcome sign extends to visitors from outside the community. No one has ever chased me away at Scott's, no one has ever told me not to print this or photograph that. In fact, Rodney welcomes visitors to tour his smokehouse, to take pictures (which he'll pose for) and ask questions (which he'll do his best to answer above the din of the stereo's speakers). "My whole business plan is to let them share my world," he told me. "Food, music, family."

This is open-source barbecue, barbecue as social leveler.

Rodney might not tell you what's in his barbecue sauce (in my opinion, some of the best that's ever come into contact with pork), but his pit hands won't stop you from daring to peek into the tall stockpot of liquid simmering on a portable propane stove. A whiff and a glance will tell you all you need to know to replicate a close approximation at home: vinegar, great scoopfuls of red and black pepper, and, the secret ingredient, lemon slices.

To showcase the transparency of his pits, the openness with which he operates, Rodney challenged me to "name one time you were standing by a grill and someone didn't ask you a question." Did you marinate it? What'd you put on it? Where you from? How do you cook where you're from? The barbecue pit was our nation's first office water cooler, a safe space for convening and conversation, a site that harkens back to our love affair with fire: gathering around the fire, seeking warmth at the fire, talking near the fire, staring contemplatively into the fire. And what better fire than this: a fire that provides enough work for at least two and usually many more men; a fire that will guarantee enough meat to feed all who could possibly gather; a fire that assures time to sit and think over enough hours in which to dissect the universe.

What better fire to unite, to bring a community together, than a whole-hog fire?

This is utopian barbecue, perfected at Scott's, where everyone is welcome, everyone belongs. That is despite the fact that until recently a sign above the pit house door warned:

NO CUSTOMERS

ALLOWED IN WORK AREA

PLEASE WAIT IN THE LOBBY

SORRY . . . INSURANCE REG.

Of course there is no lobby at Scott's Bar-B-Que. But adjacent to the pit house there is Scott's Variety, a shabby, lost highway convenience store with a few shelves holding dusty canned comestibles and gleaming rows of two-liter bottles of Red Rock strawberry soda. There are four tables and an ordering window, where Ella Scott, Rodney's mother, and a rotating cast of cousins and sisters fill orders for barbecue, which they pull from the carcass with latex-clad hands, separating meat from bone and gristle to fill sandwiches and Styrofoam clamshell trays. Mrs. Scott is as sweet as buttercream frosting and always tries to sell me a piece of homemade cake, yellow and pink slices wrapped in cellophane. Above the ordering counter a menu lists the prices: $7.50 for a pound of barbecue, $3.50 for a sandwich (fifty cents more for a jumbo), large hog $425.00, medium hog $400.00, a gallon of barbecue sauce $22.00. Price to cook a hog if you supply your own: $110.00. To the right of the menu, a sign—black and red marker on poster board—reads:

CREDIT IS "DEAD"

FUNERAL "NOON" SAT.

PLACE COUNTY JAIL

BURIAL IN "HELL"

REV "DEVIL" IN CHARGE

THE MANAGER

I take this as a signal to always arrive with enough money to pay for my purchase.

Ella's husband, Rosie, holds court out front, from a pair of recycled church pews that line the variety store's front porch, next to grocery carts full of seasonal produce for sale: watermelon, cantaloupe, and sweet potatoes. Early morning, there's usually a wooden-slatted box of freshly boiled peanuts tossing steam into the rising sun. Roosevelt Scott wears the same uniform every day, maybe even every day since he bought the old country store in 1972: a khaki-gray work shirt with his name stitched above the right pocket, dark brown pants held up by suspenders, thick-framed eyeglasses, and a gold chain. Only his ball cap changes from day to day. He nods at the steady stream of customers who come for a bite of his son's whole hog. He is a man driven to silence. "It's better to be slow to speak and slow to listen," is his motto, according to Rodney.

Rosie moved back home to Hemingway after a decade in Philadelphia, a year after his son, Rodney, was born, and purchased the

Variety. When "I was a little fella," he told me, growing up seven miles down the road, "I used to buy penny candy and cookies out of that store." The tiny storefront on the corner of Hemingway Highway, aka Highway 261, and Cowhead Road used to be a Shell gas station, then an Exxon, before becoming Scott's Variety Store, a place to stop for a soda and a bag of chips, and sometimes, very sporadically for the first decade or so, barbecue. The whole-hog side of the business picked up over time, and Rosie worked the pits with friends and family until a stroke left him unable to lift pig or shovel.

Now he sat or stood near where cars once pulled up to the gas station's pumps, beneath a marquee whose faded letters spell out SC T VARIETY and broken fragments of the missing O and T dangled loose, silently nodding to the steady line of customers, many of whom drive one-hundred-plus miles for a plate of chopped whole hog. Most locals still call this place Rosie's.

But the tourists flock here to meet Rodney, to shake his hand, and eat his barbecue. It's Rodney who has signed with a New York–based PR and media firm. It's Rodney who dreams of opening a second Scott's location in Charleston, of bringing "his world" to the big city; who joined the Fatback Collective, a team of progressively minded pitmasters, including Sam Jones of the Skylight Inn, who donate their time and raise money to invest in community-rooted businesses and organizations that find themselves imperiled by change or catastrophe. It's Rodney who did not have a passport five years ago but now travels the world, alongside the cheffiest of chefs, smoking hogs from Uruguay to Melbourne, Australia. But when Rodney leaves Hemingway to cook abroad, it's his father, Rosie, now seventy-three years old, who says, "You go. We got this."

So the question needs asking: Will success spoil Rodney Scott?

He likes to tell a story of the first time he cooked at an event outside of Hemingway. It was 2010 at the Charleston Wine and Food festival, a well-heeled engagement where the likes of Bill Murray can be found rubbing seersuckered elbows with the culinary world's elite. While Rodney roasted a hog on the sidewalk off King's Street he made friends with Nick Pihakis, a Birmingham, Alabama, restaurateur who had made a small fortune as the founder of the Jim 'N Nick's Bar-B-Q chain. Nick blanched when Rodney told him how much he charged per pound of barbecue and encouraged him to raise the price by a buck. And that's what Rodney did, on a Sunday afternoon, in the middle of lunch service: parted a line of customers at the ordering counter and, with black Magic Marker in hand, rewrote the menu.

But he'll often follow up that story with another: the tale of his first hog, a time when Rodney was very young and very much enamored with basketball. One day Rosie Scott presented his son with an option: he could attend the next night's game if he smoked his own hog. Rodney had grown up by Rosie's side, he had pushed a broom around Scott's from the age of six, but he had never cooked a hog. "He had the hog set up for me and he left," Rodney told me. He stoked the fires throughout the night with a shovel longer than he was tall, all the while completely unaware that his dad's trusted pitman Buster was keeping watch. "And when they flipped the hog over it was just where it needed to be: perfect." Rodney Scott was just eleven years old and had smoked the perfect pig.

As much as Rodney enjoys cooking hogs in exotic locales and feeding thousands of strangers, he told me that he really savors when people make the trip to Hemingway. "There's only so many things we can do to bring people into this town," where the only rival to his family's barbecue shop is Tupperware's global distribution center on the outskirts of Hemingway. Scott's Bar-B-Que has become a tourist attraction.

We were standing outside the pit house, along South Carolina Highway 261, where only the occasional big-rig trucker flashed by every ten minutes or so, hauling lumber from east to west. "Look how much traffic we got." He laughed with a sigh. As if on cue, a frog casually hopped across the road. This is the world Rodney wants to share.

One afternoon, he offered to share a bit more of that world with me. Riding shotgun, I was bounced around the cab as we drove along the unpaved, horseshoe-shaped track that formed a tight crescent around Rodney's mother's family farm. His pickup truck kicked up a mini dustbowl of the road's red dirt, which blew across low fields of tobacco and soy. For once there was no soundtrack, no music accompanying the scenery. It was beautiful here, the family compound where Rodney spent much of his childhood, stepping through fields of cotton and corn, helping his father farm tobacco and beans. "We got a cold soda and a Nab [pack of peanut butter crackers] as pay." This is where he watched litters of pigs grow into hogs before being carted away to the slaughterhouse, and where he learned to mistrust snakes.

Not used to periods of silence, Rodney broke the quiet. "I tell you what," he said, "a lotta dreaming went on, on this dirt road."

He pointed past the property line toward the two-lane highway that trailed into the distance. "On Sundays, you could spot the fancy cars rolling past, sometimes pulling big boats," en route to the beaches and well-kept colonial towns of the South Carolina coast. Young Rodney and his cousins would run to the edge of the family property and watch the world fly by, claiming rights to the biggest boats, the finest cars. "We used this place to imagine," he continued. "If a plane flew over, we'd imagine where was that plane going, who was on it." Part game, part dream, the more inventive the travel story, the more famous the passengers, the more exotic the locales the better.

Anywhere but here, anywhere but Hemingway.

We stared at the highway in silence, waiting, until a lone car putted into view before disappearing into the trees. I imagined Rodney was thinking not about where that driver was going, but where he, himself, was going next.

"It's hard to believe that you can come from here," he said, shaking his head.

———

Before Rodney Scott traveled the globe lighting a fire in the world's barbecue consciousness, there was Ed Mitchell, who emerged from

Wilson, North Carolina, a decade earlier to become a featured face in the culture of the changing South.

I first met Mitchell at a 2012 barbecue event held in Oxford, Mississippi, where he cooked a cast iron vat of tobacco-barn Brunswick stew, a mélange of chicken, beef, sausage, okra, tomatoes, corn, and butter beans that traditionally fed eastern North Carolina farmers and laborers throughout the late-summer tobacco harvest. Broad shouldered and bulky, Mitchell wore denim overalls and a baseball cap, a fluffy white beard and a toothy, plump-cheeked smile broader than the stew pot he steadily stirred that night. He looked like an African American mountain man who had joined a Santa Claus cult. Though busy greeting a succession of old friends and other well-wishers, with me he was almost excessively genial, answering my questions before I could even ask them, questions about himself, his life, his barbecue career. He answered these questions and narrated his life while speaking in the third person—"So then, after that first hog, Ed Mitchell decided to open his own barbecue place." I couldn't immediately decide if this was a charming quirk or a hint of some deeper lust for fame.

Mitchell had recently found himself without a home base to cook hogs and had been navigating the circuit of public and private cooking events for the past year. He described to me a new venture: a culinary school and museum dedicated to whole-hog barbecue housed in his now-shuttered restaurant in Wilson. He would hold weekly seminars and demonstrations, graduate potential pitmasters from his barbecue college, and enshrine generations of forgotten pit cooks and their craft. I thought it a magnificent idea, but entirely impossible. What sort of benefactors would fund a museum dedicated to barbecue? Afterward, a North Carolina–based friend pulled me aside with a warning: "*Do not* fall under the spell of Ed Mitchell."

Eight months later, I would run into Ed again, at the Big Apple

Barbecue Block Party, where he was a featured pitmaster. I immediately recognized the same uniform that he wore in Mississippi: workman's overalls and the baseball cap that read—upon peering closer—"The Pitmaster," a moniker that he consistently used to refer to himself in conversation and on his website, a title that hung palpably in the air like so much barbecue smoke. Here, in New York, he hurriedly hand-chopped pork while barking directions to his pit crew, too busy to talk to me or any of the hundreds of casual acquaintances and hard-core Ed Mitchell fans.

I paid for and was handed a barbecue sandwich prepared by the master himself. Tremendously smoky and wonderfully moist, the finely chopped whole hog was spiced in the eastern North Carolina fashion, finished with apple cider vinegar, sugar, salt, and red and black pepper. One bite of the meat convinced me that this was some of the best barbecue I'd ever eaten. I wanted to go back for another round, but the line of customers ran some three hundred deep.

Returning to my room, I scanned photos of Mitchell online, read interviews and profiles of the Pitmaster. He was everywhere, and everywhere looked the same: old-timey, sentimentally southern, with the slight whiff of fabrication, like the walls that decorate every dining room of the Cracker Barrel chain of restaurants. The ubiquitous overalls, I soon gathered, together with the cap, North Pole beard, and ego-centered speech patterns were props in a campaign of unsubtle self-branding. "This is a persona. This is an image," he once told his restaurant's staff while within earshot of food journalist Andrea Weigl. "Back in the day, they wore bib overalls. This is what the pitmaster is. This is what got me national fame. This is how I ended up on the front page of *The New York Times*." His denim overalls represented not only a typical pitmaster's traditional work wear; it was the Pitmaster's costume.

His history was just as carefully curated, manufactured into myth. Mitchell told me bits and pieces of his story over that pot of Brunswick stew in Oxford; numerous interviews filled in the rest.

Ed Mitchell was born in Wilson, North Carolina, where the call letters of the local, now defunct, AM radio station spelled out WGTM, short for the "World's Greatest Tobacco Market," a nickname earned a century ago after the town became the capital of the state's flue-cured, golden-leaf cigarette tobacco trade. Born in the summer of 1946, Mitchell was the grandson of farmers turned town folk, but on holidays the family would reunite at the farm for whole-hog smokeouts. "Barbecue has always been a fabric of our lives," Mitchell maintained, and "just as natural as natural can get in my life."

At eighteen he left Wilson for nearby Fayetteville, attending Fayetteville State University on a football scholarship. After three years, the Vietnam War called him abroad. The brotherhood of combat during his eighteen-month tour was transformative. Years later he would assert that only Vietnam and barbecue, in his experience, contained the power to transcend America's tempestuous racial history. But the barbecue half of his history would come much later.

Mitchell completed his degree and enlisted in a Ford Motor program established to groom potential minority auto dealers. After a dozen years with the company, spent primarily in Boston, he took a leave of absence and returned to Wilson to help his mother care for his ailing father. For decades his parents Willie and Doretha had run Mitchell's Groceries at the corner of Singletary and Highway 301 South. The family store was, like Rosie and Ella Scott's crossroads convenience store, a penny candy and soda kind of place, and the Mitchells "pillars of the community," according to their son.

Ed remained in town following his father's death from cancer in 1990, and his mother kept the store going. But longtime customers now avoided the place. The mom-and-pop team that always greeted everyone by name had disintegrated.

This is the point in time at which the Ed Mitchell myth begins.

One morning, soon after his father's passing, Mitchell stopped by the store only to receive his poor mother's worries: she had only pulled in seventeen dollars thus far, with nearly three-quarters of that sum purchased with food stamps. In order to comfort his mom Mitchell offered to cook her something special. "What do you want to eat?" he asked her. "I don't know," she fretted, "I've got a taste for some old-fashioned barbecue." Her son immediately understood: wood, fire, hog—the one true barbecue. Barbecue he could no longer source from Bill Ellis or Parker's, the heavyweight barbecue emporiums in town that fed hundreds each day with gas-cooked hogs.

He purchased a pig from the Super Duper supermarket. "A little small guy," he remembered, "thirty-two or thirty-five pounds." It would yield just enough pork to feed both of them. This would not be Mitchell's first hog. In one magazine interview he says that he cooked his first hog at the age of fourteen, a day that also marked the first time he indulged in a few swallows of moonshine, the day the future pitmaster, in his words, "became a man." So he knew how to provide Mom with some old-fashioned barbecue. After cooking that small bantam-weight hog for three hours, he chopped and seasoned the meat and fed his mother barbecue sandwiches. It is easy to imagine her pride, her sated hunger and full belly.

As they were eating their sandwiches, a customer stopped in for a cheap hot dog or hamburger from the grocery's deli counter. "Oh, Mrs. Mitchell," he cried out, "y'all got barbecue too?" This would be his lucky day, and that man left with a sackful of barbecue sandwiches.

By that evening, Doretha Mitchell had sold out of barbecue. Before she closed up shop her son had promised more barbecue to come the following day. Word spread: a pitmaster was cooking old-fashioned barbecue at the old Mitchell Grocery. That first thirty-something-pound pig was followed by another double its size. The shelves of dry goods made way for dining tables. Ed Mitchell cooked the barbecue and Mom fixed the sides: collards and mustard greens, candied yams and mashed rutabagas.

By late 1992, Mitchell, with his mother's blessing, was ready to go whole-hog, to transform the neighborhood grocery into a full-service barbecue restaurant. He hired James Kirby, a veteran pitmaster whom he knew from the local poker game, to tutor him in the ways of the flesh. "If you want to get into the barbecue business," the wily vet warned, "I'll put you in the water, but it will be up to you to swim." Behind Mitchell's Grocery, in a dirt-floored shed used to store old glass cola bottles, Kirby kneeled down and, as if driven by a bolt of inspiration sent by the gods, scratched out a blueprint of the pit into the ground.

Within a half-dozen years, Mitchell's Barbecue, Ribs & Chicken had outgrown the meager confines of his parents' grocery. He started expanding the building, a construction project that would stretch, progressing in fits and starts, over five years. Twice, hurricane winds toppled the unfinished walls.

But by 2001 Ed Mitchell had built himself a two-story cinder-block monument to old-fashioned whole-hog barbecue, a labyrinthine compound that engulfed the grocery like a whale swallowing a fish. It looked, in its own way, like a pit house writ large—a castle of a pit house. There was a buffet-style dining room and a second with servers, a drive-thru, and a walk-up takeout window. He dreamed up something called a "pig pickin' bar"; envisioned as an oyster bar or raw bar but dedicated to the hog, it featured lesser-appreciated delicacies like chitterlings and pigs' feet, ears, tails, and

WILL SUCCESS SPOIL RODNEY SCOTT?

snouts. There was a full-service liquor bar, instructional classrooms to teach backyard pitmasters how to grill a pig, and a trio of private party rooms. Mitchell designed the kitchen to be the Mercedes of whole-hog pit houses, a circular room of four gleaming stainless steel barbecue pits and tricked out with a state-of-the-art ventilation system. In the entryway to the kitchen, the tiled floor spelled out "Mitchell's."

Just as he had overhauled his family's mom-and-pop grocery, Ed Mitchell had remodeled himself to become the Pitmaster. But a pitmaster whose hog-smoking methods could be considered more than a little idiosyncratic.

For one, he used charcoal, twenty-pound sacks of your everyday Kingsford briquettes, to roast his pigs. Most wood-burning pitmasters, from the Carolinas down to Texas, consider the use of processed charcoal the most venial of barbecuing sins, certainly not as soul damning as cooking with gas or electricity, but a move that wouldn't earn many admirers among the set of smoked-meat aficionados. They call it plain old cheating. But Mitchell used those briquettes for the intense heat they could radiate over several hours of cooking time.

We've all heard the trite phrase "low and slow" used to designate the default temperature and time settings used to barbecue meats. Mitchell, on the other hand, liked to define his cooking style as "hot and fast." He transformed his pit into an inferno of an oven, getting the temperature up to 450 degrees, by shoveling only a single, massive, nearly mountain-sized load of charcoal under his pigs. Staying up all night to stoke the fire gradually while attempting to gauge the meat's internal temperature was never on his agenda. "If you're looking, you ain't cooking," he was fond of telling reporters. Staying up all night with the hog, he said, was nothing but an excuse to get out of the house and drink moonshine. Other whole-hog pitmasters, who stopped to watch Mitchell cook at the circuit of barbecue bonanzas, often wagged their heads in disbelief. He's finished? Going home? Those pigs are done for—scorched skins and pink insides.

So how did Mitchell get that tremendous smoke flavor into his meat with ordinary briquettes commonly known as a one-note heat source? Answer: a single oak log, maybe two, which he'd marinate overnight in a black pepper–infused vinegar bath. At public demonstrations, he'd tell spectators that this was his "trade secret," passed down from his grandfather to his father to himself. (This is a difficult story to swallow. The mass production of American charcoal didn't begin until the 1920s, and the product wasn't readily available until the late 1940s, well after his granddad would have cooked a pig. And, interestingly enough, it was Henry Ford, Mitchell's future employer of sorts, and his brother-in-law E. G. Kingsford, who invented the charcoal briquette by mixing wood scraps, remainders from the Model T production line, with potato starch glue.) Indeed, every pitmaster I asked declared Mitchell's vinegar-soaked wood formula to be a complete and utter farce, a mockery of barbecue theory and simple science. And I can't help but agree that it sounds ridiculous. But though we scoffed, as if by alchemy Mitchell's meat always contained that mellow, oaky richness imparted by wood smoke.

The burgeoning food media world would soon follow that smoke to come knocking on Ed Mitchell's door, just as they would for Rodney Scott a decade later. Just months after the official reopening of Mitchell's new and enlarged house of barbecue, the Southern Foodways Alliance, a then relatively new organization that had already proved itself not only a tastemaker but a kingmaker, invited the pitmaster to cook a hog. This earned him a picture in *The New York Times*, where on October 23, 2002, page A20—not the front page as he was fond of boasting—he appeared in his soon-to-be-familiar costume of cap, beard, and overalls: affectations all. The next year he arrived at the first annual Big Apple Barbecue Block Party as the sole representative from the Carolinas and very likely became the first man to ever smoke a hog on the sidewalks of Manhattan, a performance that would score him a call back to the event each year thereafter. Anthony Bourdain made a pilgrimage and gnawed on pickled pigs' feet. *New Yorker* staff writer and barbecue junkie Calvin Trillin wrote that Mitchell's 'que put him in "an expansive and ecumenical frame of mind." The Pitmaster had reached cult status among barbecue aficionados nationwide.

For those who would listen, Mitchell would expound on his belief that the histories of race and barbecue in America were intertwined. "African Americans," he told one interviewer, "were the labor force" in all culinary sectors throughout the South. "We did the laboring part and producing and perfecting the thing." Go back and rewatch the famous barbecue scene from *Gone with the Wind*, he urged. Scarlett O'Hara wears her best dress, a floral-print silk organza and green velveteen number that Mammy helps her put on. Her dozens of suitors are dressed in rich grays and browns, jackets and cravats. "They didn't do any preparations," Mitchell said. Rhett Butler couldn't cook no damn hog.

But he also believed that only barbecue, and war, could heal the scars and traumas of history. Only the pit house and the foxhole were sites imbued with the potential to bridge any sort of conflict. For Mitchell, barbecues, whether owned and/or patronized by black or white Americans, existed because of a common measure. "As my old math teacher used to say, there was a common denominator that you could tie the two together and the common denominator was the pig." The commonality of the pig linked birthday celebrations, holidays, and summertime cookouts across color and class lines. The common denominator engendered celebrations, provided a reason to break the proverbial bread and share a table.

With such deep thinking, Ed Mitchell had nowhere to travel but the deepest reaches of outer space, at least on a metaphoric level, to go where no pitmaster had gone before. He would turn his attention toward fixing the common denominator. He would return to the "true original taste of barbecue," as he called it, to the pigs his forefathers once cooked.

Mitchell vowed that by March 2004 he would only sell barbecue sourced from free-range hogs. Not only would this meat taste better, but the shift away from commodity pigs would put a stake in the heart of large-scale commercial farming. It might rank as just a toothpick-sized jab at the ten-thousand-ton vampire that was Smithfield, Hormel, and the rest, but it was a move that would draw blood nevertheless. For the past year he had shaken hands with the nation's leading foodists: chefs, writers, activists, and farmers, including Bill Niman, a Bay Area rancher who turned a handful of cattle into a leading brand name in the distribution of beef, lamb, poultry, and pork that is, as the company's slogan says, "Raised with Care." This could be "an opportunity for the little guy to get back into the game of raising pigs," Mitchell said in a follow-up interview, "and develop a market for him all across the country."

This was big news for North Carolina—a real effort to restore the links in the farm-to-consumer chain that had disappeared half a century ago. But Mitchell's announcement was a big gamble in the town of Wilson, where more than a fifth of residents lived below the poverty line (that number has since risen). Mitchell would have to charge more per pound of barbecue, drastically raising the price to unheard-of levels.

But it all came crashing down before Mitchell could sell his first "all-natural" barbecue sandwich. In Mitchell's telling, at the second of two press conferences to announce his switch to free-range hogs, a pair of men confronted the Pitmaster. "You're getting ready to start something," one sputtered. "You're getting ready to tell people not to buy my product."

Looking back, Mitchell said that this was the first omen in what he has called an "orchestrated turbulence"—a life interrupted by petty jealousies, a business ruined by underhanded dealings. Soon he would be audited by the state. Then his bank would foreclose on the business and property. Finally, he was accused by the state Department of Revenue of embezzling about $75,000 in state sales and withholding taxes. Within a month following that press conference, he would lose his restaurant (it would take him three years to win it back in a court ruling) and be sentenced to thirty days in jail, which he served on the weekends. His career in flames, Mitchell went on the attack, accusing his bank, commercial pork purveyors, and the local white barbecue establishment of torpedoing his career. Most damning of all, Mitchell would lose the support of many culinarians and Carolinians that he had built over the past year.

But Ed Mitchell would not relinquish his dream of bringing free-range pigs to the whole-hog barbecue scene. His pursuit of this uncommon common denominator continued in 2007, when he partnered with Greg Hatem, a Raleigh businessman and downtown developer who had spent two decades buying up, rehabbing, and putting back into use block after block of blighted buildings throughout the state capital. Born in nearby Roanoke Rapids to first-generation Lebanese American parents, Hatem had turned downtown Raleigh into a hip living and dining destination. Mitchell abandoned Wilson to join Hatem's Empire Eats restaurant group at a concept called the Pit. His title would not be pitmaster but "master chef."

It would have been easy to dismiss Mitchell and Hatem's project as simply profit-driven gentrification. Hatem was, and still is, a wealthy real-estate developer, but he counted himself a big barbecue fan. He'd been smoking hogs for at least thirty years, beginning as a volunteer pit cook for his hometown fire department's annual fund-raiser. He still hosts, each October, a massive pig pickin' party during the North Carolina State Fair. His goal for the Pit, he told me, would be to "preserve and celebrate the heritage of North Carolina barbecue."

But preservation often comes with a price; celebrations are expensive.

The Pit opened in November 2007 with a price point that undoubtedly ranked among the nation's highest. For comparison, a chopped barbecue plate, with two sides included, from the Pit cost roughly double the price of a large tray with cornbread and coleslaw from the Skylight Inn. Only in New York City, where a handful of intrepid entrepreneurs operated high-scale smoke joints, like Danny Meyer's Blue Smoke, even come close to matching Hatem and Mitchell's big-ticket barbecue. The Pit's owners spoke a new language of fancy barbecue.

Hatem and Mitchell sourced a heritage-breed hog from a farm two hours east of Raleigh that met Animal Welfare Approved standards, ensuring that they were raised outdoors and without the use of hormones and steroids. This Berkshire-Yorkshire crossbreed ensured greater fat-to-muscle marbling, tenderness, and flavor. The hogs would be cooked indoors, in a slickly modern full-service kitchen, on a pair of barbecue pits, each capable of accommodating a 180-pound pig.

Housed in a New Deal–era Armour meat-packing plant, the Pit, with its brick walls and reclaimed wood beams, concrete floor and vaulted ceiling, looked much like every chef-driven, farm-focused, artisanally aggressive restaurant that opened in the late aughts. The numerous dining rooms seated 220 customers, while an outdoor patio included room for 50 more (it wasn't rare for more than 1,000 covers to be served in a night). There was a "pig bar," where customers could sit in high-backed chairs in full view of the barbecue pits; artfully curated beer, cocktail, and wine lists (bottles from all three were displayed in a temperature-controlled floor-to-ceiling glassed vault partitioned off from the main dining room); and a menu that spanned smoked whole hog, pork spareribs, beef brisket, chicken, turkey, a grilled fish of the day, a spinach salad tossed with house-made hog jowl bacon, and—a dish I find it hard to believe passed Ed Mitchell's lips—barbecued tofu ("seasoned and grilled, topped with our famous sauce"). There was a sous chef armed with a culinary arts degree.

The Pit had just about everything to make it possibly the most ambitiously conceived barbecue restaurant—whole-hog barbecue restaurant at that—to ever open. Everything except a pitmaster. By the summer of 2011, Ed Mitchell was out as partner of the Pit. Hatem confided in public and private interviews that the Pitmaster was never really involved in the restaurant's day-to-day operations.

For the second time, Mitchell found himself without a place to cook barbecue, a pitmaster without a pit. For a while he ran with the barbecue school and museum idea, touting these vagaries to anyone who would listen, like myself, at events across the nation. Ed kept chasing the limelight.

In the spring of 2014, he finally opened Ed Mitchell's Que, a restaurant that was at least three years in the making. Located not in Wilson, nor in Raleigh, but in Durham, North Carolina, Que would not only mark Mitchell's return but the symbolic passing of the torch to his son, Ryan, who would join him in running the business.

But though a promotional campaign pushed Mitchell as a "barbecue legend" and an "iconic pitmaster," Que launched onto stormy seas. He would be going head-to-head with Greg Hatem, who opened a second Pit location in Durham, not one mile up the road. Then there was Mitchell's new menu, filled with the old standards—chopped pork, ribs, fried chicken—but also filled out with new dishes that didn't translate: A caprese salad? Deep-fried pork-rind-encrusted brie? Barbecued tempeh?

Ed Mitchell's Que closed in February 2015, less than a year after opening and before I could make a visit. But I did make a trip to Mitchell's Barbecue, Ribs & Chicken, which, closed long before my interest in whole-hog barbecue ignited, sat empty and shuttered. One early Sunday summer afternoon, determined to see the inside of the Pitmaster's former barbecue castle, I banged and rattled on the locked front doors of the building, which now, according to a dinky sign out front, was operating as Utopia Cafe and Lounge. Eventually a man who introduced himself as Tony, just Tony, ushered me inside with a terse nod. I think he knew I was there to tour the ambitiously impossible dream of a barbecue icon. Tony led me inside to what looked to be Mitchell's main dining room, now converted into a dance space with DJ booth. He told me to look around before easing himself into a massive faux leather recliner that occupied a quarter of the dance floor.

Room to room I walked in awe: the hugeness of the place was humbling and sad. I found what must have been the former pig bar, now covered in liquor bottles. I peeked into the kitchen, where a semicircle of stainless steel barbecue pits gleamed with a fingerprintless polish.

I tiptoed back to the dance floor, careful to not wake Tony as he snoozed off a hangover. A long windowless wall along the far side of the room caught my eye; it was covered in a heavy black curtain that ran parallel like a long chalkboard. I lifted the curtain's rightmost lower corner to uncover a painting there on the wall, a mural, a scene portraying a white plantation house, like Tara in *Gone with the Wind*, and in the foreground a long wooden table, shaded by oak trees, at which people sat, black faces seated next to white faces, joined in celebration, waiting for that old-fashioned barbecue. I had heard rumors of this mural. How it was painted by a Mitchell's employee, a dishwasher with a folk-artsy talent, commissioned by Ed to showcase the barbecue history he knew to be true. I saw only that last, final scene, but I knew how the story began: a tobacco harvest; a barn for curing; men slaughtering hogs, digging pits, and swigging moonshine. Here was Mitchell's bright shining dream for the whole hog: a rainbow of peoples breaking bread over barbecue. I left the aptly named Utopia hoping Ed Mitchell would one day find his very own.

But utopias have a tendency to be fragile, susceptible to the ravages of the world. All it took was a single drop of grease meeting a solitary spark of fire to reduce Rodney Scott's pit house to a heap of blistered ceiling beams, charred concrete walls, and scorched tin roofing. It looked like a tornado had blown through. The inferno occurred on the morning of November 27, 2013, the day before Thanksgiving, a business transformed by one drop, a molecule of liquid fat, from any one of the fifteen pigs on the pit, meat on its way to outshine turkey and pie on the holiday table. Rodney received the call at home, in bed, from his employee Willie Johnson at just after four AM: Boss. A grease fire. Out of control. Come quick.

Get out, he said, just get out of there.

On two occasions, Rodney had suffered pit fires. He had witnessed the inferno-like potentiality of a grease fire, had lost hogs to the heat, seen a smokehouse devoured by flames. A year earlier, he had traveled down to Humboldt, Tennessee, with his Fatback Collective teammates to donate a weekend in helping to gut and rebuild Sam's Bar-B-Q, a regionally vital smoked-shoulder joint recently ravaged by fire. But the last incident to occur at Scott's had happened under his father's watch, nearly a quarter century before. Now he contemplated the future as fifteen firefighters from five Williamsburg County stations battled the blaze that threatened to consume the adjacent building, the heart of Scott's Bar-B-Que: his parents' old convenience store. After an hour and a half, the firefighters saved the store but declared the pit house a total loss.

News of the disaster traveled fast through the circuits of the culinary world. After seeing pictures of the fire's aftermath, I remember feeling gloomy, mired in a state of preholiday hopelessness—that was, until Rodney texted to assure me that they would still be cooking for Thanksgiving. "Play with fire, you get burned," he told me. But few who get burned return to play with fire. By midafternoon, before the firefighters finished packing up their gear and while smoke still seeped from the scattered ruins of the pit house, Rodney and his tireless crew would have six pigs smoking from a set of auxiliary pits stored under a shabby lean-to structure nearby. Though he didn't have much barbecue to serve to walk-in customers come Thanksgiving morning, he later proudly told me that he filled every single prereserved order.

His friends and Fatback Collective compatriots rallied around the pitmaster, mobilizing a bootstrap rebuilding outing through the South and beyond. In late December the Scott's Bar-B-Que in Exile Tour launched in Charleston, where Rodney cooked a pair of whole hogs right on King Street, the city's posh and touristy downtown thoroughfare. Folks waited in line for an hour to purchase barbecue sandwiches at five bucks apiece. He raised $5,492 that day. In the New Year, the Exile Tour racked up more than seven thousand miles as it rambled through Atlanta, Nashville, Oxford, New Orleans, Birmingham, Charleston (again), and, in a testament to the growing popularity of whole-hog barbecue, San Francisco. In each city, local chefs assembled pop-up dinners—evening-hour bonanzas, with Rodney's whole-hog barbecue paired with cocktails and artisan sides—at $100 per plate. The tour pulled in just over $80,000, a quarter of which Rodney paid forward to the Fatback organization to aid in future rebuilding efforts. (That $20,000 assisted in the relocation of the Cozy Corner Restaurant, an iconic Memphis barbecue spot gutted by fire in January 2015.)

Five months following the disastrous Scott's fire, carbonized fragments of the pit house still littered the visibly scorched earth. The actual barbecue pits survived, and after some quick brick and cement patchwork, now sat within the confines of a massive portable carport turned makeshift smokehouse. Rodney pulled out his cell phone and showed me blueprints of the pit house to come. The plans, sketched by a Charleston architect with a knack for designing restaurants using recycled materials and featuring the work of local craftspeople, upped the number of pits from fourteen to twenty, included a high-powered exhaust system, and, if the fire marshal would allow, had patio seating along the building's exterior. (The variety store survived unscathed and Rodney promises to keep the building as is.)

The plans carried more than a whiff of Ed Mitchell, but I didn't need to tell Rodney that. He had long thought deeply about the Pitmaster's rise and fall; he was familiar with the pitfalls of success. He grimaced when telling me that a few Hemingway townspeople have slighted him for his national notoriety: the guy at the gas station who said, "You ain't nobody special," the customer at the local diner who said, "You're too good to speak to us now."

And Rodney and Ed have met on several occasions. Their first meeting didn't exactly strike chords of friendship and harmony. This wasn't Nixon meeting Mao. It might even have been worse than Nixon shaking hands with Elvis. It was 2012, and the trustees of the Big Apple Barbecue Block Party gave Mitchell's long-held spot at the corner of Madison and Twenty-Third to Rodney Scott, a first-time participant. Mitchell, who had cooked at all ten previous annual events, was transferred to a less-than-ideal location across Madison Park, which suffered from pedestrian bottlenecks throughout the weekend. Rodney had been set up by the festival's organizers to receive the fury of an understandably pissed-off Ed Mitchell. "You're stealing my spotlight," the Pitmaster told his younger rival.

I asked Rodney how the conversation proceeded from there. He frowned. "His picture still hangs in our place," was all he would say—a peacekeeping gesture, an act of barbecue détente.

Rodney's future pit house will cost $100,000 to build, meaning he has to raise an additional 40 percent of the total construction price, or roughly 12,000 barbecue sandwiches. But that didn't stop the Scott family from hosting their eighteenth annual Easter picnic, a complimentary catered party thrown in Hemingway's honor. It's a "give-back to the community," in the words of Rodney, an offering of soul food and soul music for all the years of neighborly support and all the unnumbered loads of donated firewood.

Despite the constant threat of rain, more than one thousand people—more than double Hemingway's population—lined up on the day before Easter for free plates of fried chicken, purloo (a Lowcountry rice casserole), and stewed field peas. Barbecue had to be purchased separately, but he still sold ten-plus hogs' worth. In the large empty field opposite Scott's Variety Store old men slyly sipped from pocketed half-pint bottles, as the Touch Band kept the crowd grooving to R&B and funk favorites. Local school board and House of Representative candidates set up tables and handed out flyers and buttons despite Rodney's protests ("There's no campaigning here, this is my crowd").

As the party entered its fifth hour, with no sign of slowing down, I shook hands with George Frederick, Sr., fifty-something years old and a lifelong Hemingway resident, whom Rodney introduced as a wealth of local history. As a boy, Frederick used to work at the convenience store, long before Rosie Scott purchased the business. "This area," he said, pointing to the intersection that Scott's occupies one corner of, "is called Brunson Crossroads." Named for the wealthy planter who once owned the surrounding land, the Crossroads boasted a thriving black entertainment and shopping district from the 1960s until the early 1980s. Downtown Hemingway could claim the banks and clothing stores, but here, on weekends, "the Crossroads were alive," Frederick told me. He had lived right here, "on top of Brunson," where lounges and juke joints, restaurants and pool halls, a grocery and two barbershops lined the four corners of Highway 261 and Cowhead Road. Locals nicknamed the junction "Blood and Thunder" because both could erupt at any moment. He remembered taking dates to Lawrence Coakley's for fried chicken and later dancing at the Jam Factory, where the proprietors jammed the patrons in. "That nine-piece band would make the windows vibrate," he chuckled. "And there was always a place to get barbecue," he recalled, one business operated by a local named Vander McCray and another whose name has faded with time.

The Brunson community once hosted annual summertime fairs, Frederick told me, on the same grounds where the Scotts hold their Easter picnic. But the crack epidemic, joined with the escalation of imprisonment and policing of the black community, killed every single business at the Crossroads, every business except Scott's Variety. "This brings back Brunson," he said before echoing a familiar word: "This is like a reunion."

The Easter picnic was that reunion Rodney spoke of during my first visit to Scott's Bar-B-Que. And though few (including myself) passed up the free chicken and sides to spend money on barbecue, this was, in Rodney's definition that he had passed along to me years before, the truest of barbecues: A gathering. A party. An opportunity to join in and enjoy one another's company. The meat did not make the barbecue, nor the fire, the hickory and oak logs, or that spicy vinegar sauce.

The barbecue was booming from Rodney's stereo. The barbecue was sitting around the fire. The community made this barbecue what it was. Rodney, Rosie, and Ella, George Frederick, Sr., and the campaigning politicians; Uncle Sam, Sonny Boy, and Bo Diddley; all the rest of the attendees and even myself. The barbecue was us. Each and every one of us gathered there that day, like all the parts of the pig: a whole hog of a barbecue. Everyone enjoying food and drink, music and one another—everything the world has to offer. This was peacemaking barbecue. Barbecue as utopian vision. A secular gospel of barbecue. Barbecue that could save the world.

A NEW YORK CITY CODA

At the corner of Twenty-Third, a waist-high pile of split oak timbers blocked the left lane of Madison Avenue. As I crossed the street, a yellow cab zigged to miss a stray log that had tumbled into the center lane, forcing me to leap behind a police barricade that cordoned off a barbecue pit. The cabbie looked back to steal a rearview-mirror glance at the towering burn barrel that glowed spectrally in the downpour. Scott's Bar-B-Que had made it to New York.

Tropical Storm Andrea had hit the city during the Friday-night kickoff of the Big Apple Barbecue Block Party. Overnight nearly five inches of rainfall would descend on the city, winds gusted to forty-five miles an hour. Streets flooded and subway service was suspended in Upper Manhattan. Rodney's trusty two-man crew needed to cook a half-dozen hogs by daybreak, before doing it again—we hoped with fairer weather conditions—the following night. Nearby, Rodney was making the rounds: bear hugs and handshakes with old friends, artisan cocktails and flights of fancy barbecue hors d'oeuvres at an opening night party/film festival, prepping for an appearance on a morning news show.

I arrived to find Uncle Sam and another man huddled beneath the corner of a tented tarp to escape the wind and the rain. They were wet and miserable, their flimsy rain slickers and makeshift shelter unable to shield them from the deluge, leaving them in no mood to cook a mess of hogs, much less talk barbecue with me. Uncle Sam grumbled at the sight of my smile and wave. He rose from his seat and stomped around the barricade, splashing in pools of water that hadn't been there minutes before.

Sam grabbed an armful of oak and, puddle-jumping back across the avenue, tossed the logs into the open top of the burn barrel, a smaller, modified version of the model back home. Somehow, despite the monsoon-like conditions, a fire steadily burned in the barrel's mouth. Across its front midsection, a raised script, carved with a welder's torch, spelled out something I couldn't quite discern in the wet darkness. I leaned in and flashed my cell phone's strobe. "Cut Chop Cook," it read, with Rodney's distinct signature below.

I stepped back to take in the scene. Ten blocks due north, a barely discernible, but readily obvious, architectural silhouette shimmered in the rain and fog, looming behind the burn barrel. The Empire State Building stood glooming in green and white. I took note of how their complementary shapes and sizes echoed each other in their incongruity: squat bases and cylindrical towers, luminance that burst through the sky. Fire, steel, and concrete. Skyscrapers and barbecue.

Meanwhile, Uncle Sam massaged his coals into shape with a long-poled shovel. A large black SUV slowly rolled by, a half-dozen passengers inside, their faces pressed forward to the car's open windows, mouths agape, watching Sam carry fire. Shovel and fire in hand, he trudged over to a flatbed trailer that held the pits, a series of hulking steel-welded whales that Rodney had built specifically for this weekend. With arms dripping and the coals starting to smolder, he struggled to lift the shovel up high to clear the trailer's raised surface and spilled the first load of fire into the pit. It felt as if all of New York had exhaled a great relieving gasp of breath, the stream of taxis continued unabated down the avenue. Barbecue would be served tomorrow.

As Uncle Sam continued to shovel fire, I introduced myself to his partner, who, like all of Rodney's helpers, had a peculiar nickname: Fishman. He explained that like his buddy Sam, the uncle, he is what his name says he is: the owner of the Fishnet, Hemingway's sole seafood market. Fishman, born Laurie Cooper, helps the Scott family on occasion, perpetual payback for a lifetime of financial assistance from Rosie. "That's my bank," he conceded with a shoulder shrug. Energetically chatty despite the weather, he mentioned that before fishmongering he hauled canned South Carolina peaches cross-country in an eighteen-wheeler. As I search for the nerve to ask if his friends called him the Peachman back in those days, Uncle Sam signaled him over.

"These some solid hogs," Sam said, shaking his head while motioning to a soggy cardboard box. Inside, a sextet of gutted and flayed pigs, kept cool with bags of ice, threatened to spill into the streets. A cabbie stopped his car to watch the two men bend over and attempt to heft the topmost carcass onto a nearby table. With wet hog flesh slipping from their gloved hands, they strained to hold their load.

"Where'd they get these fuckin' hogs from?" growled Sam.

"Ol' fat-ass hog," Fishman agreed. A white tag safety-pinned to the hog's hindquarters read 191, almost 200 pounds, or approximately 25 percent more than the pigs they cook back home, a hog as big as Hollywood's famous ape who cinematically scaled the skyscraper in the distance.

As Uncle Sam held the hog down on the table, Fishman grabbed a knife, cheap and dull looking, and began to hack away at the dense tendon that connects a hog's hoof to hock. The sounds of the city provided the soundtrack for a night of cooking. An ambulance sirened by, its emergency lights flooding their faces with red and blue. A line of men in suits exited the brokerage and banking firm opposite and hollered for taxis while trying their best to ignore the strangeness of a controlled fire burning on a New York sidewalk. Others gathered to watch Uncle Sam and Fishman work: first one pair, then another, until a crowd surrounded the table, murmuring in excitement, their umbrellas blocking out the sky, offering the men shelter from the storm.

CHAPTER 10

Brooklyn and Beyond

**We protest against the efforts being made by
Northern operators to steal away our barbecues. That is
"going the whole hog" to a degree beyond our taste and inclination.**
—*CHARLESTON DAILY COURIER*

*I*t was the great Summer of Barbecue, and America had quite literally gone up in smoke.

In the summer of 2013, barbecue, in all its diverse and divergent forms, had hit it big. Barbecue became more than another name for the backyard grill, a ubiquitous potato chip flavor, and something people eat in Memphis. Barbecue emerged as a lifestyle.

As with most recent food trends, dynamic, adventurous restaurant chefs led the charge. Their latest weapon, used to garner attention as much as to incite the gustatory senses, was smoke, which drifted from the savory side of the menu to appear in desserts (smoked chocolate cheesecake) and cocktails (charcoal-aged bourbons and Campari) and beers (smoked porter with chipotle). Soon, it seemed that no professional kitchen could exist without a handheld smoke infuser, called a smoke gun, and a selection of wood chips (hickory, mesquite apple, cherry, cedar) and leaves (tobacco, tea). And no backyard would be complete without a Big Green Egg or some other high-priced designer pit cooker. Of course, the smoke trend was not limited to what one could eat and drink: this was also the first full year of legalized marijuana consumption in Colorado and Washington. You could now legally smoke a joint while smoking a pork shoulder seasoned with any one of the many cannabis-laced barbecue sauce recipes available online. Dallas chef Tim Byres released *Smoke*, the cookbook companion to his restaurant, also called Smoke, where most everything—breakfast, lunch, and dinner—came smoked or included a smoked component.

Though humans had long been adding smoke to more than meats and fishes, smoke-infused food and drink suddenly became fashionable. Mescal, tequila's smoky cousin, became the latest trendy quaff. Tea sippers demanded greater access to rare Lapsang souchongs.

The nation's continued fascination became transparent in May, when *Texas Monthly* magazine hired Daniel Vaughn as its first full-time barbecue editor and critic, a position they advertised as the first of its kind in the history of American print. (An astute Carolinian pointed out that the *North Carolina Literary Review* named poet William Harmon to serve as its barbecue editor back in 1996, though for just a single issue.)

Texas not only invented the professional barbecue critic, they could also claim the nation's most lauded pitmaster. In Austin, friends and strangers bonded while queueing up for beef brisket, pulled pork and pork ribs, smoked turkey, and sausage outside Franklin Barbecue, where the line often stretched for a three-hour wait. Owner and pitmaster Aaron Franklin had recently become the culinary scene's latest wunderkind, though a cultish following had been developing long before *Bon Appétit* magazine declared his barbecue the nation's best, just two years after he launched the business out of a trailer in a rapidly gentrifying neighborhood in the outskirts of east Austin. He would become the first pitmaster to not only receive a nomination for but win a James Beard Award for best regional chef. In his acceptance speech, he dedicated the win to "all the barbecue cooks before me and the ones to come." By the middle of 2013, Franklin—thirty-five years old, handsomely sideburned, and hipster bespectacled—was quickly becoming the face of the new barbecue movement, hotter than the heatwave that descended upon much of the country that summer. He hawked the Chase Sapphire credit card in television commercials and starred in his own PBS-produced web series, *BBQ with Franklin*.

The barbecue revolution would be televised: the smoke and fire, raw meat and frequent displays of uncooked masculinity made for good copy. The travel programs *Man Fire Food*, *American Grilled*, and *BBQ Crawl* all premiered around the same time, while the Food Network's reality show *The Shed* featured the misadventures of the Orrison family, proprietors of a south Mississippi barbecue chain. And then there was *BBQ Pitmasters*, a competition show styled after *Top Chef*. It aired its fifth season in the summer of 2013, with the final episode pitting the three remaining contestants, none of whom hailed from the South, to a whole-hog cook-off.

Whole hog proved to be irresistible to fledgling pitmasters looking to tackle the world of smoked meats. The first to plant his shovel in the fire was John Currence, an Oxford, Mississippi, based chef and restaurateur who ranked as one of the town's most notable cultural luminaries since William Faulkner. After opening his first restaurant in 1992, he had built a mini-empire of eateries, from fancy to casual, in the small university and literary community that lies eighty miles south of Memphis. He is one of the few American chefs able to balance a high national profile—wide media attention, prestigious culinary awards—with the bigheartedness and bravery to combat injustices on a local level. He's a James Beard Best Chef winner but also a former president of the local arts council and appears as a guest commentator on CNN and MSNBC, making an effort to recognize the contribution of immigrants to the hospitality industry ("I cannot survive without the Latino segment of the workforce") or to protest the passing of Mississippi's Religious Freedom Restoration Act, widely seen as a piece of anti-LGBT legislation ("This isn't just about LGBT rights, this is about human rights. This is about everybody. The potential for discrimination runs completely across the board").

So when a pair of local bar owners offered to sell their watering hole to Chef Currence during the height of the Summer of Barbecue, he turned that establishment, the Lamar Lounge, into one of the nation's only not-for-profit restaurants. All annual net revenue would be donated to a different local charity, starting with Good Food for Oxford Schools, an organization dedicated to improving the cafeteria selections across area public schools while educating students to change their eating habits for the better.

Currence kept most of what the previous owners had left behind: the popular burger, the wall-mounted taxidermied hyena head, and a stunning mahogany bar they'd found on eBay, allegedly a gift from Liz Taylor to her then husband, Eddie Fisher. The only change was a two-hog block pit built out back, making the Lamar Lounge Mississippi's only place for whole-hog barbecue and the southernmost spot serving one of the most iconic of southern foods.

If asked back in 2010 to guess which major metropolitan city would be the first to become the urban capital of whole hog, I would have chosen Memphis. Its proximity to the struggling whole-hog dominions of Henderson and Lexington, the number and diversity of barbecue restaurants, and the passion that Memphians possess for smoked pork made Elvis's adopted city the natural pick. But it would be Memphis's more cosmopolitan and countrified neighbor to the east, Nashville, where the haze of hardwood smoke would first appear on the skyline.

Carey Bringle made up one-half of Nashville's nascent whole-hog stronghold. He opened his restaurant in May 2013, the kickoff to the Summer of Barbecue, out of an old warehouse across from an operable railroad yard in a rapidly gentrifying slice of downtown Nashville named the Gulch. Before he introduced himself to me as "Carey," I, like most barbecue fans and followers, knew him as Peg Leg Porker, a name that not only referred to the man but also his brand—sauces, rubs, one-of-a-kind smokers for the serious gear-head, and now, most recently, his restaurant.

I had met Carey a few times at barbecue conventions and competitions, where he always came off as endearingly uncouth and a more than a little bullheaded—I wouldn't want to argue politics with him. But what was most immediately noticeable was his limp and, if he was wearing shorts, as he often did at daytime cook-offs and the like, a prosthetic right leg. At the age of seventeen, Carey was diagnosed with osteogenic sarcoma, a particularly vicious bone cancer that claimed his leg from the knee down. But that wouldn't stop him from hefting hogs and shoveling coals. In college, he acted as his fraternity's go-to pitmaster, an expertise gained on the family farm outside Memphis under the tutelage of his uncle Bruce, whom everyone called Uncle Juice because of his nasty drinking habit. In 1991 he attended the Memphis in May cooking contest, an annual event that bills itself as the world championship on the barbecue team-competition circuit, as a guest member of the Rolling Wonder Pigs. As Carey proudly admits, the Wonder Pigs were a touch too rowdy for the organizers of the family-friendly event and were removed from the premises.

Already transfixed by the spectacle of whole-hog cooking, Carey left the event smitten with the camaraderie of competition barbecue. Over the next twenty-five years, he embarked upon a series of business ventures: T-shirt printing, clinical lab testing, mail-order vending, tech consulting, and Medicare billing, all while developing his Peg Leg Porker persona on the competition barbecue circuit and online. The prosthetic leg and gruff personality became a part of his brand, easily recognizable and marketable.

All the while, Carey longed to open his own restaurant, but his wife, Delaniah, threatened divorce each time he expressed a desire to move in that direction. That was, however, only until their college-ready children moved out of the house. When Carey opened Peg Leg Porker in May 2013, he knew how he wanted to decorate the place. Next to the ordering counter, he set up a glass cabinet, like the ubiquitous trophy cases in high school hallways, to display his competition winnings alongside his old prosthetic legs, weathered and worn. Next to the case, a blown-up black-and-white photograph showed his grandfather, Dr. Carey Bringle, Sr., a Second World War naval officer, overseeing the cooking of a pair of whole hogs on the Filipino island of Luan. In the scene, American sailors and native Filipinos stoke a pit fire and wrap a hog in what were probably banana leaves, working side-by-side to make barbecue.

The photograph acted as a reminder that whole hog not only flows through Carey's veins but runs deeper, globally, across oceans and across cultures. Though barbecue is an invention of the Americas, the language of pig and fire, the one true barbecue, is universal.

Hog, Carey told me, had been a hard sell in Nashville, even though the whole-hog hotbed of Lexington, home of Ricky Parker, lay just one hundred miles west-southwest down Interstate 40. For now, he specializes in ribs and butts, while only offering whole hog as a summertime weekend special.

"People love to romanticize barbecue places that cook over nothing but wood and only cook whole hog," Carey said, obviously referring to me, the guy sitting across from him, taking notes for a book on whole-hog barbecue. "When a writer tells me it's not barbecue unless you burn down your coals and shovel them under a pit, I tell them to go fuck off, he can start writing his articles with a quill pen again." We laughed in unison as I looked fondly upon my Japanese-made ballpoint.

"For a lot of writers," he said, "it's about the romance. But if you gotta make a living at it, you can throw romance out the window."

He was, of course, correct. Whole hog is a dicey business venture, especially when your granddad is not handing you the keys to the pit he's kept warm since the 1940s. Hogs are pricey and often difficult to source. Up to two-thirds of the carcass weight is burned up or tossed in the garbage. Fire codes and the insurance industry do not welcome live fires with open arms and full-coverage policies. The labor involved is expensive and brutally tough, unhealthy to one's economic and bodily livelihoods. But since the pitmaster's life is often the best and sometimes only viable option for employment open to pitmen throughout the rural South, choosing to cook whole hog in a city might just make a person downright insane. But romantics often are just that.

Nashville, Music City, USA, the capital of the great state of Tennessee, has always existed as a transient town, a stopover for rambling singer-songwriters, session musicians, and, now, plenty of hipsters, old and young—romantics all. Like so many country and western showmen and -women who have dreamed of playing at the Grand Ole Opry, whole hog just might one day hit it big in the big city. Its best chance might rest with Patrick Martin of Martin's Bar-B-Que Joint. If Carey Bringle is Nashville's realist, open to smoking an occasional whole hog without going the whole hog, Pat might be the city's chief barbecue romanticist.

His love affair started as a freshman attending Freed-Hardeman University in downtown Henderson, Tennessee. Freed, as its students called it, was a Church of Christ campus—"Worse than the Baptists!" Pat said, laughing—and anything but free by modern standards. The student handbook enforced a zero tolerance policy on alcohol, premarital sex, homosexuality, gambling, and offensive language of any kind. From the start, Pat disobeyed the campus curfew, often sneaking out in the middle of the night to watch pitmasters at work across the county. He remembered that there must have been a dozen whole-hog joints scattered throughout Chester County: Jacks Creek, Liz's, L & L, and Nobles, which would eventually become Chris Siler's Old Time BBQ three decades later. But his favorite was Thomas & Webb, just a mile walk from campus down South Church Street, where Harold Thomas allowed a young Patrick Martin to escape the jail-like confines of his school for the freedom the adult environment of the pit house granted. "He let me in his world a little bit," Pat reminisced—letting him hang around the pit house, huddle around the fire with the rotating trio of pitmen, and ask any question that popped into his teenage, barbecue-loving head. He still recalled asking Thomas how high to build a pit. "Right there," the old man slapped him on the thigh, "right there."

And that's how high Pat has stacked the bricks for every pit he's built ever since. When he cooked his first hogs, catering for Freed social-club parties, he stacked the bricks thigh high. His sophomore year, after getting kicked out of school for drinking beer, he moved up north to bid up and sell off soybean futures in the Chicago Board of Trade's famously chaotic commodity exchange pit, and he built his own pits the same height to smoke pigs for the wealthy senior traders, his bosses, at Merrill Lynch. He built the same sized pits after returning to Freed and, getting kicked out a second time for drinking beer, then in Nashville, where he enrolled at Lipscomb, a Church of Christ university with a more liberal attitude toward alcohol consumption, and eventually in Charlotte and Memphis. In his telling, he was becoming "a barbecue freak," smoking, testing, eating hogs wherever he settled. After moving back to the Nashville area, Pat knew how high to build his pit when he eventually opened the first Martin's Bar-B-Que in the suburb of Nolensville in 2006. Right here.

The newest of Martin's four, soon to be six, locations could not have occupied a trendier position amid the designer boutiques, innumerable coffeehouses, and artisan eateries that define the new Nashville. Stepping into this Belmont Boulevard location, built from the ruins of a former glass factory on the south-central side of town, I immediately noted a thick haze of bluish smoke hovering mere inches above the heads of any standing patrons.

The walls of the dining room and built-in bar were filled with posters and photographs, record sleeves and signed artifacts— memorabilia that had defined Pat's interests since childhood: wrestling and baseball, outlaw country music and eighties metal. In the far right corner of the room, an employee reached into a chimney with a long-handled shovel, withdrew a load of feverishly hot coals, and swiveled on his feet to face an adjacent barbecue pit: a single brick-lined and heavy-steel-lidded oven. He pushed the shovelful of fire through a trapdoor at the base of the pit, joggled the load loose, and removed the now-empty shovel before clanging the door shut. I asked him if I could steal a look under the pit's lid. He happily agreed and pressed a button that set the automatic rope-and-pulley winch into motion to uncover the one hog inside. The whole beast, head still attached, lay belly up and ripe to doneness, crisp and charred to a golden-brown lacquer. New plumes of smoke crowded the dining room, a signal to customers to rally around the pit and take a look. They filled the spaces around the wooden bar that angled around two sides of the pit, just out of arm's reach but close enough to feel the simmering touch of its radiant heat. They gasped and cheered, took pictures on their cell phones, and, with mugs of draft beer, toasted the hog, which was bound for the glory that is a barbecue sandwich.

Pat Martin had waded through fire codes and insurance regulations and found a way to transform the pit house into a legal, functioning dining room. The trick was constructing the pit on the outside of the building, knocking down an exterior wall, then rebuilding the wall around the pit. "Legally, this is outside," he laughed while slapping the top of the pit. He had fulfilled the dream of more established pitmasters like Ed Mitchell and Rodney Scott; he had taken the next step in the evolution of whole-hog barbecue. Pat had made whole hog a spectator sport, had brought the process of smoking and roasting a pig to a new audience of eaters. This was what farm-to-table advocates of all stripes, from producers to chefs, could only hope to capture: an opportunity to show their customers how barbecue is made from the raw material that is a whole animal's flesh. Pat did them all one better, visibly demonstrating how we transform the raw into the cooked to his customers while they are eating the finished product. This was the pit house as a conscientious culinary classroom. From a young age, we Americans are often told that we do not want to see or know how sausage is made, that the steps that go into the production of food, especially the flesh of animals, is ugly, disheartening, and shameful. But Pat Martin had made the process of turning meat into edibles real and palpable, and it was beautiful.

A single whole hog does not yield enough meat to supply a restaurant that is open ten hours a day, seven days a week, so the kitchen supplemented the pig with shoulders smoked on a separate pit. But the public spectacle of the dining-room-roasted hog was

enough to change the minds and alter the appetites of local diners. A downtown Nashville location of Martin's Bar-B-Que was set
to open by year's end. The blueprints called for a dining room big
enough to fit four whole-hog pits, not quite enough to feed a busy
restaurant but a further step in the right direction. He envisioned
customers gathering around the pit to watch the pitmaster feed
the fire, the succulent smell of hog fat and flesh gradually replacing the waft of smoke throughout the day. "My thought was that
they would have to be engaged with it," he told me, "so they would
finally learn to appreciate and learn about it." In a sense, he was
re-creating the cherished scenes from his younger days at Thomas
& Webb: sitting around the fire, talking to the pitmasters, studying
every facet of the whole-hog technique. He would bring the one
true barbecue to the masses.

But despite his present success and future plans, Pat Martin
missed the simple barbecue spots that he enjoyed way back when.
He spoke of completing the circular arc of his barbecuing life, of
opening a place like his cherished Thomas & Webb. "When it's all
said and done, just to be able to come back to Henderson, open up
a little five-table barbecue joint, cook, and not have to deal with
all this goddamned stress, it's pretty appealing. One day. Not now,
though; I got kids to feed."

Outside of Nashville, whole hog achieved meme-status levels
that summer of 2013, becoming especially popular with a generation of younger chefs who diligently researched and revived disappearing and underappreciated southern foodways traditions and
introduced them to a wider audience. These chefs were experimenting with benne seeds, country hams, and once-extinct watermelon
varieties. But there was something extraordinarily appealing about
cooking whole animals over fire, a bit of catnip irresistible to chefs,

many of them graduates of four-year culinary institutes who now cooked tasting-menu dinners out of spotless kitchens outfitted with stoves that could cost as much as a foreign sports car. Chefs, much like myself, were romanced by the whole hog.

In Asheville, North Carolina, I met the entrepreneur and dreamer Elliott Moss, who planned to open the first modern whole-hog establishment in the city located high in the Blue Ridge Mountains. It attracts more than its fair share of fresh-air-seeking retirees, lifestyle-searching New Agers, and weekend honeymooners. Born in Florence, South Carolina, a half-hour's drive from Scott's Bar-B-Que, Elliott was raised on smoked pork at Woody's, a long-defunct whole-hoggery: "Like families get KFC or Pizza Hut, we'd go get barbecue and a loaf of white bread three to four times a week." He began a foray into the professional kitchen life at the age of seventeen, first at Chick-fil-A, then restaurants in Columbia, South Carolina, and farther afield in Philadelphia, before settling in Asheville to open the Admiral, an adventurous dive bar meets modern bistro.

Elliott had just left his head-chef position at the Admiral when I met him there for a whiskey cocktail. He looked and talked like many chefs I'd met over the last several years. Square-rimmed glasses and tattooed sleeves, thirtyish, talented, and cocksure. His mind and mouth raced with a litany of culinary possibilities. He was weeks away from launching Ben's Tune Up, a beer garden slash Japanese *izakaya* slash sake distillery, but was clearly focused on his dream barbecue project.

Named for the old dilapidated Asheville neighborhood where it would one day be located, Buxton Hill would bring wood-smoked South Carolina–style whole hog north of the border. The restaurant's theme, in his words, would be "fifty-fifty, Boy Scout meets

Americana." There would be a range of southern-inspired char-cuterie: house-cured bacons, hams, and sausages. Pound cake sold by the pound, candied apples, and snowballs, served spiked for adults. And, finally, what he described as a three-tiered pit for cook-ing hogs. I didn't quite understand the concept, nor the proposed design for the pit. "I'm a chef who's opening a barbecue restaurant," Elliott told me, "not a pitmaster."

Buxton Hill, understandably, never materialized. Elliott moved on to a series of Asian-inflected and southern-contemporary pop-up operations as he planned his next steps.

It entered my mind that fire-cooked whole-hog barbecue ran the risk of becoming too trendy, too prevalent, a gentrified culinary art form. Would the original Scott's Bar-B-Que in Hemingway be any less authentic, any less special, if Rodney opened a second location in Charleston? Would the Skylight Inn be any less the "Bar-B-Q Capital of the World" if there was a whole-hog restaurant in every state? Would the labor that goes into cooking a night of pigs at Wil-ber's be any less special if a Michelin-starred chef threw his toque into the whole-hog ring?

In June 2013, the preeminent food journalist Jonathan Gold asked the same question about all the various forms and geographic styles included under the heading "American barbecue." "Could bar-becue be the cupcake of 2013?" he wrote in his review column at the *Los Angeles Times*, referring to the once-beloved, now-despised food trend of years past. "Squinted at in a certain way, it just might be." Though I agreed with Gold, and despite the fact that my eye-sight, even post–LASIK surgery, left much to be desired, it pleased me to know that I didn't need to squint to see that whole hog would be the absolute last in line, trailing by incalculable distances, among all the barbecue genres to oversaturate the American market. We might eventually see whole-hog barbecues in Asheville and Atlanta, but god forbid if one ever opened up in Brooklyn.

———

Thus it stretched the limits of my barbecue junkie's imagination when Tyson Ho opened the Arrogant Swine in the summer of 2014. Of course it would come to this, the naturally flowing tide of culinary happenings and openings would bring the first contemporary whole-hog restaurant to New York City. Such was the state of foodie affairs in the era that followed the Summer of Barbecue.

In a weird way, Tyson's journey into the madness of whole-hog fanaticism mirrored my own. Seen in another light, or perhaps taking place on another earth, existing on another timeline, I could have followed his path to barbecue proprietorship. We both romanticized the culinary form, roamed through the Carolinas eating barbecue, tracked down pitmasters, and kept blogs detailing our discoveries. But from there our paths deviated.

Tyson Ho's journey began, inconspicuously enough, on West Twenty-Sixth Street between Sixth and Broadway, the site of Hill Country Barbecue, one of two high-profile barbecue restaurants to open in New York City, circa 2007—the other, Southern Hospitality, was more known for being owned by Justin Timberlake than for their Memphis-style ribs. Hill Country, from its menu to its décor, carried a singular geographic and culinary focus: beef brisket, pork ribs, sausages, and sides from the south-central Texas region of the same name. Until Hill Country came along, most New York–area barbecue restaurants offered a smorgasbord of smoked meats: pulled pork from Tennessee, Kansas City–style ribs, Carolina vinegar dip and a half dozen other varieties of sauces. This was fake barbecue, franchised chain in a food court barbecue, a Disney's Epcot world culinary showcase of barbecue.

I remember excitedly subwaying into the city from my Brooklyn apartment when Hill Country opened for business. So does Tyson. "Hill Country was really unique in the sense that it was the first place where they said, 'Listen: New York has very traditional ramen joints, traditional sushi joints, old-school Naples-style pizza. We're giving you exactly what you would find down there'" in Texas. It's a long way from Austin to Midtown Manhattan, but Hill Country altered the trajectory of American barbecue by changing the way those of us who can't claim a barbecue home culture ate and thought about the various styles of barbecue.

Tyson had long maintained a deep interest in eating and cooking. He avoided a semester of classes during his senior year at Bayside High by signing up with the experimental City as School program, which found him an internship position at Chanterelle, ranked among the city's finest French restaurants over its thirty-year run. Born and raised in Flushing, Queens, to immigrant parents, a Cantonese father and Malaysian mother, Tyson possessed a vague notion of fine dining, based on "Bugs Bunny cartoons with guys in tuxedoes and domed dishes and whatnot." Following the internship, he worked at a string of high-profile New York kitchens—La Caravelle, Bouley, Telepan, and Payard—before leaving New York for college in Lubbock, Texas. Lubbock is nowhere near Hill Country—it's nowhere near anywhere—and was thus a perfect place for Tyson, a self-described "geek" and "introverted reader," to embed himself in an obsessive study of dead religions. He specialized in dusty Babylonian texts, picked up Cyrillic and a bit of ancient Greek, and scored a place in the University of Chicago's prestigious PhD program in linguistics. He could have spent the next seven years of his life studying Akkadian, an extinct Meso-potamian language, but like many brilliant minds of his genera-tion—he was born in 1979—Tyson passed up an academic career in the humanities for the financial security of Wall Street. There he worked for an analytics firm that wrote software for investment banks. But after several years of the day-to-day office drudgery, he welcomed a new obsession.

Hill Country's focus struck him as interesting, unique. If New York can sustain dozens of traditional ramen shops and even more classic sushi counters, he thought, why not try to add another ver-nacular barbecue joint to the city's dining options? "My goal was to eat at these different places around the country, pick one that I would hyperfocus on, and really make it my own." He preordained Memphis the shoo-in to win; its ribs made it the barbecue style to beat. But he elected to at least give North Carolina a shot: it was closer to New York than Tennessee, and the eastern and western halves of the state could claim distinct barbecue cultures. So Tyson planned an eating itinerary for the summer of 2011, packed up the car, and, with his wife, journeyed south.

What he had read online about Carolina barbecue filled him with trepidation: "When I started, it was like, 'Who, in their right mind, wants to eat pork dredged in vinegar?'" His first stop was the Skylight Inn. Pete Jones's capitol dome came off as goofy, the interior aesthetic left much to be desired. And the food? Tyson had never eaten minced barbecue, and he was certainly no fan of coleslaw. But that Ayden-style barbecue had a way of molding skeptics into diehards. "You know what?" he told his wife after devouring a sandwich. "I'm good. This is what I want. This is what I want to do." Tyson was ready to take a victory lap before his car's engine had even warmed up. He had found perfection, but he wandered onward, hitting Bum's and Wilber's, followed by a few spots for shoulder barbecue in the Piedmont region, eating barbecue from one side of the state to the other, tracing a route that I would repeat, just in the opposite direction, a few months later. Before returning home, he had bought a smoker, a portable unit with just room enough for a small hog, and resolved to learn how to master it.

Back in New York, Tyson's first roast became an exercise in hilarity from step one. There are pitmasters, cookbooks, and even YouTube videos that can explain the nuances of time and tempera-ture, sauce techniques and flavor profiles, but there are no how-to's on the proper way to unload a ponderous wet-slicked hog from the bed of your pickup truck. That was the first misstep in what Tyson now refers to as his "train wreck" of an evening. Then he allotted twenty-four hours—and stockpiled twenty-four hours' worth of beer for his friends who gathered—to cook the beast. But his hog only weighed one hundred pounds, and lunch was ready sixteen hours early. Finally, when it came to spicing the roasted meat, he didn't yet understand the ratio of salty to spicy to sour, and the chopped pork came out tasting like the pig had gone swimming in a vinegar bath.

The next two years went by like a Rocky Balboa training mon-tage. He cooked hog after hog, experimenting with assorted hard-woods, various breeds of pigs, and different peppers with which to spice his sauce. He went back on the road and ate his way through South Carolina. He read all of the barbecue oral histories that I had compiled for the Southern Foodways Alliance and posted online. He studied alongside the master of pitmasters, Ed Mitchell, at the 2012 Big Apple Barbecue Block Party. He attacked the art of whole hog, like he did in his collegiate study of Babylonian texts. And the following year, throughout the great Summer of Barbecue, he hosted fourteen pop-up cookouts with beer, live music, and barbecue. He quit his job to dedicate all his time and effort into opening the Arrogant Swine, the city's first barbecue joint wholly inspired by the Carolinas.

Whole hog had come north, but not for the first time. Way back in 1856, an editorial in the *Charleston Daily Courier* teased that the North had hijacked the South's barbecue culture to ill effect: "We protest against the efforts being made by Northern operators to steal away our barbecues. That is 'going the whole hog' to a degree beyond our taste and inclination, and moreover, the barbecue is so peculiarly a Southern Institution that like every other good thing stolen from us, it will degenerate at the North." The northern efforts the anonymous editorialist referred to were the era's popular political barbecues, events held to rally the true believers, buy the votes of any undecideds, and perhaps even ensure a victory. In a way, they were the antiquarian equivalent of today's pop-ups: a warm-up party heralding the big event.

In a bimonthly series of short essays for the food blog *Serious Eats*, Tyson documented his quixotic quest to bring an open-fire, wood-burning, whole-animal pit house to a city notoriously hard on restaurateurs and, during Mayor Bloomberg's long reign, unfriendly to air pollution of any sort. His essays, which at the time of this writing are still forthcoming, are amusing for their humor and, most notably, astonishing for their honesty, exposing a side of the New York restaurant and real-estate markets that outsiders aren't often privy to. He wrote about inept real-estate agents, shoddy storefronts, and cutthroat lessee agreements. One agent tried to sell him on an address directly across the street from a mosque.

"Are you fucking serious?" he yelled over the phone to the soon-to-be-fired broker. "My cuisine is a big fat middle finger to their faith and they'd have to look at it every day." And furthermore, he continued, "I can't serve beer within two hundred feet of a place of worship."

"I thought that only applied to churches," the bumbling agent answered. "So mosques are churches?"

Tyson eventually found a spot for rent in an obscure corner of Bushwick, the Brooklyn neighborhood that trend spotters had long predicted would replace Williamsburg as the city's boho-hipster zone. The Morgan Avenue location lay at the edge of an industrial business corridor, a mean set of streets straight out of Scorsese's grimmest dreamscape. First impressions were not kind. "It smelled," Tyson told me. "You could smell chemicals or whatever being pumped into the air and shit like that." On my visits, I haven't found the smell to be too terrible, no worse than other New York sidewalks I'd strolled down or once lived on. But Google Maps did remind me that across the avenue, behind the big red warehouse that sold sheet metal, meandered the Newtown Creek, one of the city's most toxic waterways. For an incipient whole-hog pitmaster, the site was perfect. There was no chance his neighbors—a plastic bag factory, several car parts warehouses, and a stuffed-animal manufacturer—would complain about the wood smoke or twilight work schedule. He might even bring better smells to this part of Bushwick, or, as they might say in modern Brooklynese, he could aromatically gentrify the neighborhood.

The building's zoning status, that most important of urban issues for new businesses, also worked in his favor. On the books,

173 Morgan Avenue was, owing to a century-old quirk, defined as a restaurant space, though, in Tyson's telling, not a soul had so much as "fried an egg here since World War One." And calling the space shabby would have been kind. Cracks sliced through the roof and cinder-block walls, craters pocked the adjoining parking lot. But seeing that poor, blighted building, Tyson imagined a high-raftered restaurant, and those cinder-block walls were perfectly, plainly austere like that of many a pit house he had visited. The dimensions of the parking lot measured just large enough to fit a barbecue pit and an open fire, with enough room to spare for a "backyard" picnic-tabled seating area. It might be ugly, but it might just work.

Tyson's temple to Carolina hog opened on October 8, 2014. He sourced Chester White hogs from a heritage breeder down in Seven Springs, the same North Carolina town that birthed Stephen and Gerri Grady. The city signed off on his burn barrel and pit smoker, designating each part and parcel of a wood-burning oven, which had become a de rigueur piece of kitchen equipment for most every new ambitious restaurant. And in a stroke of genius, he repurposed a pair of shipping containers into a safe and viable pit house—able to contain flare-ups, insulate from New York's topsy-turvy weather patterns, and look aesthetically hip.

Tyson discovered early during his pop-up days that his brick and mortar version of Arrogant Swine would require a full-time pitmaster to manage the graveyard shift. With the help of the Doe Fund, a local nonprofit dedicated to transitioning former homeless, incarcerated, and addicted individuals into stable and reliable jobs, he found Roland Smith. A middle-aged African American man from Kissimmee, Florida, Roland had most recently swept the streets of Brooklyn between picking up sporadic construction jobs. Like most everyone raised down south, Roland had grilled burgers and ribs on his backyard grill, but he'd never cooked a hog before. Almost overnight, he not only had to learn to handle live fire and smoke but had to struggle with roasting a pig in a snowstorm and occasionally solve the dilemma of how to get fire from hickory logs that had frozen solid. He quickly became, in Tyson's estimation, his "single most trusted guy." Roland told me that he wished he had discovered the life of the pitmaster earlier and looked forward to traveling down to the Carolinas for some real whole hog.

But no one would confuse this place for Ayden or even Raleigh. Tyson invited the Bushwick Collective of graffiti artists to turn the building's exterior into an outdoor gallery, featuring a rotating set of spray-painted murals. His architect talked him into the DIY installation of a pine-wood bar top charred to blackness, using an eighteenth-century Japanese preservation method called *shou sugi ban*. Chris Struck, a close friend and trained sommelier, helped him expertly curate a bar menu of boutique wines, whiskies, and draft beers (Tyson advocated pairing barbecue with a nice Belgian ale: "Reminds you of sweet tea, almost"). Meanwhile, the food menu toyed playfully with our often static notions of barbecue mains and sides. The centerpiece dish was a shout-out to the tradition he first fell in love with: "eastern Carolina whole hog," dressed in a vinegar pepper dressing and seasoned with cracklings, in the style of the Skylight Inn. The smoked pork belly, served with a spicy tamarind dip, and the spareribs, glazed with a tweaked South Carolina mustard sauce, pointed in new directions. Conventional sides, like macaroni and cheese or sweet potatoes, came waffled: pressed to a gooey crispness in a waffle iron. The menu's most obvious omission spoke as loudly as its offerings. There was no Texas brisket, no

Kansas City–style baby back ribs, no sticky-icky molasses sauce by way of West Tennessee.

"My whole goal was to introduce Carolina barbecue in the philosophical sense," Tyson told me. That philosophy started at the pit and extended to the oversized state flags of North Carolina and South Carolina that hang, with conspicuous intent, from the interior walls of his restaurant. He was trying his damnedest to market this restaurant as an authentic Carolina barbecue experience, without Disneyfying the culture or completely reimagining the culinary form. The barbecue tasted of the Carolinas without attempting to persuade me—even if only for one moment, or just one bite—that I was in the Carolinas. Rather than pretending to be authentic, his was a study in authenticity. Like his prior interest in dying religions and languages, he had found a vanishing—at least when he first discovered it back in 2011—barbecue genre.

Tyson called his business the Arrogant Swine because, in his telling, it was the only swine-centric Internet domain name not claimed by cybersquatters. But there does exist a slight shadow of arrogance surrounding him, though it is the sort of arrogance that savants carry as a burden, an arrogance I can get behind. You can't hate or fault a guy for loving something to the point of obsession, for having a pedantic mind for everything barbecue. Tyson might be a neophyte pitmaster compared to, say, Sam Jones or Rodney Scott, but he is the complete opposite of a dilettante, a charge anonymous commenters, and there are many, frequently lob at him from deep in the trenches of barbecue bloggerdom.

When detractors are not critiquing Tyson's commitment, they're misguidedly questioning his place in the greater world of professional barbecue. He's heard it several times over his short career as a pitmaster, comments and questions about his ethnicity: "Funny, there's a Chinese guy cooking Carolina barbecue," or a simple, skeptical, "Where are you from?" His response is to challenge our notions of barbecue and Americanness. "Well, I'm not from anywhere. I'm from here."

I asked Tyson to explain further how he felt when "Americans" dispute his ownership of barbecue. "Me and some dude from Shanghai have absolutely nothing in common. He gets teary eyed and nostalgic every Chinese New Year, whereas I get really excited with Christmas trees, Santa Claus, Thanksgiving dinner. And besides"—he laughed—"Asians have been cooking Carolina barbecue for a while." He was absolutely right. Years earlier, in the pit house of Stamey's Barbecue in Greensboro, North Carolina, I'd met the veteran pitmasters Pon, a member of the indigenous Degar people from the Central Highlands of Vietnam, and Bim, a Cambodian immigrant, who have cooked that restaurant's famed pork shoulders for several decades. I interviewed Put Temmerath, a Laotian migrant who batched several hundred-gallon pots of barbecue hash each week at Midway BBQ in Buffalo, South Carolina.

"I see myself as an American," Tyson told me, "cooking the oldest form of American barbecue." Rather than degenerate in the North, as the *Charleston Daily Courier* once warned, whole-hog barbecue just might find its future in those urban centers located well beyond the Mason-Dixon line. He's just another American making good old-fashioned barbecue. Or as Tyson likes to tell haters, "I've got two hundred years of history on my side."

Whole-hog barbecue would endure.

CHAPTER 11

Come July, 100 Whole Hogs

I last saw Ricky Parker on Thanksgiving Eve 2012. I was on the road, and, as always, hungry for a whole-hog sandwich.

I peered in the back gate to the pit house. No Ricky. Walked through the front door and stepped to the ordering window. No Ricky. As I placed my order, a movement caused me to look over my shoulder. There sat Ricky Parker. I had walked right past him.

He was alone at a two-seat corner table, sitting down. This was a position I had seen him occupy only once before—four years earlier, when he finally succumbed to a seated interview. I have no doubt that he sat down to eat, at least on occasion. He obviously drove his truck while seated. A church pew, the dentist's chair, his favorite La-Z-Boy recliner to watch Sunday-night football: he probably visited each once or twice since I'd known him. But I didn't believe it; Ricky Parker was at rest.

From ten feet away I could tell that he was counting numbers, recording names, tallying orders. He was shuffling papers. This was another side to the pitmaster I had never seen, a side I immediately felt wrong bearing witness to: the ordinary business owner he was and had been for more than two decades.

I took a table next to the front door, facing Ricky so that I could watch him from afar. He appeared a pale shadow of himself: swollen face and puffy hands, skin gray, altogether sick. He looked as if he could hardly stand up straight, much less flip a hog, or twelve. The man who once bragged that he ran through five pairs of shoes annually looked like he hadn't worn out a pair in more than a year.

Staring at my order, which sat unwrapped on the table, I remained unable to force myself to tear open the wax paper. Just look at him, I thought; Ricky couldn't have cooked this. I was panicked by what it would taste like. Would it still taste like Ricky's barbecue? I could have painted a still life of that wax-paper-wrapped sandwich in the time I took to unwrap my barbecue. I studied the paper's creases and folds, the toothpick spear that held it all together, the grease smudges that began to soak through the paper to gradually and subtly reveal the sandwich within.

I carefully unpacked the sandwich and, tossing aside the top bun, warily gathered a strand of fatty, white-fleshed barbecue—it must have been middlin'—from the heap of meat before me. Before completely dispatching the first bite, I crammed a larger chunk into my mouth, then a third morsel. I swallowed the remainder of the barbecue in what felt like a single gulp, chewing without tasting, but knowing that if I could taste it, it would have tasted good. The same as it always was. Ricky Parker's barbecue.

I stepped up to Ricky and said hello, as he, head down, continued to shuffle papers. Staying firmly planted in his chair, he shook my hand and, palming an unlit Swisher Sweet in his left, motioned for me to sit.

He had been counting turkeys, readying a stockpile of more than a hundred frozen, semisolidified, and defrosted birds for smoking on his barbecue pits to supply his customers' holiday tables. Without going into the details or describing his health, he told me that he would be relying on his sons to barbecue this season's turkeys and that he was thinking of taking some time off now that he could rely on Zach and Matt. We shared other news. He pulled from his wallet a photograph of his daughter, Hope, who had recently won Tennessee's Teen Princess pageant, a sort of Miss America for juniors. I told him I hoped to write a book on whole-hog barbecue. He responded with a question—"Who else cooks hogs over wood?"—as if he were still the only one. I laughed and he winked. His eyes sparkled, prismatic and dazzling.

"July," he told me, as I said good-bye. "Remember: July." He reminded me of that magic number, the slow race to one hundred smoked hogs.

But Ricky Parker would not live to see another Fourth of July. He would never smoke a pig on a New York City sidewalk. He would not fulfill his dream of cooking one hundred whole hogs.

Ricky was dying. For months Zach and Matt tried to get him to the hospital, but their dad wouldn't go. He didn't much believe in the expertise of doctors. And there was the business to consider: he would not leave his pit behind. Not yet. Though he hadn't cooked many pigs over the last year—his sons had taken on most of his duties—Ricky stubbornly held on. He continued to cook only on Mondays, the slowest day of the week.

Years of suffering for his barbecue had taken its toll on Ricky Parker, but he would suffer on. "It was liver disease," Matt told me later. "Liver disease that got up into his lungs, his kidneys. All but his heart. His heart was strong. He had a strong heart." He still came to work every morning, arriving well before his sons, and sat near the door—right where I had seen him the previous November—conversing with customers and friends. He still couldn't sleep, staying awake throughout those twilight hours, worrying over his hogs. He might now walk instead of run around the pit house, but his heart, that strong heart, would keep on running to the very end.

That heart finally gave out on April 27, 2013. Over thirty-five of his fifty-one years, Ricky Parker had smoked more hogs, burned more hickory, and worn out more pairs of shoes than any other pitmaster. His sons laid him to his eternal rest alongside his mother and father at the Natchez Trace Baptist Church Cemetery, choosing to bury him in his everyday uniform: blue work pants and a beige shirt with "Ricky" stitched across the left breast and a five-pack box of Swisher Sweets planted in the pocket. Whether or not there was barbecue in the afterlife, Ricky would take some smoke along with him.

After closing the business to bury their father, Zach and Matt would reopen Scott's-Parker's Barbecue one week later to little fanfare. The pits had never sat this quiet, this cold, for so long. But they would relight with ease. Barbecue, and whole-hog barbecue especially, has a tendency to endure, to survive the crushing stutters and stops of time and to linger in the imaginations of eaters. Ricky Parker might have been gone, but his sons still burned staves of hickory wood down to coals and fired their hogs every half hour for most of a day. The people of Lexington, Tennessee, still arrived hungry for whole hog, slaw, and hot sauce; the regulars feuded over the few orders of catfish and ribs; and the Parker boys often sold out of everything well before sundown.

I arrived two days prior to the first Fourth of July after Ricky's passing. Not a chance I would miss this. The date had become totemic, circled on my mental calendar for five years. This Independence Day, I long knew, fell on a Thursday, the start to the four-day weekend over which Ricky had wanted to cook one hundred whole hogs.

I turned up just as Zach and Matt pulled into the parking lot with a pickup truck loaded heavy with freshly killed hogs. Zach had recently discovered weightlifting and the protein-rich lifestyle and could toss a pig around like a pillow. Matt was still skinny and quiet and looked even more like his dad than in years past.

The past ten weeks had been a series of ups and downs for Ricky's young sons. Twenty-two-year-old Zach, operating under his father's auspices, took the lead in running the barbecue place. Matt, nearly two years older, stuck by his brother's side and, together with a small cluster of friends turned employees, ran the pit house, while crash-course learning the other side of any business—filing paperwork and paying the taxman. Of course there were doubters. People around town asked when the boys would install the gas lines to the pits, concluding that they would take the first available shortcut in crafting whole-hog barbecue. "A lotta family members and my girlfriend and friends, those that didn't work here, asked if we would be able to keep it open," Matt told me. "You know, being nosy."

As the brothers lifted the hogs from truck bed to walk-in cooler, they both looked to be operating at the razor's edge of collapsing from exhaustion. "I haven't had a day off since Dad passed," Zach said.

And for that reason, the brothers had decided to forgo their father's quest for one hundred hogs. Their July Fourth weekend would be spent on holiday, fishing and boating alongside their girlfriends and best pals. They would find time to drink to excess, barbecue something significantly smaller than a whole hog, and sleep in.

The brothers sold out of barbecue well before the Fourth had even dawned: 1,200 pounds, more than a half ton of meat, spread among three hundred orders, from one-pound single servings to twenty-five-pound party trays, reserved weeks in advance. I woke early on the morning of the Fourth to witness the first order go out the door at eight AM and waited until the last departed seven hours later. I watched as customer after customer hugged the Parker boys and thanked them for continuing their father's legacy. I saw many customers who had neglected to reserve their barbecue leave empty-handed and felt only half guilty when Zach handed me three pounds of white and dark, with my own squirt bottle of hot sauce on the side. I observed Zach and Matt hustle harder and faster than their dad ever had. And at day's end, I watched as they shoveled sand into each of their barbecue pits, one by one, extinguishing the fires that once kept their father, Ricky Parker, awake at night.

EPILOGUE

My One True Barbecue

Send me, Gods! a whole hog barbecued!
—ALEXANDER POPE

*F*ive years passed before I made it back to Henderson, Tennessee, and the place I fell in love with whole hog cooked over an open flame: Siler's Old Time BBQ. Pulling into the parking lot, the first thing I noticed was a new wooden sign, a childlike drawing of a vividly pink pig peering canine-like over a fence, looking for attention. Above the pig was written SILER'S OLD TIME BBQ. And beneath: OPEN 7 DAYS.

Open all week! Business must be good, I thought. I could already feel the wash of fat rolling around the cavity of my mouth.

Retracing my previous journey, I walked around back and stepped into the pit house. Once again, I gasped, immediately overtaken by the sight.

Scrubbed free of their carbonized soot, the cinder-block walls were now covered in brightly colored chalk drawings: sky blue clown faces and neon pink hashmarks, like a child's interpretation of the Lascaux caves. But there was also smoke, emanating from the pits, obviously some sort of pig product roasting away. Dizzily, I turned to face the phrase SAMANTHA LOVES CAT written in a sunny shade of yellow. More than a little confused, I felt clouded by a sort of ludicrous dread. Compelled to scramble outside, I tripped and nearly tumbled over a plastic toy truck. There, not ten feet from the burn barrels, I saw a sandbox smattering of children's toys: an Easy-Bake Oven and a kid's tool kit, a hula hoop and high chair.

On cue, Chris Siler appeared, no overalls and just a bit paunchier. I joined his side as he stomped toward the pit house and spilled a stream of questions, half of which I could only manage to mumble, all of which were mutely ignored.

What happened? Where are the pigs? And Ronnie, where's he? What's with the chalk, and why does this place looks like a barbecue/day care?

"I remember you," he said flatly. "Business has changed a lot since I first opened."

I followed him into the smokehouse, where he pulled the tarp off the rearmost pit and slid off the metal sheet roofing. We both swatted at wafts of smoke to reveal row upon row of fat-glistening, black-and-brown-barked pig shoulders. Seventy-two shoulders in all, each uniformly ellipsoidal, the unholy union of an overinflated and slightly smashed basketball with a bowling ball's heft and weight. They were beautiful, but they weren't whole hog. Siler stared at them with a prideful intensity. Shoulders were not what I came here for, but they still instantly filled me with hunger. "There's no more whole hogs," he shouted through the smoke. "Impossible to find." As he rearranged the tarp, I couldn't help but think of him as a magician, having momentarily revealed his secret, throwing the curtain back over the trick.

We regrouped in the kitchen, talking about the past five years while he prepped orders for tomorrow's Fourth of July. First, the price of sorghum tripled, from four to twelve dollars a gallon, making his rib recipe unsustainable, he said. It didn't help that the syrup had become all the rage with a generation of new-wave southern restaurants that flooded the dining scene: sorghum-sweetened cocktails could be found in Charleston, Vietnamese-style sorghum-glazed pork belly in Chapel Hill, and, for dessert, sorghum semifreddo in Atlanta.

Then the hog industry dried up. Farmers left the business, slaughterhouses shuttered. Even the local Wonder bread distributor went belly-up. Most frustrating of all, a nearby competitor—he didn't name names—cornered the hog futures market, outbidding all other local whole-hog restaurants for the prize commodity.

The final blow came with having to dismiss his right-hand man, Ronnie Hampton. The IRS finally caught up with Siler, forcing him to pay several years of back taxes. "Ronnie is semiretired," he noted with regret. "Works at the county dump."

With no hogs to cook and no pitmaster to cook them, Siler soon switched to smoking prepackaged shoulders. Weighing in at between twelve and twenty pounds, a whole shoulder could be prepped and loaded onto the pit by a single man. And because of their uniformity, shoulders made ordering easy. Siler's purveyor, Dalton Meat & Poultry out of Jackson, could immediately hotshot over a refrigerated truck full of shoulder-packed cases: "I call and say, 'Gimme twenty cases, now,' and they're here in an hour." There is little to no waste product. The shoulder can be smoked, chopped, and sold whole. Compared to the economics of the whole hog, Siler easily netted double to triple more per pound of shoulder meat. After making the switch to shoulders, he had become the head pitmaster for the local Chamber of Commerce–sponsored Chester

County BBQ Festival. The previous September, he fed the multitudes that packed downtown Henderson, seven thousand people satiated with his barbecued pork shoulder.

I gathered that the changeover must have been worth it: the financial stability, the recognition gained by cooking for thousands, and the hours freed to spend with his family instead of sawing off hogs' feet and staring at the fire.

"I miss doing hogs, I ain't gonna lie," he said before pausing for several beats while looking out the kitchen's back door, toward the pit house. "It was different."

Ten minutes later, the phone rang: a customer calling to order an entire hog for his Independence Day shindig. Siler was noticeably exasperated; this was obviously not the first request for a hog that he'd received leading up to the holiday weekend. "Hog market's dried up," he told the caller. As he explained further to his customer, I toured the dining room, where everything seemed in its place, just more of it. The devotional signage increased tenfold; the pig decorations had taken over one large table and begun to wrap the walls. I scanned the recent family photographs scattered near the cash register, noting that the Siler brood had nearly doubled in size since my last visit. "If someone says they're serving whole hog," I can hear him shout on the phone from the kitchen, "ask to see the hog first." In this tiny corner of the nation, Siler has found himself performing the role of dealer selling spare parts to a customer base that still wants to buy a brand-new car.

I ordered a chopped sandwich and ate the barbecue alone and in silence, swallowing as quickly as I could. The meat was good, relatively moist and flavorfully smoky, certainly better than hundreds of other barbecue joints that littered the state. But everything had changed. And so had my taste for barbecue.

I walked out back and shook Siler's hand good-bye while making sure to compliment his barbecue. "You don't gotta wait five more years to come back now," he shouted after me. "Ya hear!"

————

Back in Asheville, Elliott Moss had rebounded by partnering with an established local restaurateur and announcing pared-down plans for his dream barbecue venue, now renamed Buxton Hall. Set to occupy a 1930s-era skating rink, Buxton Hall should be serving whole hogs high in the Blue Ridge range by the late summer of 2015.

By that summer's July Fourth, Rodney Scott rebuilt his pit house using modern design and materials. While he continued his search for the perfect location for a second Scott's Bar-B-Que in Charleston, across the border in North Carolina, his good buddy Sam Jones quietly announced the biggest barbecue news of the past two centuries. He would become the first member of the Dennis-Jones family to open a barbecue joint outside of Ayden, where generations of his kin have been cooking and chopping hogs since 1830. Set down in Greenville, just ten miles from Ayden, Sam Jones BBQ would have three times as many seats as the Skylight Inn; a lengthy menu that aspired to go beyond barbecue, coleslaw, and cornbread to include ribs and burgers, sides and dessert; and, much to his abstaining father's immense displeasure, a full-service bar. Pastor Bruce might consider alcohol a sin, but even his father, Pete Jones, the first great Bar-B-Q King, once served beer alongside his barbecue.

The wait for these places to open was unbearable. I needed my fix, and continued my chase after the whole hog. Even in this age of supposed culinary oversaturation, when every restaurant and menu item had been documented, Instagrammed, and listicled, odds were that there was someone out there roasting pigs and selling the meat.

Occasionally, reports surfaced of places in eastern North Carolina, somewhere off in the middle of nowhere, that had been smoking hogs since the 1960s, of another old spot out in Ricky Parker's territory that had somehow been overlooked. I poked around only to find that these locations either didn't exist or, if they did, didn't meet my criteria. They cooked shoulders or hams, not hogs. They used gas or electric cookers, not hardwood fire and smoke.

I was chasing ghosts, hunting down barbecue where barbecue didn't exist.

On one road trip, while searching for new barbecue joints in North Carolina, I detoured up Interstate 95 to the town of Rocky Mount to visit Barbecue Park. Located along the muddy banks of the Tar River, where Bob Melton built the nation's first indoor, sit-down barbecue restaurant in 1924, the park is an open-air museum dedicated to celebrating barbecue's regional traditions. Plaques provided short histories of the state's whole-hog heritage and Rocky Mount, which once enjoyed five whole-hog eating houses—two were owned by African American entrepreneurs—and was called the "Barbecue Center of the South" in the 1950s. At the park's center stood the only remnants of Melton's Barbecue: a redbrick fireplace, once used to burn oak and hickory coals, and his famed cook pit, now reduced to the brick and mortar outline of its groundwork foundation. A nearby plaque declared this "hallowed ground."

One Sunday morning, still on the road in North Carolina, I rushed westward to make an eleven AM sermon. Though I've never been a regular churchgoer, I like to seek a bit of random spiritual restoration when the mood strikes. And how could I pass up an opportunity to worship in the Lord's House of Barbecue?

The Barbecue Church is a real place of worship, a Presbyterian church located at 124 Barbecue Church Road, near Barbecue Creek, and just outside the town of Barbecue. According to the church's biography, local legend says that General William Cornwallis and his battalion of British Redcoats held a barbecue cookout along the creek during the Revolutionary War and thusly named the waterway. But land grants date Barbecue Creek back before the Revolution. A second story credits Scottish settler Neill McNeill, who witnessed the early morning mist rise smokelike from the creek and, reminded of his sailor days in the Caribbean watching the islanders roasting meat over their traditional wood-framed structure, named the creek after the *barbacòa*.

I find both stories equally ridiculous: neither assign naming rights to local indigenous peoples. But the Barbecue Presbyterian Church verifiably dates back to 1758, when a group of Scottish settlers, fleeing the Highlands for America, formally organized the congregation on the banks of Barbecue Creek.

The service was my first Presbyterian experience and a bit austere for my taste: no stained glass, no iconic representations of saints, no communion. But I did feel accepted, especially when, as I exited the building, the reverend shook my hand and invited my return. Outside the church a sign read *"Ceud Mile Failte,"* a Gaelic phrase I later learned that translates to "one hundred thousand welcomes."

I was searching for just one more whole-hog welcome. And in the spring of 2015, with time for one last weeklong road trip, I found my way to several.

The first to pop up on my radar was Fuller's Old Fashioned Bar-B-Q off the interstate outside Lumberton, a town just north of the Carolinas' border. This was southeastern North Carolina's Lumbee country, regional home to the state's largest Native American tribe, the largest tribe still living east of the Mississippi River, one of the largest tribes in the nation that is still fighting for federal recognition.

At Fuller's, operated by a Lumbee family by the name of Locklear, eight dollars bought me a roundtrip lunch ticket to the buffet line, the spread of all spreads, spanning three long tables and sixty-plus items. There were traditional Lumbee specialties like thin crisp discs of fried cornbread eaten topped with collard greens; more stewed vegetables than I could count; and a whole row of steaming meats: fried chicken, pigs' feet, and freshly rendered pork rinds, along with several I couldn't identify. The barbecue, chopped in the eastern Carolina style and sauced with vinegar and pepper, inhabited a small corner of the buffet. I treated this supposedly "old-fashioned" barbecue with a large heaping of skepticism. Why spend the time and effort to cook hogs with wood if the barbecue was one of a dozen or so meats on offer?

Two days later I got to ask owner Eric Locklear that same question from the pit house located behind the family compound, where his father, Fuller Locklear, began smoking hogs when he opened his business in 1986. A great slap of smoke that greeted me at the pit house door confirmed that, yes, this was old-fashioned barbecue. Eric showed off the hogs on the grill while telling me his family's restaurant history. There were originally only four items on the buffet at Fuller's: fried chicken, a rotating vegetable of the day, coleslaw, and whole-hog barbecue. Over time, the buffet expanded exponentially—upwards of 1,500 customers pass through the line on any given Saturday—with barbecue's role as headliner diminishing year by year. But Fuller's was founded as a barbecue joint, and a barbecue joint it would remain, at least in name. The wood-cooked hogs would remain also, Eric Locklear told me. "It's wood, or no way."

I encountered more whole hog eighty-odd miles away in the pastoral surroundings of the state's southeastern corner. From the highway, the next stop on my itinerary looked like your typical 1950s-era residence because, well, it was a classic example of the period: a single-chimneyed redbrick home. Its wide grassy yard had recently been trimmed. Red- and pink-bloomed azaleas lined the wraparound driveway. A carved wooden sign, embellished with roseate white magnolia blossoms, hung from a fencepost:

THE BLIZZARDS

Ann & Sidney

455 S. Railroad Ave.

BEULAVILLE, NC

It looked like the suburban house I grew up in, the tiny abode on Pigeon Loop with the basketball hoop and the lawn I mowed every Sunday. Better yet, it looked like that stereotypical setting from just about any film in which the protagonist returns home, or unexpectedly drops into the cozy confines of an eccentric great-aunt or -uncle—the cinematic plot device where the clueless urbanite becomes stranded in suburbia.

Following the driveway back behind the Blizzard homestead and adjoining tool shed revealed a large smokehouse and equally vast restaurant, both completely unnoticeable from the approaching highway. This was Sid's Catering, where Sidney A. Blizzard had been smoking pigs since 1977, the year he quit the hog-farming business after estimating that there was more money to be made in barbecue, even if he only opened on Saturdays.

Sid's remains a bit of hidden magic: an old Wurlitzer in the back with singles by John Denver and Smokey Robinson; walls lined with taxidermied trophies, wild turkeys and boars' heads. It was 8:45 on a Saturday morning, the only day Sid's opens for business, and both dining rooms were full with patrons filling up on whole-hog barbecue, coleslaw, and freshly fried hushpuppies. I had found barbecue for breakfast—Sid's often sells out well before noon. Sid Junior answered the ceaselessly ringing phone and barked orders to the kitchen, while his father Sidney, eighty-one years old, roamed from table to table greeting his customers, his friends.

Sid's and Fuller's proved that there were still whole-hog pit houses to uncover and pitmasters to interview. A wrong turn down the right road, a question posed to the right gas-station attendant, or a curlicue of smoke spotted in the distance might bring me to the next great undiscovered barbecue. There were others, I knew, men cooking whole hogs, smokehouses hidden in plain sight, places like Scott's, not Rodney Scott's, but Ricky Scott's, located down a series of country roads, just two lefts and a right, only thirty-one miles away from the famous barbecue stop that had put Hemingway on the map.

A friend had given me Ricky Scott's cell phone number a week before I had planned to drive up to South Carolina. I called to verify that he would be open. "I think I will cook some barbecue," he said, "if I can get a pig." Like many good barbecue men, Ricky seemed a man of few words. But that would be enough to convince me to drive the eight hundred miles to this other Scott's Bar-B-Que, nestled deep in the South Carolina Lowlands, in a community called Hell's Half Acre.

This other Scott's had no listed phone number. There was no working address, no mailbox, no sign. Hell's Half Acre does not even exist on the map, at least not the Hell's Half Acre I was headed toward. Google-mapping "Hell's Half Acre, SC" brought me to a different South Carolina town with that same name, located 120 miles to the southwest. I only found this unofficial, unmapped Hell's Half Acre, home of Scott's-Not-Scott's, by plugging its coordinates into my GPS—33.591687, -79.706593—a sequence of numbers that I meditated on in the drive up to South Carolina from New Orleans, repeating them to myself as if they contained some sort of symbolic significance, some runic code. What would I find in a place called Hell's Half Acre?

What I found was a potholed dirt road leading to a wooden shack, one half of its exterior painted a pale pink, the other half remaining unfinished because, it seemed, the paint had run out. Behind that was a cinder-block structure, the pit house, brushed in the same fleshy shade. A crooked television antenna protruded from its low-slung roof. At the back of the otherwise unremarkable pit house, its chimney looked like a bit of folk art sculpture, twisted panels of rusted tin roofing held together with rebar and attached to the building with wire, a Rube Goldberg contraption that somehow funneled smoke into the sky.

There was smoke. I could hear the pop and crackle of hardwood logs burning on a fire. And I could smell a hog cooking.

Inside, I found Saul Epps, Ricky's thirty-four-year-old nephew, tending to the most rudimentary pit I'd ever seen: a twenty-foot length of cinder blocks, cracked and spiderwebbed, with a few sheets of plywood acting as cover. A shovel, cooling in the corner, was a specimen of ordinary length but with an equally long wooden stave duct-taped to the handle to double its reach. There was no fan and no ventilation besides the screened-in windows. The fireplace was indoors, just a 180-degree turn and scoop into the pit. The floor was dirt.

Saul limped across the pit house—he had broken both legs in an automobile accident years ago—and slid a slat of plywood from the top of the pit to reveal a single hog. A diminutive ninety-seven-pound pig, half the size of the hogs I'd seen elsewhere. This was the week's offering here at Scott's, where one hog is smoked every Thursday, put on the grill around eight AM, off at four in the afternoon, when cars start filling the potholed driveway and the old-timers arrive to drink beer and dawdle away the early evening, ready to grab a piece of barbecue before returning home. Often the barbecue is available only every other Thursday, and sometimes the pig isn't ready until after six. Scott's does not keep regular hours. Scott's might not even be called Scott's. Some locals I spoke to called it Scott's or used the plural form Scotts'—as in Scotts' Family Bar-B-Que—others said Ricky's, while one group of men called it simply "the Barbecue." The only guarantee that this place existed at all was that I was there.

Ricky Scott's pickup truck pulled in front of the pit house an hour later. He wore a clean black polo tucked into a pair of pressed jeans and a new black ball cap. He strode with and spoke in that

West Indies–like accent that my ears picked up back in Heming-way. For forty or so of his fifty-three years, he'd crafted barbecue alongside members of his family: his father and mother, Freddie and Lerline Scott, and a dozen siblings. Dad was a sharecropper, farming tobacco, corn, soy, and cotton; he dug water wells through-out the county and, out of earthen pits trenched at the family farm, smoked hogs as a side business. Mom made the sides and sauce, a pleasantly mild blend of apple cider vinegar and pepper. The Scotts chose to cook and sell on Thursdays only: a plate of barbecue to help launch the weekend.

Home was this unincorporated territory ten miles outside the town of Kingstree, an area local residents termed Hell's Half Acre. "Back in the day," Ricky's brother Freddie Jr. told me, "you couldn't come back here." I wasn't sure if he was referring to my whiteness, my outsiderness, or both. But it was clear he meant to imply that this area was a half-acre-sized no-man's-land, the Devil's cross-roads, a small slice of hell.

The community certainly seemed tamer now, not completely accessible to the outsider but perfectly safe. Especially with Ricky Scott as my guide. For thirty years he'd worked for Williamsburg County, moving his way up to director of public works, oversee-ing the upkeep of every unpaved road and wooden bridge within a thousand-square-mile area. He also volunteered at the fire depart-ment, spun records as a DJ for hire (country and western, R&B), and drag-raced his 1972 Chevy Vega at the local track. The barbecue business became his after Freddie and Lerline started ailing twenty or so years ago, so on Thursdays he heads straight from the office to the pit house. He said he'll slide "into a coma" if he ever takes the opportunity to slow down. He planned on retiring four years from now, he told me, and had been thinking of taking to the pit house full-time in the hopes of making Hell's Half Acre a barbecue destination. He was just waiting for it to be discovered.

Or I should say rediscovered, because Ricky's had been discovered several times over. Two decades ago, Scott's had been broadcast to the barbecue-rabid world in a book and documentary film called *Smokestack Lightning*, respectively written and produced by my friend Lolis Eric Elie. I had twice read his book, I owned a copy of the film in which Scott's-Not-Scott's is prominently featured, but still I failed to track the place down. Later, on at least one occasion, Rodney Scott had told me that he heard customers whisper of another whole-hog barbecue, another unrelated pitman named Scott, in the area surrounding his family's farm. Asking around, he found out that his longtime girlfriend, now wife, Coco, was the niece of this mysterious barbecue man, but he never followed the lead. This other Scott's Bar-B-Que had remained within reach all along. It was as if Hell's Half Acre had wanted to remain undiscovered.

One month before my visit to Hell's Half Acre, Ricky, subbing for a double-booked Rodney Scott, who was off cooking a hog halfway around the world in Melbourne, Australia, starred as the main attraction at the Charleston Wine and Food festival's $175-a-plate barbecue dinner. Fame might soon come pouring Ricky Scott's way. Smoke seekers could fill his pockmarked parking lot. But I have my doubts—I was the only outsider who came to Hell's Half Acre for barbecue this Thursday.

As Ricky and I talked outside the pit house, waiting for the hog to finish, he pointed across the two-lane country road: "That's another barbecue place there by the name of McKnight." Sure enough there was a smoke shack, not one hundred yards from where we sat. He barbecued hogs every now and then, especially in the summer. Just "up at the head of the road," Ricky told me, a McClary smoked every other Thursday. And there was another pit house "at the end of the road." Four barbecue establishments, on the same road, within a mile of one another. I thought I had located the truest of the one true barbecues, worked by a pitmaster who operates at the end of the world, but what I had discovered was the center of a whole-hog universe.

My mind ran rabid with dreams of moving to Hell's Half Acre for a month, maybe even a whole summer, to track down each of these pitmasters and keep them company by their fires. It didn't matter that they all likely purchased their hogs from the same farmer, cooked out of similar pits, and prepared their barbecue in the same fashion. It didn't matter if they all used similar sauce recipes, or if the taste of one was indistinguishable from the next—though I doubted this possibility. They might all smoke a hog the exact same way, but each and every one of their stories would be different.

I waited until a dozen or so customers were served before ordering my pound of roast and smoked pork flesh. I will not say how Ricky Scott's barbecue tasted that evening. My words could never do his work justice. But I will confirm that I cleaned every lick of meat and fat from that Styrofoam tray. I will admit to tipping the tray upward to drink down the vinegar and pepper-laced barbecue sauce. Ricky offered another pull of pork, but I had eaten until I could eat no more. I was satiated, belly and mind.

I remembered a conversation I had with Tyson Ho one year earlier, over coffee in New York City's Koreatown. I asked why he chose to specialize in whole hog and not, say, ribs or brisket. "I found that most people don't pick a barbecue style," he said. "I think most people have a barbecue style that helps them discover who they are. Different people kind of lean toward one thing or the other. It's almost like they didn't pick it. It picked them."

I nodded in excited agreement, recognizing myself in his words: I hadn't chosen whole hog, it had chosen me. Back in 2008, when I started this journey, I was searching for a place, a time, and the right people to share their stories. Any stories. I craved, needed a community of stories set in the present but couched in the past. The pitmasters provided the narrative; the art of slow cooking fueled and afforded us countless hours to talk and sit silently in the pit house and by the fire, twin sites that acted as communal hearths. Whole hog not only attracted me, it defined me, articulated my being, expressed a needful longing for conversation with people and communion with history.

This is what initially attracted Tyson to the hog; with the Arrogant Swine, he now has two hundred years of American history on his side. History is what brought Sam Jones back to the Skylight Inn after writing a family biography for a college class, and history is what has encouraged him to move forward with his own endeavor. A dedication to whole-hog history is what drove Larry Dennis, Stephen Grady, Rodney Scott, and Ricky Scott to cook pigs alongside their fathers. At Wilber's, Pop Ward not only learned under his dad's tutelage but followed in the footsteps of near-forgotten Goldsboro pitmasters like Adam Scott and Guy Parker. History is what makes Chris Siler long for the days he still cooked hogs. And it was his single-minded pursuit to make history that brought down Ricky Parker.

I often think back to my brief encounter with Ed Mitchell's mural that lay covered with black sheeting in his defunct monument to whole-hog barbecue: the wooden table stretching under the oak trees, filled with eaters, black and white, hungry for old-fashioned whole hog. My waking dream is for that table to be filled with everyone I encountered over my whole-hog journeys. Yvonne

Parker would be seated next to her husband, Guy, again. Dennises could break bread with their crosstown cousins, the Joneses. All the Bessinger brothers would be present. I'd even let old Maurice take a seat, and I'd sit right next to him and force him to shake hands with the Gradys and Scotts and the other Scotts. The table would stretch on, infinitely, to include all those pitmasters captured in John Hemmer's lenses, and all the rest whose names have been lost to time. Ricky Parker would be there, finally able to sit and rest at peace. And maybe Pete Jones and Adam Scott could cook the hog, two kings side-by-side, before taking their seats at the heads of the table. Together we'd eat and find room to talk about anything but barbecue.

Acknowledgments

$\mathcal{M}$y ardent gratitude goes, first and foremost, to everyone whose name populates this book. You shared your time, your food, and your stories. Thank you.

Thank you to the first champions of this story and my role in imagining it: Amy Evans and John T. Edge. Amy brought the serious pursuit of oral histories to the Southern Foodways Alliance and unleashed this tenderfoot Terkel upon the barbecue trail back in the summer of 2008. SFA founder John T. has been a mentor and guiding light. He has taught me, and many others, how to write, live, and even dress for going on a decade.

Two decades ago, my barbecue guru, Lolis Eric Elie, wrote a book that provided the inspiration for this one. I will never forget his words of advice, an icebreaker that has turned many an awkward interview into an insightful conversation: "Ask them what music they listen to while they work." Brett Martin took my book proposal and helped me find an agent; he is the big brother I never had, the friend I will forever cherish. Agents Tim Wojcik and Daniel Greenberg found this book a home. I thank them for their continued encouragement. Matthew Benjamin and the team at Touchstone and Simon & Schuster helped turn eight years of driving, eating, and documenting into *The One True Barbecue.* Thank you, thank you, thank you.

And, finally, a thousand thanks of praise to Denny Culbert. In November of 2011, we set out for the chilly climes of eastern North Carolina hardly knowing each other. We have since worked on many stories together—first as writer and photographer, then as cocreators and conspirators, and now as very best buds. More thank-yous go to Denny's wife, Katie, my oldest, dearest friend, and the only other person to survive a trip on the Barbecue Bus.

Thanks also to those across the nation who fed me, bed me, and read me: Rachel Arons, Barney Atkinson, Jami Attenberg, Harry Barton, Wes Berry, Sean Brock, Ashley Christensen, Jennifer Cole, Howard Conyers, Kimberly Corbett, Wayne Curtis, Shome Dasgupta, Burton Durand, Elizabeth Engelhardt, Chloe & Tommy Fertel, Matt Fertel & Alexandra Castillo-Kesper, Owen Fertel, Randy Fertel, Melissa Hall, Kira Henehan, Vivian Howard & Ben Knight, Dorothy & Tom Howorth, Pableaux Johnson, Sarah Jones, Nathalie Jordi, Julie & Bill Knox, Blair Langlinais, Mary Beth Lasseter, Dan Levine, Ted Maclin, Sarah Malphrus, Terri Martin, Phil McCausland, Dean McCord & Family, Allston McCrady, Dave Mezz, Sara Camp Arnold Milam, Robert Moss, Ted O'Brien, Stacey Ornstein & David Turner, Nicholas Pihakis, Nick Pihakis, Kathleen Purvis, Simone Reggie, Sara Roahen, Drew Robinson, Matt Sartwell, Michael Shemtov, David Shields, Andy Smith, Randy Sparks, Bobby Ticknor, Michael Twitty, Daniel Vaughn, Jim Veteto, Dale Volberg & John Shelton Reed, Allie Wall, Robb Walsh, Nach Waxman, Maggy & Chris Wheeler, Maggie White, Sara Wood, and Joe York.

A special big thanks to the Memphians who sheltered and fed me way back when: the Coleman Family, the Travis Family, their plucky progeny Jay Coleman and Elizabeth Travis, and, last but

ACKNOWLEDGMENTS

never least, my first barbecue buddy, Jonathan Large. Thank you to my parents, who trusted me with their brand-new RV, encouraged their three sons to explore, and might have become even bigger fans of Scott's-Parker's Barbecue than myself. And to Susie Penman, my first reader, who pokes and scratches each and every draft I write into polished shape. This book is all the better, I am all the better, as a result of your attention and love.

Selected Sources

*I*n the research and writing of this book, I owe an enormous debt to my friend Lolis Eric Elie, whose *Smokestack Lightning: Adventures in the Heart of Barbecue Country* (1996) paved the way for all serious barbecue journalism, scholarship, and writing to follow (a film of the same name, produced by Elie, is also worth hunting up). A more recent release along the lines of Elie's masterpiece is Robb Walsh's *Barbecue Crossroads: Notes & Recipes from a Southern Odyssey* (2013), which, like *Smokestack Lightning*, covers a lot of geographic ground. Both of these authors and I were inspired and motivated to hit the road by the superlative work of John Egerton. His *Southern Food: At Home, on the Road, in History* (1987) remains crucial in understanding the history, culture, and, some might say, our national, perhaps even global, obsession with barbecue and other southern foodways.

In my regrettably few conversations with him, John Egerton, who passed away in 2013, was the most friendly, compassionate, and liberal-hearted man. In 1999, Egerton assembled fifty food-minded individuals; together they created the Southern Foodways Alliance. That organization put me on the road that eventually wound its way to become *The One True Barbecue*. Come join, learn, and have fun with us; read more at www.southernfoodways.org.

Over the years, the SFA introduced me to a host of barbecue

SELECTED SOURCES

authors and activists whose work has been instrumental in the composition of this book. The organization's *Corn Bread Nation* anthology, now in seven volumes, often covers barbecue; the series' second volume (2004), edited by Lolis Eric Elie, is completely dedicated to "The United States of Barbecue." I met Andrew Warnes at an SFA symposium back in 2007. His talk, excerpted from his forthcoming *Savage Barbecue: Race, Culture, and the Invention of America's First Food* (2008), angered many in the audience. But his scholarly brilliance and courage emboldened me. There is no better book on barbecue. (Additionally, much of what I learned about the photographer John Hemmer comes from Warnes.) The SFA also put me in touch with Robert Moss and his *Barbecue: The History of an American Institution* (2010), an invaluable chronicle of roasted, smoked, and sauced meat, and its role in the nation's past and present.

Recently, a host of regional barbecue studies have been issued. The most valuable in the writing of this book was *Holy Smoke: The Big Book of North Carolina Barbecue* (2008) by John Shelton Reed, Dale Volberg Reed, and William McKinney. *A History of South Carolina Barbeque* (2013), by Lake E. High, Jr., is, let's just say, an interesting read. The most cleverly titled essay collection of all time, *The Slaw and the Slow Cooked: Culture and Barbecue in the Mid-South* (2011), by James R. Veteto and Edward M. Maclin, is a good interdisciplinary look at varied barbecue forms. And finally, although I'd have trouble finding Texas and Kentucky on the barbecue map, Elizabeth S. D. Engelhardt's *Republic of Barbecue: Stories Beyond the Brisket* (2009), Daniel Vaughn's *The Prophets of Smoked Meat: A Journey Through Texas Barbecue* (2013), and Wes Berry's *The Kentucky Barbecue Book* (2013) tell me that people do, in fact, eat what they call "barbecue" in those states. Though I remain skeptical, I trust all three and their excellent books.

When I started my whole-hog journey eight years ago, I was

struck by the very weird, very funny, and very smart *Searching for the Dixie Barbecue: Journeys into the Southern Psyche* (2005). I dearly hope to share a meal with its author, Wilber W. Caldwell, someday. Need to study up on issues of pit liability and sauce recipe theft (or *Bessinger v. Bi-Lo*) as I did? Well, *The Little Book of BBQ Law* (2013), written by Cecil C. Kuhne III, and graciously given to me by Bradley Black, Esq., is for you.

There are dozens—too many!—barbecue guidebooks. But I would like to give a shout-out to the first, *Hog Heaven: A Guide to South Carolina Barbecue* (1979), by Allie Patricia Wall and Ron L. Layne. It was an honor to eat barbecue with Ms. Wall. Biographies of pitmasters and other barbecue bosses are, unfortunately, quite rare. *Adam's Ribs: The Success Story of Adam Scott, the 'Barbecue King'* (1977), by Moses Rountree, is a flattering profile of the nation's first King and a very difficult little booklet to source. In my opinion, there are too many copies of the autobiographical *Defending My Heritage: The Maurice Bessinger Story* (2001). Not many readers will want to waste their time with this one.

But enough about barbecue, let's hear it for the hog. I enjoyed reading William Hedgepeth's *The Hog Book* (1978) and Mark Essig's *Lesser Beasts: A Snout-to-Tail History of the Humble Pig* (2015) for different reasons. If the former is a bit wild, rooting around here and there through history, the latter is domesticated but never boring, a solid piece of scholarship on the swine. S. Jonathan Bass's essay, " 'How 'bout a Hand for the Hog': The Enduring Nature of the Swine as a Cultural Symbol in the South," from volume 1, number 3 of the journal *Southern Cultures* (1995), is indispensable in understanding the importance of pigs in the South.

I devoured Linda Flowers's sweet and sad *Throwed Away: Failures of Progress in Eastern North Carolina* (1990) when writing about that region. *Back Roads America: A Portfolio of Her People* (1980), composed by the writing/photography team of Thomas O'Neill and Ira Block, helped in sourcing the true story of Pete Jones and the Capital myth. (Hey, *National Geographic*, want to send Denny Culbert and me on a trip to retrace their steps?) And Jason Sokol's *There Goes My Everything: White Southerners in the Age of Civil Rights, 1945–1975* (2007), a necessary read in understanding the modern South, helped to get at the story of Ollie McClung and other barbecue segregationists.

Smoke. Fire. Sweat. Pitmasters look damn good on film, and filmmaker Joe York is the Herzog of barbecue documentarians. *Capitol Q*, on the Skylight Inn, *Cut/Chop/Cook*, on Rodney Scott, and *Whole Hog*, in which you can watch Ricky Parker in voice and action, are all available on the Southern Foodways Alliance's website, as is *Thursday in Hell's Half Acre*, a profile of Ricky Scott, directed by 1504 Pictures.

Three individuals deserve special mention, for their distinguished contribution to the creation of *The One True Barbecue*. Calvin Trillin writes about barbecue, and so many other things, like no other. He should be America's favorite author. The poet Jake Adam York could turn smoke and sauce and the pitmaster's passion into the most beautiful and heartbreakingly rendered verse. He passed away in 2012, and his unparalleled voice is missed mightily. Last, for better or worse, I read a bunch of James Agee—journalism, fiction, and letters—when writing this book. I admire the man tremendously.